RETAILERS AND THE LOCAL AUTHORITY

AUSTRALIA AND NEW ZEALAND
The Law Book Company Ltd.
Sydney : Melbourne : Perth

CANADA AND U.S.A.
The Carswell Company Ltd.
Agincourt, Ontario

INDIA
N.M. Tripathi Private Ltd.
Bombay
and
Eastern Law House Private Ltd.
Calcutta and Delhi
M.P.P. House
Bangalore

ISRAEL
Steimatzky's Agency Ltd.
Jerusalem : Tel Aviv : Haifa

PAKISTAN
Pakistan Law House
Karachi

RETAILERS AND THE LOCAL AUTHORITY

by

Ceri R. Morgan, LL.B. (Lond.), M.I.E.H., M.Inst. W.M.
Barrister of Gray's Inn,
Borough Environmental Health Officer,
Ogwr Borough Council

LONDON
SWEET & MAXWELL
1989

Published in 1989 by
Sweet & Maxwell Limited of
183 Marsh Wall, London E14.
Computerset by Promenade Graphics Limited, Cheltenham.
Printed and bound in Great Britain by
Butler & Tanner Ltd., Frome and London.

British Library Cataloguing in Publication Data
Morgan, Ceri
    Retailers and the local authority.
    1. Great Britain. Retail trades. Law
    I. Title
    344.103'887

    ISBN 0-421-34790-2

To Beryl, Andrea and Louise

PREFACE

There are two main purposes of this book. One is to inform retailers of their statutory obligations in respect of various commercial activities in which they are involved or which they may contemplate pursuing, while the other is to bring together those legal responsibilities of occupiers of shops to their employees and members of the public.

The realisation of the need for this book came to me while I was a principal officer specialising in health and safety and enforcement of the Shops Act 1950. This was about five years ago. Pressure of work and subsequent promotion, first to Deputy and then to Borough Environmental Health Officer, considerably reduced the time that I could spend on the venture. In fact I suggested to the publishers about two years ago that it should be abandoned, but I have to thank them for persuading me to continue and giving me encouragement to complete the project.

It was my intention to approach the subjects from a practical viewpoint without, as far as possible, restricting the academic side. To further this approach many cases heard at magistrates' court level have been taken from "The Inspector," a magazine not normally associated with law reporting. The cases have filled gaps where no High Court examples exist and have put "flesh on to the bones of the law" in these areas but, of course, they do not create any precedent.

The first person that I wish to acknowledge for his help and encouragement not only with regard to this book but also in respect of our many hours spent together at University College, Cardiff on Saturdays studying and lecturing on law is Mr. Trefor Pedrick, barrister. His love of the law was infectious. Also I would like to express my gratitude to Mr. Howard Johnson, who is a friend and senior lecturer in law at the University of Wales College, Cardiff, as it is now known. He very kindly read through the proofs of the manuscript and made several helpful suggestions which I was able to incorporate. Mr. C. A. Cross read the whole draft too and made some constructive comments. Of course, I take sole responsibility for the opinions expressed and for any errors or omissions left undetected.

It would be ungracious of me not to acknowledge a debt to members of the staff of the Environmental Health and Planning Departments at Ogwr, some of whom made useful comments in respect of the disciplines in which they specialise. I must, however, particularly mention my secretary, Mrs. Doreen Redmond, who, in her own time with great fortitude, patience and humour transmitted a mass of scribbling into an exceptionally neat and tidy manuscript. Lastly, but certainly not least, I wish to give special thanks to my wife Beryl for sharing the burden with such understanding.

Ogwr   C. R. Morgan
July 1989

CONTENTS

CHAPTER 4: HOURS OF CLOSING AND SUNDAY TRADING

CHAPTER 5: HEALTH AND SAFETY OF SHOP ASSISTANTS AND MEMBERS OF THE PUBLIC

CHAPTER 6: WELFARE ARRANGEMENTS FOR SHOP EMPLOYEES

CHAPTER 7: HOURS OF EMPLOYMENT OF SHOP ASSISTANTS

CHAPTER 8: PREPARATION, STORAGE AND SALE OF FOOD

CHAPTER 9: MOBILE SHOPS, STALLS, DELIVERY VEHICLES AND STREET TRADING

APPENDICES

INTRODUCTION

The content of the book is only concerned with the legislation that is enforced *in the main* by district councils. Trading standards, for example, is not included. I have, however, included peripheral topics such as planning and highway law where it is of interest and concern to retailers. In fact, Chapter 1 is devoted entirely to planning law as it is of prime importance to the shopkeeper who is considering improvement or alteration to his business. It must be noted that planning conditions attached to a planning permission may restrict the hours and/or days of opening of shops.

The activities that require licensing or registration have increased in recent years principally as a result of the enactment of the Local Government (Miscellaneous Provisions) Act 1982. The responsibility for the issuing of music and dancing licences (now known as public entertainment licences) has passed from the magistrates to local authorities and the Act has given power to the local authorities to control street trading and sex establishments by licensing, and skin piercing by registration, the hygienic control of the latter activity being extremely important in preventing the spread of blood transmitted diseases such as AIDS and hepatitis "B". There are two types of registration. One where the local authority has the power to refuse or cancel registration and the other where, although it is an offence to carry on the activity without registration, the local authority cannot refuse or cancel registration.

The Shops Act 1950 was passed to protect the working conditions of shop employees. There has been much criticism of the Act by the press, the trade and some Members of the House of Commons. The criticism has been directed, generally, towards the anomalies on Sunday trading and the failed Private Members Bills only serve to highlight the problem. Certainly the provisions relating to hours of employment and hours of closing of shops are complicated and the ordinary shopkeeper must have some difficulty in understanding the extent of his obligations. However, I am sure total de-regulation of closing hours would adversely affect the quality of life of those people living near shopping centres and allow freedom for the exploitation of shop workers.

The sections of the Shops Act 1950 relating to the welfare of shop assistants have been repealed and replaced by the Offices, Shops and Railway Premises Act 1963. This Act, in turn, has been complemented and overshadowed to a certain extent by the Health and Safety at Work etc. Act 1974. Extensive duties are placed on the shopkeeper both in respect of shop workers and members of the public. One example is the care needed on the storage and use of cannisters and cylinders filled with liquefied petroleum gas. The whole of the Guidance Note CS8 from the Health and Safety Executive has been included in Appendix VIII so that there is no uncertainty on the precautions needed. Also, from October 1, 1989 specific duties are placed on retailers under the Control of Substances Hazardous to Health Regulations 1988.

The preparation, storage and sale of food raises particular problems and the retailer should be aware of the need for registration and licensing of certain functions as well as his duties under the Food Act 1984 and the Food Hygiene (General) Regulations 1970. The Institution of Environmental Health Officers have long campaigned for some form of prior approval or registration of food premises and there has been a guarded welcome by the Institution to the review of food law that is currently taking place.

Registration of food premises is one of the proposals contained in the government's White Paper "Food Safety—Protecting the Consumer." A Bill is to be introduced to "adapt the law to tomorrow's needs" and included in the White Paper are changes in the legal defences with the withdrawal of the statutory warranty defence and the introduction of a due diligence defence for main offences. Also included are the extension of enforcement powers to *possession* of unfit food and food which is not of the nature, substance or quality demanded by the purchaser, speedier closure of food premises where there is an immediate risk to health and statutory regulation of the training of food handlers.

Mobile shops have special consideration in Chapter 9. It appears that they are exempt, by reason of judicial interpretation, from the Offices, Shops and Railway Premises Act 1963 and the Shops Act 1950, but not so stalls regularly erected on the same piece of land. Highway law may be used by appropriate authorities in the case of obstruction or danger and there is some control, under the Control of Pollution Act 1974, of noise emitted for the purpose of plying trade. Hygiene requirements where food is sold are contained in the Food Hygiene (Market, Stalls and Delivery Vehicles) Regulations 1966.

TABLE OF CASES

TABLE OF STATUTES

TABLE OF STATUTORY INSTRUMENTS

Chapter 1

ACTIVITIES THAT MAY REQUIRE PLANNING PERMISSION

General

A commercial retailer wishing to alter his premises, whether the alter- **1.01**
ation be structural in character or perhaps simply a change in the type of
business being carried on, must first consider the need to apply to the
district council for planning permission. If the use of a premises has
commenced before 1964 without permission it is immune from enforcement action[1] and application may be made for an established use certificate in order to have its status certified.[2] Planning control of this nature
revolves around the definition of "development" which is the carrying
out of the building, engineering, mining or other operation in, on, over
or under land, or the making of any material change in the use of any
buildings or other land.[3] "Land" includes a building.[4]

It can be seen that two separate types of activities are involved:

    (a) an operation, which normally in relation to a shop will be a
        building operation; and

    (b) a material change of use.

Lord Parker of Waddington C.J. in *Cheshire County Council* v.
Woodward[5] said, when explaining the definition of "development":

> "For my part, I feel that the concept behind that definition is two-
> fold; first, in regard to change of use, you take the land as it is and
> ascertain if it has been put to a different use, and secondly, and this
> is quite regardless of use, you have to ascertain whether the land
> itself has been changed by certain operations. I go further and say
> that, having regard to the preposition describing the operations as
> 'in, on, over or under land,' the concept in regard to that limb must
> be, first whether the physical character of the land has been
> changed by operations in or on it, secondly, whether the physical
> characteristics of what is under the land have been changed, for
> example by mining operations under the land, and thirdly, whether
> the physical characteristics of the air above the land have been
> changed by operations which can be described as operations over
> the land."

Some activities are deemed not to constitute development. These are

---

[1] Town and Country Planning Act 1971, s.87(1).
[2] *Ibid.* ss.94, 95.
[3] *Ibid.* s.22(1).
[4] *Ibid.* s.290.
[5] [1962] 2 Q.B. 126.

1

contained in section 22(2) of the Town and County Planning Act 1971 and those prescribed by the Town and Country Planning (Use Classes) Order 1987.[6] Other activities may be deemed to have planning permission granted, with or without conditions and limitations, under certain statutory instruments.[7]

Works of Maintenance, Improvement or Alteration

1.02 Any works of maintenance, improvement or alteration to the interior of a shop will not require the approval of the planning authority, unless, of course, it involves a change of use. Also works of maintenance, improvement or alteration to the exterior of a shop will qualify for exemption as long as it does not materially affect the exterior of the building.[8]

If a retailer intends to carry out repairs or alterations to the exterior of his premises he will want to know the kind of works that will be exempt from planning permission. For example, he would probably assume that painting the external part of his shop doors and windows to prevent deterioration of the woodwork would be allowed without the need to consult the council. But would he be permitted to paint them an obtrusive colour as this would certainly materially alter the external appearance of the shop and may not blend in with the immediate vicinity?

Another example is the installation of floodlights. Could the shopkeeper instal floodlights without redress from the council so that the whole building can be lit up in the evening at the touch of a button and thereby bring prominence to his business by making it stand out amongst the shops in the district?

The answer to both questions is yes. These activities do not require planning approval (if not in a conservation area) and yet they may materially affect the external appearance of a building. The painting of the exterior of any building, as long as it is not for advertisement, announcement or direction is deemed permitted development.[9] In *Kensington and Chelsea Royal London Borough* v. *C.G. Hotels*,[10] the owners of a West London hotel installed floodlights without planning permission and the local authority served an enforcement notice on them requiring their removal. It was reported at the planning inquiry that:

> (1) the works were not considered to amount to building, engineering or other operations; and

---

[6] S.I. 1987 No. 764.
[7] *e.g.* (a) Town and Country Planning General Development Order 1988 (S.I. 1988 No. 1813); (b) Special Development Orders—orders affecting specified areas; (c) Enterprise Zone Schemes.
[8] Town and Country Planning Act 1971, s.22(2)(g).
[9] T. & C.P.G.D.O. 1988 (S.I. 1988 No. 1813), Sched. 2, Part 2, Class C.
[10] (1980) 41 P. & C.R. 40.

(2) in any case the floodlights were unnoticeable and virtually invisible from the street during daylight so they could not be said materially to affect the external appearance of the building. Donaldson L.J., in dismissing the appeal of the council, said: "It was not necessary to resolve that the running of cables and placing of lights was 'development' . . . on no view as I see it, did the works, which were the only works, materially affect the external appearance . . . the Act was never intended to cover this situation."

The owner of any premises can also construct a gate or wall up to a height of one metre where it is abutting a roadway or up to two metres elsewhere with impunity. If it is proposed to alter or maintain existing fences or walls the height cannot be raised above the limits already mentioned. These works are deemed permitted development.[11]

However, should it be decided to construct a new window in order to, perhaps, provide extra ventilation and/or natural lighting the owner will probably need to seek planning permission. It is all a matter of fact and degree whether the works will materially affect the external appearance of the building. The replacement of a window of the same design as the existing one will probably be satisfactory, as will the installation in the external wall of a small ventilator. The only test that the owner will encounter, unless of course he appeals, is the subjective view of the local planning authority.

When considering whether or not the external appearance of the building is materially altered for the purposes of section 22(2)(*a*) of the 1971 Act, it seems that it is the appearance of the building at the time the proposal is considered or an application is made under section 53 of the 1971 Act[12] that must be considered and not some years prior to that date. For example, if a building is in a derelict condition with no slates on the roof and no doors or windows, and the proposal is to re-slate the roof and provide windows and doors, it is no good pleading that the suggested works will not materially alter the appearance of the building as it looked when it was in a good state of repair perhaps some 10 years prior to the date of application.[13]

If the intention is to take down walls and rebuild to the same design in the course of alterations, no development will probably occur, but it depends on the extent of reconstruction. In *Street* v. *Essex County Council*,[14] a demolition order on a house was stayed on the acceptance by the council of an undertaking that all the necessary repairs would be carried out. When the repairs were complete the only part of the orig-

---

[11] T. & C.P.G.D.O. 1988 (S.I. 1988 No. 1813), Sched. 2, Part 2, Class A.
[12] A person may, under this section, make application to the local planning authority to determine, in the case of doubt, whether planning permission is required in respect of any proposed operation on land, or proposed change in the use of land.
[13] See also [1979] J.P.L. 117.
[14] (1965) 193 E.G. 537.

inal structure still standing consisted of two walls which enclose the original kitchen. An enforcement notice was served to restore the building to its former condition. On appeal, the Divisional Court held that the question whether or not constructional works amounted to "maintenance" or "re-building" must be a question of fact and degree. In this case little remained of the original structure; development had taken place without permission, and the appeal was dismissed.

If there is need to erect a temporary building in land whilst any building operations are being carried out (being building operations for which planning permission has been granted or deemed to have been granted) or if heavy plant or machinery is required for such works such works are deemed permitted development.[15] This is subject to the condition that such temporary buildings, plant, etc., are removed when the building operations are finished and the land reinstated. However, this deemed permitted development does not apply to the erection of temporary buildings or plant, etc., on land in connection with a building where the planning permission is for the use of the building rather than building operations.[16]

PROVISION OF KIOSKS, VENDING MACHINES, ETC.

1.03   The construction of an extension to retail premises will obviously be development but there may be circumstances when a retailer may wish to place some form of structure, such as a kiosk which is easily moved, onto his land. This may fall outside the definition of "building" and therefore not represent development. It must be emphasised, however, that when considering one part of the definition of development, *i.e.* building operations, it is necessary to distinguish and exclude the other part, *i.e.* material change of use. A converted caravan selling food on a retailer's land may not be a building operation but it is a separate question whether it involves a material change of use of the land upon which it is situated. If either or both parts of the definition is satisfied then it constitutes development.

A "building" is defined as including "any structure or erection and any part of a building, as so defined, but does not include plant or machinery comprised in a building" and "building operations" as including "rebuilding operations, structural alterations of or additions to buildings, and other operations normally undertaken by a person carrying on business as a builder."[17]

In *Cheshire County Council* v. *Woodward*[18] it was stated that no simple test is sufficient in deciding whether or not an object comes within the definition of "building." A degree of permanence is relevant

---

[15] T. & C.P.G.D.O. 1988 (S.I. 1988 No. 1813) Sched. 2, Part 4, Class A.
[16] *Sunbury-on-Thames Urban District Council* v. *Mann* (1958) 56 L.G.R. 235.
[17] Town and Country Planning Act 1971, s.290(1).
[18] [1962] 2 Q.B. 126.

and an analogy was made with the problem encountered when deciding what fixtures pass with the freehold. Regard must also be had as to whether the physical character of the land or the air space above it has been changed by the operation.

According to Jenkins J. in *Cardiff Rating Authority* v. *Guest Keen Baldwin's Iron and Steel Co.*[19] there are three prime factors to be considered:

(1) Size. Normally it will be constructed on the site as opposed to being brought already made to the site;

(2) Permanence. The building or structure should make a physical change of some permanence. In *James* v. *Brecon County Council*[20] the Divisional Court decided that the erection of a battery of fairground swing boats, capable of being lifted and taken away complete by six men or dismantled in about one hour, did not constitute development;

(3) Physical attachment. Not in itself conclusive but, considered with the other facts, it may be sufficient for the courts to decide either way. Examples are:

    (a) a wheeled coal hopper and conveyor between 16 and 20 feet high brought onto a site was not regarded as development[21];

    (b) the erection of a large scale tower crane running along rails even though it was capable of being dismantled and being erected elsewhere was regarded as development.[22]

Although this was a case dealing with rating the test was approved by Bridge J. in *Barvis Ltd.* v. *Secretary of State for the Environment.*[23]

The placing of a portakabin with services connected on land constitutes a development even though it is not affixed to the land.[24] Also, the Secretary of State agreed with the conclusions of the Inspector when he ruled that a kiosk mounted on industrial type castors represented development. He said that account had to be taken of the degree of permanence and all other relevant circumstances and since the kiosk was too heavy to be moved readily, he considered that it was a "building" within the meaning of section 290(1) of the 1971 Act.[25] Even the erection of very small buildings may amount to development if they are fixed to the land. Buildings forming a model village have been held to constitute development.[26] However, where the kiosk is in reality a converted caravan and is unattached to the land it does not come within the definition

---

[19] [1949] 1 K.B. 385.
[20] (1963) 15 P. & C.R. 20.
[21] *Cheshire County Council* v. *Woodward* [1962] 2 Q.B. 126.
[22] *Barvis Ltd.* v. *Secretary of State for the Environment* (1971) 22 P. & C.R. 710.
[23] *Ibid.*
[24] See also [1978] J.P.L. 571.
[25] APP/5383/c/76/5470 and A/76/10483 Becket House.
[26] *Buckinghamshire County Council* v. *Callingham* [1952] 2 Q.B. 515.

of "building."[27] This also applies to moveable kiosks or stalls that are moved into their trading positions daily and into another position at night. They cannot be described as a building nor their erection as building operations.[28]

An erection of a canvas tent on tubular steel frames, 30 feet deep by 14 feet wide by a maximum height of 10½ feet, for storage (non-residential) purposes has been held to involve development as building operations. It was distinguished from "a tent or other temporary erection" because it was intended permanently to withstand weather conditions to a greater degree.[29]

The laying of hardcore to form a hardstanding or private roadway will generally amount to a building operation[30] and the formation or laying out of a means of access to a highway is automatically development because it is included in the definition of "engineering operations" in section 290(1) of the 1971 Act.

There have been some ministerial decisions on whether or not vending machines are regarded as building operations. Large milk vending machines installed on the forecourt of shops and secured by bolts to the ground have been held to be an operation constituting development.[31] Also, the erection of automatic cigarette machines which are to be permanent fixtures amount to development[32] but if the machines are moved out onto the forecourt of a shop daily and taken in at the end of the day's trading it is suggested that this would not be regarded by the courts as constituting a building or building operations.

DEMOLITION AND RE-BUILDING THE SHOP PREMISES

Demolition of the whole building

1.04   Demolition *per se* is not regarded as development.[33] An owner of retail premises who contemplates demolition of the entire building without re-building on the site does not require planning permission. This was expressed in Ministry of Environment Circular No. 67/49, para. 4(1) and in Development Control Policy Note No. 7 para. 3, dated 1969:

> "Demolition as such does not constitute development within the meaning of the Planning Acts and does not therefore need planning permission."

A demolition may, however, be sufficiently large or complex as to be

---

[27] *Guildford Rural District Council* v. *Fortesque* [1959] 2 Q.B. 112.
[28] See also [1954] J.P.L. 463/2.
[29] See also [1969] J.P.L. 592.
[30] See also: [1964] J.P.L. 358; [1966] J.P.L. 237; [1968] J.P.L. 168; [1972] J.P.L. 109 at 337.
[31] See also: [1960] J.P.L. 64; [1960] J.P.L. 443; [1963] J.P.L. 58; [1969] J.P.L. 415.
[32] See also [1960] J.P.L. 66.
[33] See, *e.g. Iddenden* v. *Secretary of State for the Environment* [1972] 1 W.L.R. 1443 where the demolition of some nissen huts was held not to constitute development.

properly regarded as an engineering operation. There is no precise answer to how large or complex it has to be to come within this definition. In *Coleshill and District Investment Co. Ltd.* v. *Minister of Housing and Local Government*,[34] walls and embankments around six buildings, four of which were 79 feet long, 38 feet wide and 11 feet high together with the two other smaller walls and embankments, were demolished. It was decided by the House of Lords that it amounted to an engineering operation.

Even though demolition is not generally covered by planning control, any person who intends to demolish the whole or part of a building (other than internal works, buildings of less than 1,750 cubic feet, greenhouses, conservatories and like buildings attached to larger buildings and agricultural buildings) must notify the local authority before commencing the work. Under section 80 of the Building Act 1984, the notice must be in writing specifying the works with a copy sent to:

> "(a) the occupier of any building adjacent to the building;
> (b) the British Gas Corporation; and
> (c) the Area Electricity Board in whose area the building is situated."

Demolition in pursuance of a Demolition Order made under the Housing Act 1985 is exempt from notification.

The local authority may serve a notice under section 81 of the 1984 Act on the person undertaking the demolition listing works to be done, such as, for example, shoring up adjacent buildings, sealing drains, and removing material or rubbish resulting from the demolition. The notice must be served within six weeks of the giving of the notice of demolition under section 80 of the 1984 Act, and demolition must not commence until either this notice is received or the six weeks has lapsed.

Specific controls exist over listed buildings and buildings in a conservation area.

Demolition and rebuilding
Demolishing and rebuilding the premises may be regarded as devel- **1.05**
opment if it can be contemplated as one operation (*London County Council* v. *Marks and Spencer*[35]). If not, the demolition work may not amount to development, assuming, of course, that it is not large or complex enough to come under the definition of engineering operation.

Demolition of part of a building
Demolition of part of a building may be considered as an alteration of **1.06**
the building as a whole and therefore, because it could be considered as a structural alteration to the building, it could be defined as a building

---

[34] [1969] 1 W.L.R. 746.
[35] [1953] A.C. 535.

operation and constitute development. This may be the case even where a whole large section of a building is demolished.

CHANGING THE TYPE OF BUSINESS BEING CARRIED ON

1.07   This comes under the second leg of the definition of development, material change of use. The general test is whether or not the proposed change in the use will completely alter the character of the land or building. In *Marshall* v. *Nottingham Corporation*[36] Glyn Jones J. said:

> "if the business of a retail dealer is being carried on in any building it may be that there is a change of use if, for example, the business of a baker is substituted for a different business, for example, that of a grocer; but I am unable to see why or how such a change can be material from any point of view which could legitimately be taken by a planning authority."

The Town and Country Planning (Use Classes) Order 1987[37] which revoked and replaced the Town and Country Planning (Use Classes) Order 1972[38] (as amended) lists different use classes. Where a building or other land is used for a purpose of any class mentioned, its use for any purpose of the same class is deemed not to involve development. Class A1 of the Schedule to the Order refers to shops and to nine types of retailing business where changing from one to another is not to be taken as redevelopment of the land. They are:

    (a) the retail sale of goods other than hot food;
    (b) a post office;
    (c) the sale of tickets or a travel agency;
    (d) the sale of sandwiches or other cold food for consumption off the premises;
    (e) hairdressing;
    (f) the direction of funerals;
    (g) the display of goods for sale;
    (h) the hiring out of domestic or personal goods or articles;
    (i) the reception of goods to be washed, cleaned or repaired

where the sale, display or service is to visiting members of the public.

In the 1972 Order pet shops, cats meat shops and tripe shops were excluded but these have now been included under (a) above and although premises used for the reception of goods for washing and cleansing are included, launderettes and dry cleaners are specifically excluded under article 3(6) of the 1987 Order. Also excluded under article 3(6) are shops used for the sale of motor cars and the use of

---

[36] [1960] 1 W.L.R. 707.
[37] S.I. 1987 No. 764.
[38] S.I. 1972 No. 1385.

premises as an amusement arcade or centre. Class I, para. 17 of Circular No. 13/87[39] states that:

> "in considering where individual uses fall it is the primary purpose that should be considered; a sandwich bar does not cease to be in the shops class merely because it also sells hot drinks, or if a few customers eat on the premises."

Class A3, the food and drink class, relates to the use of premises for the sale of food or drink for consumption on the premises or, if hot food, for consumption off the premises. Grouped together under this class are restaurants, wine bars, take-away shops, cafes, public houses and snack bars that serve hot food. It enables occupiers of such shops to react quickly to changing trends and demand. Also the effect on the surrounding environment by the use of premises within this class are similar *i.e.* similar problems with noise, litter and possibly the smell from the cooking of food may arise.

Under the Town and Country Planning General Development Order 1988[40] the following changes of use are permitted development, *i.e.* the changes are regarded as development but there is no need to apply to the local planning authority for planning permission:

(a) a change of the use of a building from Class A3 to Class A1;
(b) a change of use from the use for the sale or display of motor vehicles to Class A1.

The essential difference between the Use Classes Order and permitted development is that, under the latter, a planning authority has power under Article 4 of the General Development Order 1988[41] to direct at any time that certain permitted development rights conferred by Article 4 of the 1988 order be removed. This is with the Secretary of State's approval in certain circumstances. However, no such power exists under the Use Classes Order.

The sub-division of a planning unit into smaller units of the same class does not constitute a material change of use. An example of this would be the trend nowadays of dividing large retail stores that have become uneconomically viable into smaller shops or arcades. Until the Housing and Planning Act 1986 revised the wording of section 22(2) of the 1971 Act there was some uncertainty on this issue stemming principally from the decision in *Winton* v. *Secretary of State for the Environment*.[42] Now, provided that the resulting parts of the building or land are used for the same purpose as was the whole of the building or land prior to sub-division, it will not be regarded as development. Dwelling houses are not included in this exemption.

[39] Changes of Use of Buildings and other Land: Town and Country Planning (Use Classes) Order 1987.
[40] S.I. 1988 No. 1813.
[41] S.I. 1988 No. 1813.
[42] (1983) 46 P. & C.R. 205.

ADDING A NEW LINE OF BUSINESS

1.08 In the process of deciding whether or not a material change of use has occurred, a local authority must identify the planning unit. Normally this would be the whole of the area in the same occupation or ownership but if this is applied universally you would have a situation whereby a change of use in a small area of a very large planning unit would not be regarded as material whereas the same area of change in a small planning unit would; for example, changing a small part of a large departmental store into an office compared to converting a small shop into an office.

As a result, the courts have a flexible approach. In *Burdle* v. *Secretary of State for the Environment*,[43] Bridge J. suggested that it would be presumed that the unit of occupation is the appropriate planning unit but this presumption can be rebutted if there are separate "units of activity" within the primary unit. These must be shown to be geographically distinct and the activities unrelated to the adjoining area. Unrelated uses will not produce separate units without the sufficient degree of geographical separation. In *Brooks* v. *Gloucestershire County Council*[44] part of a manor house was used as a shop and restaurant. The whole was treated as a single unit even though the commercial activities were confined to certain rooms. Where there are, for example, three distinct areas of activities and one is intensified at the expense of another then there may be a material change of use of the premises.[45]

If a single primary use can be identified, such as a "retail shop" or a "hotel," then any number of ancillary or incidental uses may be included within that primary use. Any such use must be regarded as an activity which is ordinarily ancillary to a particular primary use such as the limited preparation for sale of articles in a retail shop. However, in *Hussain* v. *Secretary of State for the Environment*,[46] the ritual slaughter of chickens was held not to be incidental to such a use and in *Lydcare Ltd.* v. *Secretary of State for the Environment*[47-48] cubicles in a shop which were used for the viewing of films by inserting coins into automatic machines were not regarded as connected to the primary incidental use as a shop.

An ancillary use will not be regarded as such if the use is intensified or grows to such an extent as to become a separate unit. The provision of amusement machines can be taken as an example. Three or four may be ancillary, but if more were provided a separate unit may have been created. It must be remembered that a permit is required for amusement machines that give out prizes.[49-50]

[43] [1972] 1 W.L.R. 1207.
[44] (1967) 19 P. & C.R. 90.
[45] *Wipperman* v. *Barking London Borough Council* (1965) 17 P. & C.R. 225.
[46] (1971) 23 P. & C.R. 330.
[47-48] (1985) 84 L.G.R. 33.
[49-50] See Chap. 2, p. 43.

The placing of vending machines on the forecourt to a shop raises particular problems. The question of whether or not such machines come under the definition of "building operations" has been discussed earlier.[51] The point at issue here is whether the use of the machines in the forecourt is a material change of use. The answer, it seems, depends on the use of the premises to which the forecourt is attached. The installation of a milk-vending machine on the forecourt of a shop is not a material change of use, but if fixed and substantial, must be development as a building.[52] An egg-vending machine on the forecourt of a garage is a material change of use. It was considered at the inquiry that this type of machine should be contained within its fundamental retail sales category of a shopping use. The machine was moveable although of substantial size but it was not intended to be moved about the site and it would attract customers not necessarily concerned with the motoring service and introduce a noticeable different element of the use of the premises.[53]

CLOSING DOWN THE SHOP FOR A PERIOD AND THEN RESUMING

A retailer must be aware of the consequences of abandoning the use of **1.09** premises. The word "abandonment" does not appear in planning legislation but a doctrine has been established through case law that where all the evidence points to the fact that existing rights use (*i.e.* rights other than those arising under planning permission) has been abandoned the premises are left with a "nil" use and any resumption of the previous use will require planning permission. The vast majority of uses derive from planning permission, therefore it must be emphasised at this point that the doctrine and practice of abandonment is virtually non-existent; see *Pioneer Aggregates (U.K.) Ltd.* v. *Secretary of State for the Environment* [1985] A.C. 132.

Lord Denning explained the doctrine in *Hartley* v. *Minister of Housing and Local Government*[54]:

> "The question in all such cases is simply this: Has the cessation of use (followed by non-use) been merely temporary or did it amount to an abandonment? If it was merely temporary, the previous use can be resumed without planning permission being obtained. If it amounted to abandonment, it cannot be resumed unless planning permission is obtained. . . . Abandonment depends on the circumstances. If the land has remained unused for a considerable time in such circumstances that a reasonable man might conclude that the

---

[51] See p. 6.
[52] See also [1960] J.P.L. 443.
[53] See also [1962] J.P.L. 749.
[54] [1970] 1 Q.B. 413.

previous use had been abandoned, then the tribunal might hold it to have been abandoned."

In this case, premises had been used up until 1961 for two purposes, as a petrol filling station and for the display and sale of cars. The owner died in 1961 and his widow and son aged 19 continued the business but sold petrol only, not cars. The part previously used for selling cars remained unused and in 1965 the property was sold and the new owner started a car sales business, selling approximately 350 cars a year. The local authority served an enforcement notice stating that there had been a material change of use in the land. It was held by the court that by 1965 the former use of the site for car sales had been abandoned.

The court took the following into account:

(1) the period of discontinuance and non-use;
(2) the physical condition and fittings of the building; and
(3) the evidence as to the intention of its owners.[55]

The intention of the owners is an important factor to be considered, nevertheless it must be looked at from an objective and not a subjective point of view. The fact that the court takes cognisance of a subjective change of intention in altering a person's planning rights, albeit that they must look at it from a reasonable man's point of view, seems to deviate from the general scheme of development control that planning rights are altered by actual physical events.

The doctrine does not apply to a situation where one use has been followed by another without interruption.[56] A reversion to the old use may be a material change of use and require planning permission except where the reversion is as a result of compliance with an enforcement notice in respect of the new use.[57]

Further, as mentioned earlier the doctrine does not apply to rights gained as the result of planning permission. Section 33(1) of the 1971 Act provides that, without prejudice to any revocation or modification, planning permission to develop land, once granted, will enure for the benefit of the land, unless the permission itself otherwise provides. Planning permission is subject to statutory time limits[58] and such rights can only be lost if these limits are expired or:

(1) the permission has been revoked by an order under section 45 of the 1971 Act; or
(2) if the carrying out of some earlier development under a differ-

---

[55] See also [1978] J.P.L. 651.
[56] *Young* v. *Secretary of State for the Environment* [1983] J.P.L. 465 at 468, *per* Watkins L.J. This was a Court of Appeal decision which was upheld in the House of Lords: [1983] A.C. 662.
[57] Town and Country Planning Act 1971, s.23(9).
[58] *Ibid.* ss.41–44; Sched. 24, paras. 18–22.

ent permission has made it impossible to carry out the development permitted by the permission under consideration.[59]

Lord Frazer of Tullybelton in *Pioneer Aggregates (U.K.) Ltd.* v. *Secretary of State for the Environment*[59a] said, "Planning control is the creature of statute . . . It is a field of law in which courts should not introduce principles or rules derived from private law unless it be expressly authorised by Parliament, or necessary, in order to give effect to the purpose of the legislation." Referring to section 33(1) of the 1971 Act he said, "the clear implication is that only the statute or the terms of the planning permission itself can stop the permission enuring for the benefit of the land and of all the persons for the time being interested therein."

DISPLAY OF ADVERTISEMENTS

Control by the district council over the display of advertisements is by **1.10** means of the Town and Country Planning (Control of Advertisement) Regulations 1989[60] and sections 63, 64, 109 and 109A of the 1971 Act. Although the use for the display of advertisements on any external part of a building which is not normally used for that purpose is to be treated as a material change of use of that part of the building,[61] section 64 of the 1971 Act provides that the requisite planning permission is granted, provided the advertisement complies with the 1989 Regulations *i.e.* planning permission is not required. The content or subject matter of advertisements cannot be controlled under the 1989 Regulations. This is implied by regulation 4 which states that advertisements are subject to control only in the interests of "amenity" and "public safety."

"Advertisement" is defined in section 290 of the 1971 Act as meaning:

> "any word, letter, model, sign, placard, board, notice, device or representation, whether illuminated or not, in the nature of, and employed wholly or partly for the purpose of, advertisement, announcement or direction and (without prejudice to the preceding provisions of this definition) includes any boarding or similar structure or any balloon used, or adapted for use, for the display of advertisements, and references to the display of advertisements shall be construed accordingly."

Anything employed wholly as a memorial or a railway signal is excluded.[61a]

The 1989 Regulations apply to the display of all advertisements on

---

[59] *Pilkington* v. *Secretary of State for the Environment* [1973] 1 W.L.R. 1527.
[59a] [1985] A.C. 132.
[60] S.I. 1989 No. 670.
[61] Town and Country Planning Act 1971, s.22(4).
[61a] 1989 Regulations, reg. 2(1).

land (which includes buildings, and land covered with water) other than advertisements[61b]:

(a) displayed on enclosed land and not readily visible from outside the enclosure, or from any part of it over which the public have a right of way or right of access;

(b) displayed within a building (this is subject to the special control over certain advertisements inside a building but visible from outside the building;

(c) displayed on or in a vehicle or vessel, unless it is being used primarily for the display of advertisements (rather than for conveying people or goods);

(d) displayed on a balloon being flown at a height exceeding 60 metres above ground level for a maximum of 10 days in any calender year as long as it is not in certain designated areas;

(e) incorporated in, and forming part of, the fabric of a building (*e.g.* incised stonework lettering);

(f) relating to goods for sale, their containers or dispensers (these advertisements are exempt from control only if they are not illuminated and not more than 0.1 square metres in area)

Also exempt are advertisements relating to elections, those required by Standing Orders of either House of Parliament or by any enactment, traffic signs, and the display of any national flag.

Apart from the foregoing advertisements that are not subject to control, all other advertisements, in areas other than areas of special control[62] must either have "deemed consent" or "express consent" granted by a local planning authority or by the Secretary of State.

Schedule 3, Part 1 to the 1989 Regulations contains a list of specified classes of the advertisements together with conditions and limitations which may be displayed with "deemed consent," with no necessity to apply for a local planning authority's "express consent." Briefly they are:

Class 1   Functional advertisements of local authorities, statutory undertakers and public transport undertakers, *e.g.* public footpath signs, bus stop signs and railway station signs, etc.

Class 2   Miscellaneous advertisements relating to premises on which they are displayed, *e.g.* direction signs, warning signs, trade plates, etc.

Class 3   Advertisements of a temporary nature, *e.g.* "for sale" signs.

[61b] All exempted classes of advertisements are contained in the 1989 Regulations, Sched. 2.

[62] Local planning authorities are under a duty to consider, from time to time, whether any part of their area should be defined in an area of special control: 1989 Regulations, (reg. 18). In these areas, conservation areas, National Parks and areas of outstanding natural beauty the display of advertisements is restricted.

Class 4   Illuminated advertisements on business premises in retail parks and elsewhere where the advertisement refers wholly to the business carried on and the name and qualifications of the person carrying on a business from those premises. Where, for example, one company's product is sold from premises, as with a main dealer, the name of the company can be advertised under this class. However, if goods supplied by different companies are sold from premises such as a newsagent or tobacconist, a product-sponsored advertisement of any one of the companies will require the local planning authority's "express consent."
No advertisement is permitted under this class within a conservation area, an area of outstanding natural beauty, a National Park, an area of special control or the Broads.

Class 5   Advertisements (other than illuminated advertisements) on business premises. These advertisements must refer wholly to the business carried on, the goods sold or services provided and the name and qualification of the person carrying on the business or activity, or supplying such goods or services on those premises. Also, no advertisements may be displayed on a wall of a shop unless the wall contains a shop window, and the advertisement cannot be displayed so that the highest part of the advertisement is above the level of the bottom of any first floor window in the wall on which it is displayed.

Class 6   An advertisement displayed on any forecourt of business premises, wholly with reference to all or any of the matters specified in Class 5.

Class 7   Flag advertisements. A flag bearing only the name or device of the person occupying the building. This is to be attached to a single flagstaff fixed in an upright position on the roof of the building.

Class 8   Certain advertisements displayed on hoardings enclosing building operations.

Class 9   Advertisements on highway structures.

Class 10   Advertisements for neighbourhood watch and similar schemes.

Class 11   Directional advertisements.

Class 12   An advertisement displayed inside a building which does not fall within Class J in Schedule 2 of the 1989 Regulations.

Class 13   An advertisement displayed on a site which was used for the display of advertisements without express consent on April 1, 1974 and has been so used continually since that date.

Class 14   An advertisement displayed with express consent, after the expiry of that consent, unless
(a) a condition to the contrary was imposed on the consent; or
(b) a renewal of consent was applied for and refused.

Standard conditions attached to consents granted or deemed consents are contained in Schedule 2, to the 1989 Regulations. These relate to keeping the advertisements safe, reasonably clean and tidy and where express consent is not required the advertisement may only be displayed so as not to conflict with a signal or traffic sign of any sort, or otherwise to endanger the use of any road, railway, waterway or airfield. On an application for express consent these factors will be taken into account. Also, in an attempt to deal effectively with fly-posting, a standard condition has been included that no advertisement is to be displayed without the permission of the owner of the site or any other person with an interest in the site entitled to grant permission.

A booklet entitled "Outdoor Advertisement and Signs" is produced by the Department of the Environment and is available from local planning authorities' offices. It is a useful and comprehensive guide to the advertisement control system.

CHAPTER 2

ACTIVITIES REQUIRING A LICENCE OR PERMIT
SELLING MILK

General

Activities requiring a licence or permit are both numerous and **2.01** diverse. They range from the selling of milk to the selling, hiring etc. of "sex articles," and the requirements necessary in providing music, dancing and other entertainment for the public.

This section will concentrate on that area of the law which affects the shopkeeper and which is administered by district councils, *i.e.* that part of consumer legislation relating to milk, milk production and processing is not covered. The law is contained in the Food Act 1984 and the following regulations made thereunder and under the Food and Drugs Act 1955, *i.e.* the Milk and Dairies (General) Regulations 1959,[1] and the Milk (Special Designation) Regulations 1988.[2]

The Milk and Dairies (General) Regulations contain provisions regarding the general conditions under which milk can be sold, handled, stored and conveyed and includes a section which specifies that all dairies and distributors of milk must be registered. The Milk (Special Designation) Regulations define milk of special designation and outlines the types of licences required in order to deal in or distribute such milk and the conditions applicable thereto.

Definition of milk

There are no less than five definitions of milk contained in the rel- **2.02** evant legislation:

Legislation	*Definition*	*Activity to which the definition refers*
Food Act 1984, s. 33(2)(*b*)	In the foregoing subsection except in paragraph (*o*) "milk" means[3] milk intended for sale or sold for human consumption, or intended for manufacture for sale for human consumption.[4]	The hygienic handling storage and conveyance of milk.

[1] S.I. 1959 No. 277 as amended by S.I.s 1962 No. 1288, 1973 No. 1064, 1977 No. 171, 1979 No. 1567, 1983 No. 1703 and Circ. 85/68.
[2] S.I. 1988 No. 2204.
[3] It has been held that the word "means" has the effect of excluding everything apart from that mentioned. *R.* v. *Kershaw* (1856) 6 E. and B. 999, *per* Erle J.
[4] The subsection referred to lists the activities that may be the subject of regulations called the "Milk and Dairies Regulations." The Minister made the Milk and Dairies (General) Regulations 1959 under a similar section contained in the Food and Drugs Act 1955.

Legislation	Definition	Activity to which the definition refers
Milk and Dairies (General) Regulations 1959, reg. 2	In these regulations, unless the contrary intention appears "milk" means cow's milk intended for sale or sold for human consumption and includes cream, skimmed milk and separated milk.	The hygienic handling storage and conveyance of milk.
Food Act 1984, s. 47	In ss. 39, 40, 41, 42, 43, 44, 45 and 46, in this section (s. 47) and in Scheds. 4 and 5, except where the context otherwise requires— "milk" means cow's milk, excluding not only condensed milk and dried milk, but also cream and separated, skimmed and evaporated milk, and buttermilk.	Use of special designation in the sale of milk in specified areas (now the whole of England and Wales).
Milk (Special Designation) Regulations 1988, reg. 2(1)	In these regulations unless the context otherwise requires "milk" means cow's milk, but does not include cream, or separated, skimmed, dried, condensed or evaporated milk or buttermilk.	The granting of licences and dealing and distributing milk of special designation.
Food Act 1984, s. 132(1)	In this Act, unless the context otherwise requires, and without prejudice to s. 47 of this Act, "milk" includes cream and separated milk but does not include dried milk or condensed milk.	All other activities mentioned in the 1984 Act relating to milk, e.g. sale of milk from diseased cows (s. 35) and adulteration of milk (s. 36).

The principal difference in the definitions is that with regard to the regulations relating to the hygienic handling, storage and conveyance of milk, milk includes cream, skimmed milk and separated milk but under

the regulations relating to the granting of licences for dealing and distributing milk of special designation, cream, separated, skimmed, dried,
condensed, evaporated or butter milk are not included.

Milk is not excluded from the definition of "food" under section 131(1)
of the 1984 Act and, therefore, the general requirements of the Food
Hygiene (General) Regulations 1970[5] apply to milk in addition to the
specific regulations referred to.

Registration of milk distributors

There is a separate chapter in this book on activities requiring registra-   **2.03**
tion but it is felt that registration of milk distributors can be more conveniently dealt with in this section.

Any person who wishes to be a distributor of milk must make an application in writing to the local authority to be registered, and he must not
carry on the trade of distributor unless he is so registered.[6] The 1959
Regulations also state that premises within their district being used as
dairies, not being dairy farms, must be registered by the local authority,
but although a retailer of milk is included within the definition of distributor,[7] a shop is not included within the definition of dairy. Therefore, a
shopkeeper wishing to sell milk need only make an application for registration of himself as distributor.

Subject to the provisions of Part I of the Second Schedule to the Food
Act 1984, the local authority shall register such persons. Part I contains
provisions regarding the procedure to be adopted where it appears to
the registering authority that public health is, or is likely to be endan-
gered by any act or default of a person who has applied to be or is registered by the authority. The act or default must be in relation to the
quality, storage or distribution of milk and it is considered that the registration of the *dairyman* be refused or cancelled as the case may be. This
part of the schedule refers to a dairyman but it can be seen from the following definitions that it refers to a distributor of milk and therefore the
retailer of milk.

"Dairyman" includes an occupier of a dairy, a cow-keeper and a *purveyor of milk*.[8] "Distributor" means a *person trading as a dairyman* elsewhere than from premises in relation to which he is registered as a dairy
farmer under these Regulations but does not include:

(1) the Milk Marketing Board, except where they are trading at or
from premises where milk is handled by them; or
(2) any purveyor of cream in the hermetically sealed containers in
which it is delivered to his premises provided that such a purveyor is not otherwise a purveyor of milk.[9]

---

[5] S.I. 1970 No. 1172.
[6] M. & D. (Gen.) Regulations 1959, reg. 8.
[7] *Ibid.* reg. 2(1).
[8] *Ibid.*
[9] *Ibid.*

The sale of milk of special designation

2.04   After registration with the local authority as a distributor of milk, the shopkeeper has to decide what special designation milk he intends to sell. The special designations[10] are:

(1) Untreated;
(2) Pasteurised;
(3) Sterilised;
(4) Ultra Heat Treated.

The shopkeeper must apply in writing to the licensing authority for a licence to use a special designation.[11] The authority may refuse to grant a licence (whether in renewal of an existing licence or not) if they are not satisfied that the applicant's arrangements and processes for the handling, treatment, storage or distribution of milk are such as to comply with all relevant provisions contained in any Milk and Dairies Regulations and the Milk (Special Designation) Regulations.[12]

Section 40 of the Food Act 1984 provides that the use of special designations is obligatory with regard to retail sales in "specified areas," but as the whole of England and Wales now comprises of specified areas, milk cannot be sold by retail unless it is milk of special designation. Where milk or milk products are sold as, or as part of, a meal this is regarded as a catering sale[13] and, under section 41 of the 1984 Act, it is lawful only if the caterer bought the milk under a sale for the purpose of which a special designation was used, or if he holds a licence authorising him to use a special designation in connection with the milk, whether the designation is used for the purpose of the catering sale or not.

There are two forms of licence; (a) a dealer's licence; and (b) an untreated milk distributor's licence. Every dealer's licence granted before December 31, 1990 can only run until this date. The expiry date after this is every fifth succeeding year, *e.g.* December 31, 1995, December 31, 2000, so that licences granted within these five year periods will all expire on the same date.[14] Every untreated milk distributor's licence granted continues until October 31, 1991 and expires every third year from that date, *e.g.* October 31, 1994, October 31, 1997.[15]

Breach of any condition contained in Schedule 5 to the 1984 Act makes a holder of a licence guilty of an offence under section 45 of the 1984 Act. There is a restriction on liability in certain cases under section 46 of the 1984 Act. Provisions regarding refusal, suspension and revocation of dealers' licences and untreated milk distributors' licences are

---

[10] M. (S.D.) Regulations 1988, reg. 3.
[11] *Ibid.* reg. 4.
[12] *Ibid.* reg. 5.
[13] Food Act 1984, s.47.
[14] M. (S.D.) Regulations 1988, reg. 15(1).
[15] *Ibid.* reg. 13(1).

contained in Part VII of the Milk (Special Designations) Regulations 1988.

General conditions subject to which licences are granted

The business must be so operated so as to comply with the Milk and **2.05** Dairies Regulations and the Milk (Special Designation) Regulations, and the milk shall not be referred to for purpose of sale or advertisement by any such description (other than the special designation authorised by the licence) as is likely to suggest that it is tested, approved or graded by any competent person.

The shopkeeper must keep accurate records of the quantities of milk purchased and sold otherwise than by retail and the name and addresses of the persons from whom the milk was purchased. These records must be kept for a period of 12 months from the date of the transaction, and any person duly authorised by the licensing authority, usually the local environmental health officer, is permitted to inspect the premises and the records and take samples of the milk.[16]

Dealer's licence

"Dealer's licence" means a licence granted to any person to use the **2.06** special designations "Pasteurised," "Sterilised" or "Ultra Heat Treated" in relation to milk sold by him; not being milk sold, or appropriate to be sold, by him in accordance with the terms of a producer's licence or of an untreated milk distributor's licence; and "licensed dealer" means a person to whom a dealer's licence has been granted.[17]

Every dealer's licence shall be granted under the Milk (Special Designation) Regulations by the local authority for the area within which are situated the premises from which the milk is to be sold and in the application the applicant shall state the name and address of each person from whom he proposes to obtain the milk.[17a] The licensed dealer shall be subject to the condition that should he receive untreated milk from a producer he must either immediately subject that milk to heat treatment or, if he has not the facilities at his premises, dispatch it, either by sale or otherwise to such premises that have the proper facilities. Also, the licence must contain a condition that when milk is transferred from one container to another, the milk must be subjected to heat treatment as soon as practicable after the first container is opened. The latter condition would not normally affect the average shopkeeper.[18]

In addition of the general conditions, special conditions applicable to the use of pasteurised, sterilised and ultra heat treated milk are set out in Schedule 4 to the 1988 Regulations. Detailed conditions as to sampling and labelling are contained in Schedules 5 and 6 respectively.

[16] *Ibid.* Sched. 1, reg. 6.
[17] *Ibid.* reg. 2(1).
[17a] *Ibid.* reg. 14(2).
[18] *Ibid.* Sched. 3.

Untreated milk distributor's licence

2.07   This licence is defined in regulation 2 of the 1988 Regulations as meaning a licence granted to any person to use the special designation "untreated" in relation to farm bottled milk sold by him, not being sold, or appropriate to be sold, by him in accordance with the terms of a dealer's licence or of a producer's licence; and "licensed untreated milk distributor" means a person to whom an untreated milk distributor's licence has been granted.

The licence is in respect of farm bottled milk which is also defined in regulation 2 as meaning untreated milk which has been produced from a herd owned or controlled by a licensed producer and bottled, or placed in cartons, or other containers at the place of production.

There has been much concern in recent years about outbreaks of communicable diseases that have been attributable to raw, unprocessed milk and the sale of this milk has been generally prohibited in Scotland. However, the licence is subject to restrictive conditions and a recent circular letter (August 1989) from the Ministry of Agriculture, Fisheries and Food stated that in order to further minimise the risk to public health amendments to the 1988 Regulations are proposed in 1990. These will principally concern labelling and sampling.

The distributor cannot sell the milk from a shop or sell it as, or part of, a meal or refreshment and it is only allowed to be sold to the ultimate consumer who is defined under Schedule 6 to the 1988 Regulations, as any person who buys otherwise than: (a) for the purpose of resale; (b) for the purposes of a catering establishment; or (c) for the purposes of a manufacturing business. Therefore, a shopkeeper would not be interested in this type of licence.[20]

Other specific conditions applicable to this licence are that the licensed untreated milk distributor must only sell the milk from the producer mentioned in his licence and prepacked by that producer in containers not exceeding 1.25 litres capacity. Also the milk must be sold in the containers in which he receives it with the bottle caps or other fastenings unbroken.[21]

In addition, Schedule 2 to the 1988 Regulations, contains conditions applicable to producer's licences and untreated milk distributors' licences which include *inter alia* that the milk must come from an accredited herd[22] and that it must not have been treated by heat or in any manner likely to affect its nature or qualities.

---

[20] *Ibid.* Sched. 2.

[21] *Ibid.*

[22] "Accredited herd" means a herd which to the satisfaction of the Minister has either: (a) been found to be free from brucellosis by means of a series of diagnostic tests carried out by him or on his behalf and has been, since the date of commencement of the tests, the subject of adequate precautions against the introduction or re-introduction and consequent spreading of brucellosis; or (b) been wholly constituted by the transfer of animals from other accredited herds in Great Britain or from such similar herds outside

The handling, storage and conveyance of milk

Standards of hygiene are laid down in the Milk and Dairies (General)   **2.08**
Regulations 1959 (as amended) and the licences mentioned above are
issued subject to the condition that such standards are complied with.

Milk must not be handled or stored in any place where it is liable to
become contaminated or infected and in particular it is not to be handled or stored:

    (a) in any room used as a kitchen, scullery, living-room or sleep-
        ing-room; or

    (b) in any room or part of a building which communicates directly
        by door, window or otherwise with:

        (i) any sanitary convenience, cesspool or receptacle for ashes
            or other refuse, or a boiler house or fuel store or a room in
            which an internal combustion engine is operated unless
            the exhaust is discharged into the external air;

        (ii) any room which is used as a sleeping-room or any room
            which is occupied by a person suffering from a notifiable
            disease; or

    (c) in any room or part of a building in which there is any direct
        inlet to a drain which is not suitably and properly trapped.[23]

The interior furniture and fittings of any building or room in which
milk is handled or stored should be kept thoroughly clean. Except in a
building or part of a building used solely or mainly for retail sale, floors
should be impervious and sloped to a trapped drain and walls subject to
splashing should be smooth and impervious. These should be cleansed
with water at least once in every day.[24] No foul or noxious matter or
soiled bed or body clothing shall be conveyed through any part of a
building used for the keeping or storage of milk.

No articles other than the following may be deposited in a milk room,
i.e. a room where milk is handled or stored *but excluding shops*:

    (a) milk and milk products;

    (b) articles used in connection with the handling, storage and dis-
        tribution of milk and milk products;

    (c) ice-cream.

No milk room should be used for any purpose other than the handling
of milk, milk products, ice-cream and ancillary food products in their
final retail containers.[25] Animals and poultry must not be kept in a milk
room or a room where milk is handled or stored or any connecting

---

Great Britain as the Minister may either generally or in any special case allow, and has
been, since being so constituted, the subject of such precautions as aforesaid. M. (S.D.)
Regulations 1988, reg. 2(1).

[23] M. & D. (Gen.) Regulations 1959, reg. 21.
[24] *Ibid.* reg. 14.
[25] *Ibid.* reg. 21.

room.[26] Bandages, dressing and antiseptics must be provided for first aid treatment.[27]

The National Dairymen's Association and the Institution of Environmental Health Officers have approved guidelines, based on the 1959 Regulations, to ensure that high standards of hygiene and service are maintained and improved within the distributive side of the milk industry. As milk retailers now tend to deliver to the door other goods besides milk such as potatoes, eggs and fruit juice, the guidelines have allowed for the storage of ancillary food products, pre-packed in their final retail containers in a milk store.

The provisions relating to the cleansing and storage of vessels, utensils and appliances are contained in Part IX of the 1959 Regulations. A point of general interest to retailers who are also distributors of milk was discussed in *United Dairies (London) Ltd.* v. *Beckingham Corporation and E. Fisher and Sons Ltd.*[28] Regulation 27(1) of the 1959 Regulations states that every dairy farmer or distributor shall ensure that every vessel (including the lid) used for containing milk shall, immediately before such use by him, be in a state of thorough cleanliness. In this case, an untreated milk distributor bought "farm bottled milk" from a farmer who had, in accordance with the regulations, bottled and capped the milk on the farm. It was raw, untreated milk and one of the bottles was found to contain ash, probably from a cigarette. This was distributed to a customer and the distributor was charged under regulation 27(1) with failing to ensure that a bottle used for containing milk immediately before such use by them was in a state of thorough cleanliness.

There were two points of issue. First, if a milk container which is sold by a distributor is unclean, is the distributor liable under regulation 27(1), and, secondly, if he is liable could the distributor use the third party proceedings under section 113 of the Food and Drugs Act 1955 (now section 100 of the Food Act 1984)?[29]

Although the distributor preferred an information under section 113 of the Food and Drugs Act 1955 against the farmer, the justices dismissed the information and convicted the distributor. The distributor appealed and it was contended by the respondents that the word "use" in regulation 27(1) of the 1959 Regulations had a wider meaning than merely use for containing milk and that it applies to any point of time when the bottle is being used for whatever purpose. It was submitted that the appellant used the bottle at all times from the moment the driver collected the full crate containing the bottles from the third parties' yard until it was delivered to the customer, and that the obligation as regards cleanliness persisted throughout that period.

This contention was not accepted by the court. Lord Parker of Wadd-

---

[26] *Ibid.* 24(2).
[27] *Ibid.* reg. 22(5).
[28] [1963] 1 Q.B. 434.
[29] See p. 160.

ington C.J. stated that the words in regulation 27(1) appear to have a plain meaning. They are, in his view, dealing with the point in time immediately before the bottle is filled, and the obligation is placed upon the person responsible for the filling of the bottle.

The conviction was quashed and therefore it was unnecessary to consider whether third party proceedings applied to a charge under the regulation. However, as the matter was fully argued Lord Parker expressed an opinion, *obiter dicta*, that there is a clear difference between proceedings brought for offences against the Food and Drugs Act 1955, and proceedings brought for offences against regulations made under the Act, and the third party procedure under section 113 of the 1955 Act, unless specifically incorporated into the regulation in question, does not apply to proceedings brought charging offences against the regulations.

In *South Coast Dairies Ltd.* v. *Halstead*,[30] regulation 27(1) was again considered in relation to a milk bottle containing a sterile foreign body, *i.e.* a broken foil cap. The appellant company who were distributors of milk were convicted of an offence under regulation 27(1) in that they did not ensure that a milk bottle was, immediately before use by them, in a state of thorough cleanliness. The appellant company submitted that regulation 27(1) was inapt to deal with the presence of a foreign body and that if any offence had been committed in this case it would be an offence under section 2 of the Food and Drugs Act 1955.[31] The court did not accept that argument and held that the justices were right in convicting the company. Lord Parker stated:

> " . . . As a matter of common sense it seems to me that you cannot say a bottle is thoroughly cleansed if it contains some foreign body, albeit that that foreign body is itself clear in the sense of being free from germs. . . . "

In the sale, conveyance or distribution of milk, the retailer must ensure, as far as is practicable, that the milk is not exposed unnecessarily to heat and protected from contamination by dirt, dust and rainwater. In particular, he must not leave, or cause[32] to be left, bottles or cartons of milk on a public highway except on final delivery and if he is leaving the milk for a length of time awaiting collection or further conveyance he must protect it from the direct rays of the sun.[33]

When a vehicle is being used for conveying milk it must be kept clean and no live animal or bird likely to contaminate the milk must be conveyed in the vehicle at the same time. If the vehicle has been used for

---

[30] (1963) 128 J.P. 242.

[31] Now Food Act 1984, s.2 (see p. 151).

[32] "The word cause was to be given its ordinary common sense meaning and any attempts to introduce refinements was to be depreciated," McCullough J. in *Wrothwell (F.J.H.)* v. *Yorkshire Water Authority* [1984] Crim.L.R. 43, C.A.

[33] M. & D. (Gen.) Regulations 1959, reg. 31.

the conveyance of offensive matter it must be thoroughly cleansed and purified before being used for the conveyance of milk.[34]

If milk is sold, or offered or exposed for sale, from a stall or vehicle in a street or place of public resort, the name and address of the retailer must be conspicuously displayed on the vehicle or stall. If it is not displayed he will be liable to a penalty not exceeding £200 if convicted of this offence.[35]

If any person contravenes or fails to comply with any of the provisions of the Milk and Dairies (General) Regulations 1959 he shall be guilty of an offence, and shall, except where a smaller penalty is provided by the regulations, be liable on summary conviction to a fine not exceeding level 3 on the standard scale or to imprisonment for a term not exceeding three months, or to both. In the case of a continuing offence, he shall be liable to a further fine, not exceeding level 3 on the standard scale, for each day during which the offence continues after conviction.

Goat's milk

2.09   No licence is needed for the sale, handling or storage of goat's milk. However, as it is a food it is subject to the hygiene and other relevant consumer protection provisions of the Food Act 1984 and the Food Hygiene (General) Regulations 1970. The reason why no licence is required is probably because the milk is not produced at present on a sufficiently large enough scale to attract specific legislation. A useful booklet containing a Code of Practice on the Hygienic Control of Goat's Milk may be obtained free of charge from the Department of Agriculture and Fisheries for Scotland, Chesser House, Gorgie Road, Edinburgh EH11 3AW.

SELLING GAME

2.10   A licence is required from the district council, the London borough councils or the Common Council of the City of London, as the case may be, to sell game. Not only must the retailer obtain a game licence from the local authority under section 18 of the Game Act 1831 but he must also obtain an excise licence under section 14 of the Game Licenses Act 1860. The excise licence is also issued by the local authority and is normally issued by the Post Office as agent for the authorities and is valid for 12 months.

Originally, when the 1831 Act was passed, the responsibility of issuing licences rested with the local justices of the peace but this jurisdiction was given to the local authorities by section 179 of the Local Government Act 1972, the Local Government Act 1894, section 27 and the London Government (Public General Acts) Order 1965.[36]

---

[34] *Ibid.* reg. 32.
[35] *Ibid.* reg. 33.
[36] S.I. 1965 No. 602.

"Game" is defined under section 2 of the 1831 Act as deemed to include hares, pheasants, partridges, grouse, heath or moor game and black game. The licence must be renewed annually, expiring on July 31 in every year.[37]

Section 18 of the 1831 Act lists persons who may be granted a licence and those who may not. A licence can be issued to a householder or any person who keeps a shop or stall within the district council's area. Those who may not be granted a licence are:

    (a) inn-keepers (except that they may sell it for consumption on the premises as long as he has obtained it from a person holding a licence)[38];

    (b) victuallers, *i.e.* grocers;

    (c) persons licensed to sell beer by retail; and

    (d) the owner, guard or driver of any mail coach or other vehicle employed in the conveyance of the mail of letters, or of any stage coach, stage wagon, van or other public conveyance, not being a carrier or higgler, nor being in the employment of any of the above-mentioned persons.

The licence holder must buy the game from a person who can lawfully sell it and must affix to some part of the outside of the front of the shop, house or stall a board with his christian name and surname on it together with the words, "licensed to deal in game."[39]

Any person who unlawfully sells game or offers game for sale is liable to a fine not exceeding level 1 on the standard scale for each head of game plus costs,[40] and any person who deals in game without holding an excise licence may be liable to a fine not exceeding level 2 on the standard scale.[41]

SELLING PET ANIMALS

General requirements

The Pet Animals Act 1951 (as amended by the Pet Animals Act 1951 **2.11** (Amendment) Act 1983) enables local district councils to control the welfare of animals, so that no person shall keep a pet shop except under the authority of a licence granted under the Act.

The selling or keeping of animals as pets is construed in the case of cats and dogs as selling or keeping wholly or mainly for domestic purposes and, with regard to other animals selling or keeping for ornamental purposes. An "animal" includes any description of vertebrate.[42]

The keeping of a pet shop involves the carrying on at premises of any

---

[37] Game Act 1831, s.18.
[38] *Ibid.* s.26.
[39] *Ibid.* s.18.
[40] Game Act 1831, s.25, as amended by the Criminal Justice Act 1982, ss.38, 46.
[41] Game Licences Act 1860, s.14, as amended by the Criminal Justices Act 1982, ss.38, 46.
[42] Pet Animals Act 1951, s.7.

nature (including a private dwelling) the business of selling animals as pets, and it includes keeping animals in such premises with a view to their being sold in the course of such a business, whether by their keeper or any other person. It does not, however, include a situation where a person is breeding pedigree animals for sale as pets or where such a person has pedigree animals which have become unsuitable for breeding or showing, as the case may be, and which are sold as pets.[43]

In *Chalmers* v. *Diwell*,[44] the respondent ran an exporting business from his home. He exported birds, mainly birds of the parrot family, and although he kept them at his home for a time before exporting (this period rarely exceeded 48 hours), members of the public did not come to his house to buy birds. The local authority charged him with keeping a pet shop without a licence, but the justices took the view that he was not operating a pet shop and dismissed the information. The local authority appealed and the appeal was allowed. Lawson J. said:

> " . . . It is to be noted that the question does not in fact recite what the offence is. It is not operating a pet shop, and it may well be that the justices misled themselves by looking at the question whether a shop was being operated rather than the question of whether a shop was being kept. . . . In my judgment on the facts found by the justices it is quite clear that the defendant here is in fact carrying on a business of selling animals and pets. He is in fact keeping those pets on the premises for the purposes of his business, even though it be for a limited time. . . . "

In determining whether or not to grant a licence, the local authority must have regard to certain considerations. The considerations are the need for securing that:

(a) animals will at all times be kept in accommodation suitable as respects size, temperature, lighting, ventilation and cleanliness;

(b) the animals will be adequately supplied with suitable food and drink and (so far as necessary) visited at suitable intervals;

(c) animals, being mammals, will not be sold at too early an age;

(d) all reasonable precautions will be taken to prevent the spread among animals of infectious diseases;

(e) appropriate steps will be taken in case of fire or other emergency.[45]

Any of the above may be specified as conditions on the licence if the local authority considers it necessary. This may arise as a result of an inspection and recommendations of an environmental health officer, a

---

[43] *Ibid.* s.7(1)(*a*), (*b*).
[44] (1975) 74 L.G.R. 173.
[45] Pet Animals Act 1951, s.1(3).

veterinary practitioner or a surgeon. They must be authorised in writing by the local authority to enter such premises to make inspections.[46]

Even if the local authority is satisfied that the above considerations are fulfilled it is still open to them to refuse to grant a licence on any other ground.

If a local authority refuses to grant a licence, the applicant may appeal to a court of summary jurisdiction having jurisdiction over the area in which the premises are situated and the court may give such directions, with respect to the issue of the licence or conditions attached to the licence, as they think proper.[47]

The licence remains in force from the beginning of the day on which it is granted to the end of that calendar year.[48]

Offences and penalties

It shall be an offence to keep a pet shop without a licence and to **2.12** breach any condition attached to the licence granted. It is also an offence to sell an animal as a pet to a person, if the person selling the animal has reasonable cause to believe the purchaser to be under 12 years of age.

Any person guilty of an offence shall be liable, on summary conviction, to a fine not exceeding level 2 on the standard scale or to imprisonment for a term not exceeding three months, or both. If a person is convicted of an offence under this Act, or of any offence under the Protection of Animals Act 1911, the court may cancel his licence and disqualify him from keeping a pet shop for such period as the court thinks fit.[49]

Pet Animals Act 1951 (Amendment) Act 1983

This Act came into force on November 9, 1983 and amended the Pet **2.13** Animals Act 1951 so as to prohibit the sale of pet animals in street markets. It altered section 2 by substituting the word "or" for the word "except." Originally the section made it an offence to carry on the business of selling animals as pets "in any part of a street or public place, *except* at a stall or barrow in a market." The section now reads: "If any person carries on a business of selling animals as pets in any part of a street or public place, *or* at a stall or barrow in a market, he shall be guilty of an offence."

Some local authorities have avoided this by defining the stall in the market as a shop if it is of a permanent nature and the animals are normally permanently housed in the structure.

---

[46] *Ibid.* s.4(1).
[47] Pet Animals Act 1951, s.1(4).
[48] *Ibid.* s.1(5).
[49] *Ibid.* s.5.

SELLING, HIRING ETC. OF "SEX ARTICLES"

2.14 A local authority cannot restrict the selling, hiring, etc., of "sex articles" unless they pass a resolution under section 2 of the Local Government (Miscellaneous Provisions) Act 1982. The problem of sex shops is peculiar to large towns where the siting or even existence of the premises often causes great annoyance to residents who fear for the corruption of the young and the devaluation of their property. Such difficulties cannot be solved with the implementation of planning law if an existing shop premises is used and the change of use comes within Class A1 of the Schedule to the Town and Country Planning (Use Classes) Order 1987.[50]

If a local authority[51] is experiencing or anticipating this problem and if they feel they should have some control over the situation they must pass a resolution stating that Schedule 3 to the 1982 Act is to apply to their area. This must come into operation on the day specified in the resolution which must not be within one month of the date of the resolution. The fact must be advertised in the local press for two consecutive weeks, the first advertisement being in the newspaper not later than 28 days before the day specified in the resolution (*i.e.* the day that Schedule 3 comes into force in the area).[52]

In *R.* v. *Swansea City Council, ex p. Quietlynn Ltd.*,[53] the council had given notice of the making of a resolution outside the time limit. The company applied for an order to quash the council's refusal to grant their application for a licence and a declaration that the resolution had not been brought into force within the area of Swansea. Woolf J., sitting in the Queen's Bench Division, said that the requirement in section 2, to give notice of a resolution, was designed to give users of premises the opportunity of avoiding the commission of a criminal offence, and an opportunity of applying to a local authority for a licence before Schedule 3 came into force and to continue to use the premises until determination of their application. He said that non-compliance with the section renders a resolution ineffective, even though no prejudice had been suffered by the applicants as in the present case. Mere trifling and typographical errors would not normally invalidate a resolution.

This was followed in *R.* v. *Birmingham City Council and Others, ex p. Quietlynn Ltd.*[54] where Forbes J., in a long and detailed judgment, explained the procedure under Schedule 3 to the 1982 Act and the requirements that local authorities must take into account. It was held that the resolution under section 2 of the 1982 Act was mandatory and

---

[50] S.I. 1987 No. 764 (see p. 8).
[51] Local authority means: (a) the Council of the district; (b) the Council of a London borough; and (c) the Common Council of the City of London: Local Government (Miscellaneous Provisions) Act 1982, s.2(5).
[52] Local Government (Miscellaneous Provisions) Act 1982, s.2.
[53] (1985) 83 L.G.R. 308.
[54] (1985) 83 L.G.R. 461.

its requirements had to be precisely obeyed. There was no room for any suggestion that a breach of the requirements of the section might be overlooked if there was no prejudice to the applicant.

Basically, Schedule 3 to the Act contains relevant definitions, the procedure for granting, refusing or revoking licences, conditions which may be attached to licences and the procedure for appeals.

Paragraph 6 provides that no person shall in any area in which this Schedule is in force use any premises, vehicle, vessel or stall as a *sex establishment* except in accordance with the terms of a licence granted under the Schedule by the appropriate authority. It does not apply to articles for sale, supply or demonstration which are manufactured for use primarily for the purposes of birth control or are primarily related to birth control. A person may apply to the local authority to waive the requirement of a licence. A reasonable fee determined by the local authority shall be paid by the applicant for a licence.[55]

Meaning of sex establishment

A sex establishment means a sex cinema or a sex shop; they are **2.15** defined in paragraphs 3 and 4 of Schedule 3 to the 1982 Act respectively.

A shop is classed as a sex shop if it is used for a business which consists to a significant degree of selling, hiring, exchanging, lending, displaying or demonstrating (a) sex articles[56] or; (b) other things intended for use in connection with or for the purpose of stimulating or encouraging sexual activity, or acts of force or restraint which are associated with sexual activity.

The meaning of the word "significant" in relation to the selling of sex articles, for example magazines in a newsagent, was considered in *Lambeth London Borough Council* v. *Grewal.*[57] The shop sold a wide variety of articles which included newspapers, magazines, children's books, comics, cards, toys, groceries and toiletries. On the top shelf of a display unit, magazines, that came under the definition of "sex article," were displayed. The annual turnover of these articles was 1.5 per cent. of the turnover of the business and amounted to approximately £2,000 to £2,500. The owner of the shop was prosecuted for using the premises as

---

[55] Local Government (Miscellaneous Provisions) Act 1982, Sched. 3, para. 19.
[56] "Sex article" is defined in para. 4 of Sched. 3 to the 1982 Act as meaning; (a) anything for use in connection with, or for the purpose of stimulating or encouraging (i) sexual activity; or (ii) acts of force or restraint which are associated with sexual activity; and (b) anything to which the following applies; (i) to any article containing or embodying matter to be read or looked at or anything intended to be used, either alone or as one of a set, for the reproduction or manufacture of any such article; and (ii) to any recording of vision or sound, which (1) is concerned primarily with the portrayal of, or primarily deals with or relates to, or is intended to stimulate or encourage, sexual activity or acts of force or restraint which are associated with sexual activity; or (2) is concerned primarily with the portrayal of, or primarily deals with or relates to genital organs, or urinary or excretary functions.
[57] (1985) 150 J.P. 138.

a sex establishment without a licence contrary to paragraph 20(1)(*a*) of Schedule 3 to the 1982 Act.

He was convicted by the stipendiary magistrates but the Crown Court allowed his appeal and the local authority appealed to the Divisional Court. Mustill L.J. agreed that the word "significant" has more than one meaning. He stated that it is capable, in some context, of meaning "more than trifling." It does not have this meaning in the present context; a higher standard is set. How much higher cannot be prescribed by any rule of thumb. The ratio between the sexual and the other aspects of the business, the absolute quantity of sales, the character of the remainder of the business and the nature of the display of the articles will always be material. The court held that it was for the trial court to decide which considerations were material and what weight was to be attached to them and since the Crown Court had come to a decision which they were entitled to reach on the evidence, there was no ground on which the Divisional Court could intervene.

Grant, renewal and transfer of licences for sex establishments

2.16   The provisions relating to the above are contained in paragraphs 8 to 11 of Schedule 3. The licence remains in force for a year unless the local authority considers that a shorter period is necessary. The applicant for grant, renewal or transfer of a licence must publish the fact of the application in a local newspaper circulating in the district not later than seven days after the date of the application, and display the notice for 21 days beginning with the date of the application on or near the premises proposed to be used as a sex establishment and in a place where the notice can conveniently be read by the public. The notice shall be in such form as the local authority may prescribe and shall identify the premises, vehicle, vessel or stall as the case may be. A copy of the application must be sent by the applicant to the chief officer of police not later than seven days after the date of the application.

Any person objecting must give notice to the local authority in writing not later than 28 days after the date of the application and must give, in general terms, the grounds of the objection. The local authority, before considering the application, shall give notice in writing to the applicant of the general terms of the objection.

The Court of Appeal considered in *R.* v. *Watford Borough Council, ex p. Quietlynn*[58] a situation where the Council notified the applicant of an objection before the application was actually made. It was submitted by the appellant that although no unfairness had resulted, the provisions of Schedule 3 were mandatory and exhaustive and the local authority were in breach of the provisions. The Court did not accept this submission and held that paragraph 10(5) of the Schedule did not restrict the giving of notice of objection before the application but it did restrict

---

[58] (1985) 83 L.G.R. 308.

the giving of a later notice of objection. The provision was not exhaustive and no breach had been made out.

The local authority must not reveal the name and address of the person making the objection to the applicant without his consent, and in considering an application for a grant, renewal or transfer of a licence, the authority must have regard to observations submitted to them by the chief officer of police and any objection received. An opportunity must be given to the applicant, holder of the licence, or the person to whom the licence is to be transferred, as appropriate, to appear before the committee or sub-committee considering the application. The Schedule does not state that the local authority must give the opportunity to objectors to appear before them but nevertheless they may hear the objections orally. Three local authorities, *Preston, Trafford,* and *Chester*[59] allowed objectors an oral hearing, and it was contended in the Court of Appeal that since Schedule 3 did not specifically afford the opportunity of an oral hearing the authorities were in breach of the mandatory and exhaustive provisions of the Schedule and that the decision should be quashed. The Court of Appeal said the provisions were not exhaustive and since unfairness was not alleged the appeal was dismissed.

The principles of natural justice apply and in particular *audi alteram partem* (hear the other side). The committee or sub-committee that hears objections, or the applicant, must consider the application and make the decision themselves. In *R.* v. *Chester City Council, ex p. Quietlynn*,[60] the authority set up a licensing committee which was a sub-committee of the Environmental Services Committee. They heard applicants but had no power to decide applications. Recommendations were made to the Environmental Services Committee and it was that Committee that granted or refused the applications. Stephen Brown L.J. accepted that administrative functions covered a very wide spectrum and that it applied to the various licensing functions which fell on local authorities but there was an element of judicial process in this particular function that states that opportunity must be afforded for the applicant, etc., to be heard. Members of the Environmental Services Committee knew the characteristics of the locality and they could have asked, had they so wished, for details from members who had heard the applicant's representations. However, there was a breach of the procedural rules which did vitiate the decision of the Committee and the appeal was allowed and the decision quashed.

---

[59] *R.* v. *Chester City Council, ex p. Quietlynn*; *R.* v. *Havant Borough Council, ex p. Quietlynn*; *R.* v. *Preston Borough Council, ex p. Quietlynn*; *R.* v. *Swansea City Council, ex p. Quietlynn*; *R.* v. *Trafford Borough Council, ex p. Quietlynn*; *R.* v. *Watford Borough Council, ex p. Quietlynn.* (1985) 83 L.G.R. 308, C.A.; affirming *The Times*, October 19, 1983.

[60] (1985) 83 L.G.R. 308 at 316.

In *R.* v. *Reading Borough Council, ex p. Quietlynn*,[61] a councillor had expressed publicly his bias against sex shops. He was one of two on the licensing panel of three that belonged to the majority political group that had decided that they were not in favour of sex shops. An application for judicial review by way of order of *certiorari* to quash the decision of the panel was turned down. It was held that the panel's decisions could be vitiated for bias, only if it could be shown that the council had acted in such a way that it was clear that, when the panel came to consider the applications, its members could not exercise proper discretion and that the council had not so acted merely by appointing to the panel a councillor who held or had expressed views about whether sex establishment licences ought in general to be granted.

If a local authority refuses to grant, renew or transfer a licence and the applicant asks for the reasons for refusal they must give him a statement in writing of the reasons within seven days of the request.[62] An application made for a renewal or transfer of a licence before the expiry date ensures that the licence remains in force until the application is determined by the local authority even if the expiry date has passed.[63]

Refusal of licences

2.17   Paragraph 12 of Schedule 3 to the 1982 Act lists persons or body corporates to whom local authorities cannot grant licences, for example persons under 18 years of age, body corporates that are not incorporated in the United Kingdom and, subject to the applicant's rights of appeal, the grounds for refusal are contained in paragraph 12(3) of the Schedule.

One of the reasons that a local authority may refuse a licence is that the number of sex establishments in the relevant locality at the time the application is made is equal to or exceeds the number which the authority consider is appropriate for that locality. Another reason is that the grant or renewal of the licence would be inappropriate having regard to the character of the relevant locality.

"Relevant locality" was an issue to be decided in *R.* v. *Peterborough City Council, ex p. Quietlynn*; *R.* v. *Tunbridge Wells Borough Council, ex p. same*; *R.* v. *Cheltenham Borough Council, ex p. same*.[64] It was held that the expression "locality" carried no connection of precise boundaries and the relevant locality did not have a clearly pre-defined area, but an entire town, or the whole of a local authority's administrative area was too large to be the relevant locality within the meaning of the 1982 Act.

---

[61] (1987) 85 L.G.R. 387.
[62] Local Government (Miscellaneous Provisions) Act 1982, Sched. 3, para. 10(20).
[63] *Ibid.* Sched. 3 para. 11(1).
[64] (1987) 85 L.G.R. 249.

Standard condition

Paragraph 13 of Schedule 3 to the 1982 Act gives local authorities the power to make regulations setting out standard conditions to which licences granted, renewed or transferred are subject. These conditions will apply even if they are not contained in or attached to the licence itself unless they are expressly excluded. These may regulate, for example, the hours of opening and closing, advertisements, and visibility of the interior to passers-by. **2.18**

Copies of licences and any standard conditions subject to which the licence is held must be displayed in a suitable place and the local authority must send a copy of any licences granted to the chief officer of police responsible for the area where the premises are situated.

Licences may be revoked or varied in accordance with paragraphs 17 and 18 of Schedule 3 to the 1982 Act respectively.

Offences and penalties

A person found guilty of any offence mentioned in paragraphs 20, 21 and 23 of Schedule 3 to the 1982 Act shall be liable on summary conviction to a fine not exceeding £10,000. The offences mentioned include knowingly using or knowingly causing or permitting the use of any premises, etc., contrary to paragraph 6, *i.e.* as a sex establishment without a licence. **2.19**

In *Westminster City Council* v. *Croyalgrange*,[65] the first defendant company owned premises that were continuously used with its consent as a sex establishment and the second defendant was a director of the company.[66] No application for a licence had been made and it was the defendants' submission that they had honestly believed that an application for a licence had been made by or on behalf of the sub-tenant of the premises. The House of Lords turned down the appeal by the council and held that knowledge on the part of the defendant is an ingredient of the offence: knowledge not only that the premises were being used as a sex establishment, but also knowledge that they were being used contrary to paragraph 6, that is to say, in the absence of a licence.

Lord Brightman stated:

" . . . But although such knowledge is an ingredient of the offence under paragraph 20(1)(*a*), and although the onus of establishing all the ingredients of the offence must lie on the prosecution, this does not impose on the prosecution an undue burden: if (1) all the other ingredients of the offence are proved, and (2) the defendant (or the

---

[65] [1986] 1 W.L.R. 674.
[66] Para. 26 of Sched. 3 to the 1982 Act provides that where an offence under the Schedule committed by a body corporate is proved to have been committed with the consent or connivance of, or to be attributable to any neglect on the part of any director, manager, secretary or other similar officer of the body corporation, or any person who was purporting to act in any such capacity, he, as well as the body corporate, shall be guilty of the offence.

responsible officer of a corporate defendant) chooses not to give evidence of his absence of knowledge, and (3) there are no circumstances which sufficiently suggest absence of knowledge, the court may properly infer without direct evidence that the defendant did indeed possess the requisite knowledge. . . . "

Appeals[67]

2.20 An appeal may be made to the magistrates' court from a decision of the local authority regarding the refusal of this application, the imposition of a term, condition or restriction by which he is aggrieved, or the revocation of his licence. It must be lodged before the expiration of 21 days beginning with the relevant date. The relevant date is the date on which the person in question is notified of the decision of the local authority. If the person in question is sitting in the committee room and hears the chairman announce the decision of the committee it would appear that this is the relevant date and not the date on which the person receives official notification and reasons for the decision under paragraph 10(20). It was decided thus by magistrates on an appeal by *Quietlynn* v. *Oldham Borough Council* on July 6, 1984.[68]

An appeal against the decision of the magistrates' court may be brought to the Crown Court but the decision of the Crown Court is final. Paragraph 27(7) states that on an appeal to the magistrates' court or the Crown Court, the *court may make such order as it thinks fit*. The wording of this paragraph is exactly the same as in paragraph 17(4) of Schedule 1 which relates to appeals in respect of entertainment licences. In *R.* v. *Huntingdon District Council, ex p. Cowan*,[69] Glidewell J. considered this latter paragraph and stated that the appeal is by way of rehearing and the powers of the magistrates' court to inquire into relevant matters and of the Crown Court on appeal from there are not in any way trammelled. Therefore, the cases are reheard and the parties may adduce new evidence. By analogy, the same procedure applies to appeals under Schedule 3.

PROVIDING MUSIC, DANCING AND OTHER ENTERTAINMENT FOR THE PUBLIC

2.21 If a shopkeeper wants to provide entertainment for his customers he must obtain a licence from the local authority. Before the coming into force of the Local Government (Miscellaneous Provisions) Act 1982 on January 1, 1983, music and dancing licences were issued, outside Greater London, by magistrates' courts. This duty has now been transferred to district councils and "music and dancing licence" has been replaced by "public entertainment licence."

---

[67] Local Government (Miscellaneous Provisions) Act 1982, Sched. 3, para. 27.
[68] *Plymouth City Council* v. *Quietlynn; Portsmouth City Council* v. *Quietlynn; Quietlynn* v. *Oldham Borough Council* [1987] 3 W.L.R. 189.
[69] [1984] 1 W.L.R. 501.

Meaning of "public entertainment"

This is defined in Schedule 1 to the 1982 Act. Public entertainment is **2.22** public dancing or music or any other public entertainment of a like kind except:

(a) any music;
    (i) in a place of public religious worship; or
    (ii) performed as an incident of a religious meeting or service;
(b) an entertainment held in a pleasure fair; or
(c) an entertainment which takes place wholly or mainly in the open air.

"Public entertainment" is also any public contest, exhibition or display of boxing, wrestling, judo, karate or similar sport but excluding such events either in pleasure fairs or in the open air.

The entertainment must be open to the public and guests and members of a bona fide club are not members of the public. Therefore a public entertainment licence is not required for entertainment in a club.[70] In deciding whether an entertainment is public or not it is immaterial that there is no entrance fee.[71] The test is whether on the evidence any reputable member of the public, on paying for admission could come in.[72]

Public musical entertainment in the open air, such as pop festivals, can only be controlled by licensing if the local authority makes a resolution to adopt the provisions in the 1982 Act relating to such entertainment.[73] The land upon which the entertainment is held must be on private land (*i.e.* land to which the public has access only by permission of the owner/occupier or lessee). However, excluded from the adoptive provisions are:

(a) a garden fete, bazaar, sale of work, sporting or athletic event, exhibition, display or other function or event of a similar character, whether limited to one day or extending over two or more days; or
(b) a religious meeting or service merely because music is incidental to it; or
(c) entertainment held in a pleasure fair.[74]

Terms and conditions under which a licence may be granted

A local authority may grant a licence for a period of up to one year **2.23** and may renew the licence for a similar period.[75] An occasional licence may also be granted for a particular occasion as specified in the

---

[70] *Severn View Social Club and Institute* v. *Chepstow (Monmouthshire) Justices* [1968] 1 W.L.R. 1512.
[71] *Archer* v. *Willingrice* (1802) 4 Esp. 186; *Frailing* v. *Messenger* (1867) 31 J.P. 423.
[72] *Gardner* v. *Morris* (1961) 59 L.G.R. 187.
[73] Local Government (Miscellaneous Provisions) Act 1982, s.1(2).
[74] *Ibid.* Sched. 1, para. 3.
[75] *Ibid.* Sched. 1, para. 5(1).

licence.[76] Terms, conditions or restrictions may be attached to the licence as the local authority thinks fit[77] but with regard to public *musical* entertainments in the open air the conditions which may be attached are laid down in the Act. These are conditions relating to:

(a) safety of performers and the public;
(b) access for emergency vehicles;
(c) sanitary appliances; and
(d) preventing disturbance by noise.[78]

The local authority may make regulations setting out standard conditions which will apply to all licences unless they are expressly excluded or waived.[79]

A notice of not less than 28 days of an intention to make an application must be given to the district council, the chief officer of police and the fire authority. The district council may grant the licence if they think fit after consultation with the police and fire department.[80] In most authorities, applications are heard before a licensing sub-committee with a representative from the Environmental Health Department, the police authority and the fire authority in attendance. Observations are given on the application by their representatives and other objections may be heard.

In *R.* v. *Huntingdon District Council, ex p. Cowan*,[81] the district council did not inform the applicants that there had been objections to the application for a licence. They heard the application without giving the applicant an opportunity to comment on what the objectors had said either by way of oral hearing or in writing. The application was refused by the council.

Schedule 1 to the 1982 Act does not lay down a stipulation that the applicant had to be made aware of the substance of objections and does not give the applicant the right to make comment on any objections, although these rights are contained in Schedule 3 relating to the licensing of sex establishments. Glidewell J. said, at 508:

" . . . The question which has exercised my mind is: does the fact that, in the other parts of the Act to which I have referred, specific provision is made for those features, whereas no such provision is made in Schedule 1 mean that Parliament intended that the rule of natural justice should not here apply? I have come to the conclusion that I ought not to draw that deduction . . . a local authority is under a duty, when dealing with entertainments licences, first, to

---

[76] *Ibid.* Sched. 1, para. 1(5).
[77] *Ibid.* Sched. 1, para. 1(4).
[78] Local Government (Miscellaneous Provisions) Act 1982, Sched. 1, para. 4.
[79] *Ibid.* Sched. 1, para. 11.
[80] *Ibid.* Sched. 1, para. 6.
[81] [1984] 1 W.L.R. 501.

inform the applicant of the substance of objection or of any representation in the nature of an objection (not necessarily to give him the whole of it, nor to say necessarily who has made it, but to give him the substance of it); and, second, to give him an opportunity to make representations in reply. . . . "

An order of *certiorari* was granted and the decision of the local authority was quashed.

Objections from local residents usually take the form of complaints of noise and disturbance from the high level of sound emitted from within the function room. The Environmental Health Officer should investigate and make his observations to the licensing sub-committee. Occasionally the complaints also include the conduct of patrons entering or leaving the premises. Usually the police authority will report to the committee on this and the committee is entitled to take it into account when deciding whether or not to grant a licence. Under the old system of "music and dancing" licensing administered by the magistrates, the Court of Appeal, in *Lidster* v. *Owen*,[82] held that magistrates have a wide discretion in the "regulation" of premises used for public dancing, music or other entertainment and are entitled to take into account considerations which are both internal and external to the premises when deciding whether to grant or renew a "music and dancing" licence for particular premises. Thus, in exercising their discretion, magistrates are entitled to have regard to the character and location of the premises and to refuse a licence for premises even though they are well conducted, if persons leaving the premises create an unacceptable degree of public disorder when they leave. It is assumed that this reasoning would apply to public entertainment licences.

A reasonable fee may be charged by the district council for the granting, renewal or transfer of licences but no fee is payable in relation to church, village and community halls, or similar buildings, or where the entertainment is of an educational nature or is given for charitable purposes.[83]

Provisional granting of licences

If premises are in the process of, or going to be, altered, an application may be made for a provisional licence.[84] Probably this is to give the applicant an idea of whether his application is likely to be successful before spending too much money. The district council must be satisfied that the premises will be satisfactory if constructed in accordance with the plans submitted and provisional licences will not be effective until subsequently confirmed. **2.24**

---

[82] [1983] 1 W.L.R. 516.
[83] Local Government (Miscellaneous Provisions) Act 1982, Sched. 1, para. 7.
[84] *Ibid.* Sched. 1, para. 15.

Offences and penalties

2.25   There are two offences set out in paragraph 12 of Schedule 1 to the 1982 Act, namely, using premises for public entertainment without a licence and breaching conditions or restrictions attached to a licence. Both offences attract a fine not exceeding Scale 5 on the standard scale of conviction in a court of summary jurisdiction.

In the case of the first offence, any person concerned with the organisation or management of the entertainment is liable together with any person who, knowing or having reasonable cause to suspect that such an entertainment would be so provided; (i) allowed the place to be so used; or (ii) let the place, or otherwise made it available, to any person who used the place for public entertainment without a licence.

Where a condition of a licence is breached the holder of the licence is liable as well as any person who knowing[85] or having reasonable cause to suspect that the place would be so used; (i) allowed the place to be so used; or (ii) let the place, or otherwise made it available to any person by whom an offence in connection with that use of the place has been committed.

There is a defence under paragraph 12 for any person charged with any of the above offences and this is that he took all reasonable precautions and exercised all due diligence[86–87] to avoid the commission of the offence. Subject to a right of appeal, the local authority may revoke the entertainments licence if the licence holder is found guilty of breaching the attached conditions.

Variation of licences

2.26   An application may be made, by the holder of the licence, to the district council to vary the terms, conditions or restrictions attached to the licence and the council may make the variations applied for, make such variations as they think fit or refuse the application.[88]

Right of appeal

2.27   Under paragraph 17 of Schedule 1 to the 1982 Act, there is a right of appeal against the refusal to grant a licence, refusal of variation of terms or conditions, etc., unreasonable terms, conditions or restrictions and revocation of a licence. The appeal must be entered before the expiration of 21 days beginning with the relevant date in the magistrates' court. The relevant date is the date on which the person in question is notified of the decision of the local authority.[89]

An appeal against the decision of the magistrates' court may be

---

[85] *Westminster City Council* v. *Croyolgrange* [1986] 1 W.L.R. 674 (see p. 35).
[86–87] See p. 160.
[88] Local Government (Miscellaneous Provisions) Act 1982, Sched. 1, para. 16.
[89] *Plymouth City Council* v. *Quietlynn*; *Portsmouth City Council* v. *Quietlynn*; *Quietlynn* v. *Oldham Borough Council* [1987] 3 W.L.R. 189 (see p. 36).

brought to the Crown Court. The court may make such order as it thinks fit. Therefore, the appeal is by way of rehearing.[90]

LATE OPENING OF A REFRESHMENT HOUSE

A shop may be a refreshment house and the shopkeeper may find that **2.28** most of his customers attend his premises after the closing time of the local licensed premises. In such circumstances he would probably want to keep his premises open late. This may cause a nuisance to local residents and if the premises comes within the definition of a "late night refreshment house" he will require a licence from the district council.[91]

Meaning of "late night refreshment house"

"Late night refreshment house" is defined in section 1 of the Late **2.29** Night Refreshment Houses Act 1969, as amended by section 7(2) of the Local Government (Miscellaneous Provisions) Act 1982, as a house, room, shop or building kept open for public refreshment, resort and entertainment at any time between the hours of 10 p.m. and 5 a.m. the following morning, other than exempt licensed premises.

Exempt licenced premises are those premises licensed for the sale of beer, cider, wine or spirits that are not kept open between the period from half an hour after the end of permitted hours in the evening (or from 10 p.m. if there are no permitted hours in the evening) and 5 a.m. the following morning.[92]

The important words in the definition are "public *refreshment, resort* and *entertainment*." All three words must be satisfied before a premises can be regarded as a late night refreshment house. The Late Night Refreshment Houses Act 1969 is a consolidating Act and it is presumed that Parliament when passing the Act intended the law to remain unaltered. The definition is originally reproduced from section 6 of the Refreshment Houses Act 1860 and case law from that date can be applied to the present Act.

"Entertainment" does not necessarily mean music and dancing but is, as suggested in *Taylor* v. *Oram*[93]: "whatever might be reasonably required for the personal comfort of guests." Lush J. in *Muir* v. *Keay*[94] said:

"I think entertainment is something connected with the enjoyment

---

[90] *R.* v. *Huntingdon District Council, ex p. Cowan* [1984] 1 W.L.R. 501 (see p. 36).

[91] The licensing authorities under the Act are district councils and, in the case of Greater London, the councils of London borough and the Common Council of the City of London: Late Night Refreshment Houses Act 1969, s.2(2).

[92] Late Night Refreshment Houses Act 1969, s.1, as amended by the Local Government (Miscellaneous Provisions) Act 1982, s.7(2). Now establishments such as licensed restaurants that open between normal closing time and 5 a.m. the next morning require both a liquor licence and a late-night refreshment house licence.

[93] (1862) 1 H.C. 370.

[94] (1875) L.R. 10 Q.B. 594.

of refreshment rooms, tables and the like; it is the accommodation provided."

Therefore, such establishments as "take-away" food shops do not come within the definition unless facilities are provided for eating at the premises. A shop consisting of one room provided lemonade and ginger beer, having no accommodation for visitors to sit down, and nothing but a table or counter at which they stood only for a few minutes, was held in *Howes* v. *Inland Revenue Board*[95] to be a refreshment house within the meaning of this section. Another example is where tripe was supplied on plates in a shop where neither seats, knives nor forks were provided; this was held to be a refreshment house in *Cooper* v. *Dickenson*.[96] Power has been given to district councils to control the hours of opening of "take-away" food shops not coming within this definition. (See Chapter 4).

Power to impose conditions as to opening after 11 p.m.

2.30   A person cannot operate a "late night refreshment house" unless he has a licence granted by the district council on payment of a fee which the council considers appropriate. The licence lasts until March 31 of each year and is renewed annually on payment of the fee. The council must keep a register of such licences and give a copy of the list to the clerk to the justices for their area, if requested.

In order to avoid unreasonable disturbance to residents of the neighbourhood, the district council may, when granting or renewing a licence, impose conditions as to the times of opening after 11 p.m. If the applicant is not satisfied with these conditions he may appeal to the magistrates' court and the court may give such direction as it thinks proper with respect to the condition subject to which the licence is to be granted or renewed. There is a right of appeal from the decision of the magistrates to the Crown Court.[97]

Conditions of licence as to charges and touting

2.31   The district council may grant or renew a licence subject to condition that:

(a) no charges be made for entering late night refreshment houses for, or in connection with, entertainment (except cloakroom or toilet facilities) unless these are prominently displayed outside the premises; and

(b) there must be no touting for custom outside or in the vicinity of the refreshment house.

---

[95] (1876) 1 Ex.D. 385.
[96] *The Times*, January 23, 1877.
[97] Late Night Refreshment Houses Act 1969, s.7.

If, and only if, one or both of these conditions are attached to the licence will an offence be committed if these activities are carried on.[98]

Illegal and disorderly conduct

A licensee is guilty of an offence if he:

2.32

- (a) knowingly permits unlawful gaming (*i.e.* gaming in contravention of the Gaming Act 1968);
- (b) knowingly permit prostitutes, thieves or drunken and disorderly persons to assemble at, or continue in or upon, his premises.

Any person is guilty of an offence if he is drunk, riotous, quarrelsome or disorderly in a late night refreshment house and he refuses to leave when asked by the manager or occupier, or his agent or servant or by any constable.[99]

A constable has power of entry to a late night refreshment house and is authorised and required, on the demand of the manager or occupier (or their servant or agent), to assist in expelling drunken, riotous, quarrelsome and disorderly persons.[1]

Punishment of offences

A person found guilty of the following offences in a summary trial is liable to a fine not exceeding level 4 on the standard scale or to imprisonment for a term of not more than three months, or both:

2.33

- (a) keeping a late night refreshment house without a licence;
- (b) breach of a condition limiting the opening hours after 11.00 p.m.;
- (c) an offence in relation to charges and touting for custom;
- (d) knowingly permitting prostitutes, illegal gaming, etc., on the premises;
- (e) obstructing the entry of a police constable.

A licensee who fails to notify the district council of a change of his house address and a person who is found guilty of being drunk, riotous, quarrelsome or disorderly and refuses to leave a refreshment house when asked, are both liable on summary conviction to a fine of not more than level 1 on the standard scale.[2]

PROVIDING GAMES BY MEANS OF MACHINES

The legislation relevant to providing gaming machines in shop premises is Schedule 9 to and section 34 of the Gaming Act 1968. Before a shopkeeper can instal gaming machines he must obtain a permit under sec-

2.34

---

[98] *Ibid.* s.8.
[99] *Ibid.* s.9.
[1] *Ibid.* s.10.
[2] *Ibid.* s.11.

tion 34 of the 1968 Act from the appropriate licensing authority. Section 35 of the 1968 Act prohibits the use of gaming machines unless the use falls within sections 31 to 34. The authority is the district council in which the premises are situated and, in the case of Greater London, the council of the London borough and the Common Council of the City of London. If an "on licence" (other than a Part IV licence)[3] is in force in respect of the premises, the authority for granting or renewing permits is the licensing justice for the area.[4]

There has been much cause for concern lately about the addiction of young people to the playing of gaming machines. Petty theft, burglary and other serious crimes have been attributed to this problem and in circumstances such as these a local authority would be quite in order to adopt a policy in the granting of permits under paragraph 3 of Schedule 9 to the 1968 Act.

Type of prizes allowed from the machines and charge for play[5]

2.35   In any one game, no player shall receive any article, benefit or advantage other than one (and only one) of the following:

(a) a money prize or token(s) not exceeding £2.00;

(b) a non-monetary prize or token(s) exchangeable for a non-monetary prize not exceeding £4.00;

(c) a money prize not exceeding £2.00 together with a non-monetary prize of a value which does not exceed £4.00, less the amount of the money prize, or a token exchangeable only for such a combination of a money prize and a non-monetary prize;

(d) one or more tokens which can be used for playing one or more further games by means of the machine and, in so far as they are not so used, can be exchanged for a non-monetary prize or non-monetary prizes at the appropriate rate.

A player may be allowed, however, after inserting the permitted charge for play (*i.e.* coin(s) or token(s) to the value of 10p) and playing the game successfully, an opportunity by automatic action to play one or more further games without inserting any further coin or token, if in respect of all those games:

(a) he does not receive, and is not entitled to receive, any articles other than a money prize not exceeding £2.00; and

(b) he does not receive, and is not entitled to receive, any other benefit or advantage apart from the opportunity to play the further game or games.

---

[3] Licensing Act 1964.
[4] Gaming Act 1968, Sched. 9, para. 1.
[5] *Ibid.* s.34 as amended by the Gaming Act (variation of monetary limits) Order 1986 (S.I. 1986 No. 1981).

Resolution by local authority as to grant or renewal of permits[6]

A district council may pass a resolution that they will not grant, or **2.36**
renew, permits in respect of a class of premises specified in the resolution. They may also pass a resolution that all permits granted or
renewed be subject to a condition limiting the number of machines to
the number specified in the resolution. Local authorities do not have
this power in relation to premises used wholly or mainly for the provision of amusements by means of machines.

Lord Denning M.R., said *obiter dicta*, in *R. v. Herrod, ex p. Leeds
City District Council*[7]:

" . . . such resolutions can be passed by the local authority without
hearing the persons affected and without giving them any right of
appeal. In short, the local authorities are authorised to pass resolutions by which they can give a "blanket" refusal to grant or renew a
permit without hearing the applicant and without any appeal from
their decision. This would seem contrary to natural justice, even in
the case of an application for the 'grant' of a permit. All the more
so where it is the refusal to 'renew' an existing licence. Once having
been granted a permit, the applicant may have invested much
money in his venture. A refusal to 'renew' his permit may cause
him serious economic loss. Yet Parliament has authorised the local
authorities to give a 'blanket' refusal. This may be so unfair in its
result that the courts should confine this power within strict limits.
They should confine it to those circumstances which are clearly
covered by the statute, and not extend it one whit beyond. . . . "

Local authorities must use this power within the strict confines of the
statute in order to avoid a successful appeal. Taking Lord Denning's
point about the unfairness of refusing to renew a permit, it may be
equitable when considering adopting a policy to limit the refusals to the
granting of new permits only.

Grounds for refusal to grant or renew permit[8]

The local authority cannot refuse an application for a grant or renewal **2.37**
of a permit without first giving the applicant the opportunity of a hearing
before the appropriate committee. If the premises is of the class specified in a resolution made under paragraph 3, of Schedule 9 to the 1968
Act, the local authority is under a duty to refuse to grant or renew the
permit, as the case may be. In all other cases (except premises used
wholly or mainly for the provision of amusements by means of
machines), the decision is at the discretion of the local authority. The
permit shall not be granted or renewed for less than three years.

[6] Gaming Act 1968, Sched. 9, paras. 3, 4.
[7] [1976] Q.B. 540 at 560.
[8] Gaming Act 1968, Sched. 9, paras. 7, 8.

Right of appeal[9]

2.38 Notice must be given to the applicant forthwith of a decision to refuse an application for a permit and also the grounds on which it is made. There is a right of appeal to the Crown Court and this is done by notice to the chief executive of the council. The notice must be forwarded by the chief executive as soon as is practicable to the appropriate officer of the Crown Court together with a statement of the decision against which the appeal is brought and of the name and last known resident, or place, of business, of the appellant. The appeal is entered and at least seven days' notice in writing is given to the appellant and the local authority of the date, time and place appointed for the hearing of the appeal.

If the court is satisfied that the local authority was under a duty to refuse the permit in accordance with paragraph 7 of Schedule 9, the court shall not allow the appeal. Where the appeal is against a condition that the number of machines is limited to a specified number contained in a resolution under paragraph 3 of Schedule 9, the court shall not reverse or vary the decision so as:

(a) to grant or renew the permit unconditionally; or
(b) to grant or renew the permit subject to a condition limiting the number of machines to a number exceeding the number specified in the resolution of the local authority.

Offences and punishment

2.39 Section 38 of the 1968 Act contains the offences. If a condition to which the permit is subject is contravened the holder of the permit is guilty of an offence under section 38(6). He has the defence under subsection (11) if he can prove that the contravention occurred without his knowledge and that he exercised all such care as was reasonable in the circumstances to secure that the provisions in question would not be contravened.

If a machine is used for gaming on premises in contravention of section 35 of the 1968 Act any person who allowed the machine to be on the premises is guilty of an offence unless he proves that the contravention occurred without his consent or connivance and that he exercised all due diligence[10] to prevent it.[11] Additionally, where any of the provisions of sections 34 or 35 of the 1968 Act are contravened in relation to a machine, a supplier or vendor of the machine will be guilty of an offence if he knew[12] or had reasonable cause to suspect that the provisions of the sections would be contravened in respect of the machine supplied or sold by him.[13]

Any person guilty of an offence under section 38 of the 1968 Act shall

---

[9] *Ibid.* Sched. 9, paras. 11, 12.
[10] See p. 160.
[11] Gaming Act 1968, s.38(7).
[12] See p. 35.
[13] Gaming Act 1968, s.38(10).

be liable on summary conviction to a fine not exceeding the prescribed sum which is £2,000[14] unless some other sum is substituted by order of the Secretary of State. On conviction or indictment a person found guilty will be liable to a fine or to imprisonment for a term not exceeding two years or both. If a person is convicted under section 38(6) of a contravention of a condition to which the permit is subject the court may also, if it thinks fit, make an order cancelling the permit.[15]

[14] Magistrates Courts Act 1980, s.32(9).
[15] Gaming Act 1968, s.39.

CHAPTER 3

ACTIVITIES WHERE REGISTRATION IS REQUIRED

INTRODUCTION

3.01 The registration of milk distributors is conveniently dealt with under "selling milk" in Chapter 2. All other activities carried on in commercial retail premises that require registration can be separated broadly into two types. One, where special risks to health are involved and, as such, the local authority is vested with the power to refuse or cancel registration. The other is where the main purpose of registration is to inform the local environmental health department of the existence of the activity so that regular inspections can take place, to ensure compliance with relevant regulations. In the latter case, although it is an offence to carry on the business without registration, the local authority cannot refuse or cancel registration.

Section 18 of the Food Act 1984 covers the procedure for the application to the local authority for registration, where both the purpose for registration and the premises proposed to be used must be specified.

The provisions relating to cancellation of registration of food business, where deficiencies in the premises create a risk to public health, have been superceded somewhat by the procedure of obtaining a Closure Order or an Emergency Closure Order under sections 21 to 25 of the Food Act 1984.[1] These orders apply to the majority of food businesses (including both premises and stalls) and can be obtained after a lapse of only three days in the case of an Emergency Closure Order, compared with the long drawn out procedure of cancellation of registration which may take weeks.

The Government White Paper, *Food Safety—Protecting the Consumer* issued in July 1988, has proposed a scheme of registration for food premises so that local authorities will have knowledge of all food premises within their area. There is lack of detail in the White Paper but it is assumed that local authorities will not be given the power to cancel or refuse registration.

SECTION 16 PROVISIONS

3.02 Manufacturing, storing and selling[2] ice-cream[3] and preparing[4] and manufacturing sausages or potted, pressed, pickled or preserved foods intended for sale are grouped together because they are contained in

---

[1] See p. 174.
[2] "Sale" means sale for human consumption, Food Act 1984, s.16(1).
[3] "Ice-cream" includes any similar commodity, Food Act 1984, s.132(1).
[4] "Preparation" includes manufacture and any form of treatment, *ibid.*

section 16(1) of the Food Act 1984. It is laid down that registration is required for these functions, and exemptions specified in the section apply to them all. Premises[5] where it is proposed that these undertakings be carried on must be registered with the local authority. It must be noted that persons are not registered, and that these businesses can be conducted on stalls and vehicles without the necessity for registration under this section. The Ministers may, by order, direct that the provisions of section 16 apply to the sale, preparation or storage of other food for human consumption[6] but no order, as yet, has been made.

The section does not apply to premises used for the preparation, etc., of articles other than of animal or vegetable origin or to premises used wholly or mainly[7] as catering premises, schools or clubs. Catering premises means premises where, in the course of a business, food is prepared and supplied for immediate consumption on the premises.[8] However, because the preparation of meat or fish by any process of cooking shall be deemed to be the preservation of that meat or fish,[9] all fish and chip shops and other takeaway food shops that cook meat or fish must be registered.[10]

Other exemptions are:

(a) domestic premises where the food is prepared, etc., by and for the benefit of a society registered under the Industrial and Provident Societies Act 1965; and

(b) premises of any description where the person preparing, etc., the food is not doing it in the course of a trade.

These exemptions came about by an amending Act, the Food and Drugs (Amendment) Act 1981, section 1, in order to allow such groups as the Women's Institute to, for example, pot jam on domestic premises, and charitable bodies to prepare or preserve food on any premises for sale at charitable functions without the need for registration.

In a theatre, cinema, music hall or concert hall no registration is necessary for the sale or storage of ice-cream but registration is required if there is an intention to manufacture ice-cream.

Modern methods of hygienic packaging and storage make the possibility of contamination highly unlikely. There may, however, be serious consideration given and investigations made with regard to applications for the preservation of meat or fish by cooking and the manufacture of sausage. In a small butcher's shop, sausages are usually manufactured in

---

[5] "Premises" means a building or part of a building, and any forecourt, yard or place of storage used in connection with a building or part of a building, *ibid.*

[6] Food Act 1984, s.17.

[7] "Wholly or mainly": probably if more than half of the premises are so used, *Miller* v. *Ottilie (Owner)* [1944] 2 K.B. 188; but see also *Re Hatschek's Patents, ex p. Zerenner* [1909] 2 Ch. 68; *Berthelemy* v. *Neale* [1952] W.N. 92.

[8] Food Act 1984, s.132(1).

[9] *Ibid.* s.16(1), (11).

[10] *Ibid.* s.17.

a small room at the rear away from the public eye and these rooms are often insanitary with the resultant risk of contamination.

If it appears to the local authority, usually based on a report from the environmental health officer, that conditions at the premises are in contravention of the Food Hygiene (General) Regulations 1970 (S.I. 1970 No. 1172) or that the premises are otherwise unsuitable, *i.e.* it is unhygienic having regard to the situation, construction or activities carried on there, they will serve a notice on the applicant, stating a time and place at which the matter will be considered.[11] An opportunity will be given for the applicant to be represented at this meeting and to call witnesses and show cause why the local authority should not cancel or refuse registration as the case may be. If the local authority is not persuaded by this evidence, registration may be cancelled or refused, notice given forthwith of this decision to the applicant and, if required by him, within 14 days the reasons for the authority's decision. A person aggrieved by a decision of the local authority may appeal to a magistrates' court. "A person aggrieved" could include the successor of a person whose premises were removed from the register if he had taken over the decision to cancel the registration.[12]

It is an offence for a person to carry on the activities laid out in section 16, other than those specifically exempted, on any premises without being registered by a local authority.

The Selling of Food by Hawkers

3.03 The law was originally contained in sections 18 and 19 of the Local Government (Miscellaneous Provisions) Act 1982. These sections have now been repealed and are consolidated in Part IV of the Food Act 1984.

The sections are adoptive. The local authority[13] must pass a resolution stating that Part IV is to apply to their area and naming a day (at least a month after the date of the resolution) on which it comes into force and the resolution and general effect must be publicised for at least two weeks in a local newspaper.

Registration

3.04 In a local authority area where Part IV has been adopted, no person shall hawk food unless he is registered, and no premises shall be used as storage accommodation for any food intended for hawking unless the

---

[11] There must be 21 clear days between the day when the notice is given and the day of the hearing; see *Re Hector Whaling Ltd.* [1936] 1 Ch. 208; *McQueen* v. *Jackson* [1903] 2 K.B. 163.

[12] *Prosser* v. *Mountain Ash Urban District Council* [1931] 2 K.B. 132.

[13] Section 72 of the 1984 Act defines "local authority" as meaning the common council of the City of London, the Inner and Middle Temples and district and London borough councils.

premises are registered. An assistant must be registered unless he is normally supervised or if he is only a temporary replacement.

The local authority must register the person and/or the premises and issue to the applicant a certificate of registration. There is no power to cancel or refuse registration.

The meaning of "food"

For the purposes of Part IV only, "food" is defined in section 67 as **3.05** meaning "food and the ingredients of food for human consumption," including:

(a) drink (other than water);

(b) chewing gum and like products;

but it does not include:

(i) milk and cream;

(ii) live animals or birds; or

(iii) articles or substances used only as drugs.

It should be noted that this definition differs from the general definition of food under section 131(1) of the Act in that milk and cream are not included.

"Drug" includes medicine for internal or external use[14] and where there is a case of doubt it will be a question of fact and the decision of the court may rest on whether the substance was sold for use as a medicine or not. In *Fowle* v. *Fowle*[15] it was held that beeswax sold by a *grocer* was not a drug but it was stated that if a *chemist* had sold the substance a different decision may have resulted. Lord Goddard C.J. in *Armstrong* v. *Clark*[16] said that a drug means: " . . . a medicant or medicine, something given to cure or alleviate or assist an ailing body."

The meaning of "food hawker"

A person comes within the definition of "food hawker" if he moves **3.06** from place to place selling food or offering or exposing food for sale, or if he sells food in the open air or offers or exposes food for sale in the open air. He must be doing this for private gain and not ancillary to a trade or business carried on by him or some other person on an identifiable property.[17] For example, a person would not require registration if he sold food from door to door in aid of a charity or if he was a butcher delivering meat from a local butcher's shop.

---

[14] Food Act 1984, s.132(1).

[15] (1896) 60 J.P. 758.

[16] [1957] 2 Q.B. 391.

[17] Food Act 1984, s.64. In *Dodds* v. *Spear*, *The Times*, October 31, 1985, a trader who set up a stall in a Sunday market in return for a fee to the occupier was held to be exempt from registration as it was "ancillary to a trade or business carried on by him or some other person."

Exemptions

3.07   Registration is not necessary where food is for sale, offered for sale, or exposed for sale:

(a) in or from domestic premises where the food is prepared, etc., by and for the benefit of a society under the Industrial and Provident Societies Act 1965 and premises of any description where the person preparing, etc., the food is not doing it in the course of a trade. Part IV of the 1984 Act does not apply to any food prepared or manufactured on such premises. These premises are also exempt from registration under section 16 of the Food Act 1984;

(b) at a market or fair, the right to hold which was acquired by virtue of a grant (including a presumed grant) or acquired or established by virtue of an enactment or order;

(c) at a notified temporary market[18];

(d) at a notified pleasure fair[19];

(e) by registered street traders;

(f) in containers of such material and so closed as to exclude all risks of contamination.

Part IV of the 1984 Act does not apply to the storage of the food for sale in the premises mentioned ((a) to (e) above).

Offences and penalties

3.08   A person who, without reasonable excuse, hawks food or uses premises as storage accommodation for food intended for hawking without being registered is guilty of an offence. He may be liable to a fine, on summary conviction, not exceeding level three on the standard scale. There is a defence mentioned in the Act, *i.e.* if he can prove that he took all reasonable precautions and exercised all due diligence to avoid committing the offence.[20]

ACUPUNCTURE, TATTOOING, EAR-PIERCING AND ELECTROLYSIS

3.09   There was concern for some time in environmental health circles, before the enactment of Part VIII of the Local Government (Miscellaneous Provisions) Act 1982, about the lack of hygienic control over skin piercing practices because of the possibility of the transmission of blood diseases, in particular hepatitis and AIDS. Blood, serum or small pieces of tissue, that do not have to be visible, may contain the virus and will

---

[18] "Notified temporary market" means a temporary market, notice of which has been given to the local authority in accordance with the Local Government (Miscellaneous Provisions) Act 1982, s.37(2) or any other enactment regulating such markets (Food Act 1984, s.67).

[19] "Notified pleasure fair" means a pleasure fair, as defined in the Public Health Act 1961, s.75(2)(*a*), notice of which has been given to the local authority in accordance with by-laws under that section. (Food Act 1984, s.67).

[20] Food Act 1984, s.65. (See p. 160 for the defence of "due diligence.")

adhere to the needle and could be transferred to towels, the practitioner's hands or other instruments. The next customer could contract the disease by contact with these contaminated objects.[21]

Some operations are often carried out as a part of or in conjunction with another business, for example ear-piercing and/or electrolysis in hairdressers and ear-piercing in jewellers. In such premises the risks of cross-infection are increased.

The need for control of the different practices varies throughout the country and the 1982 Act has made the provisions adoptive by a resolution of district and London borough councils. For the purposes of making a resolution, the practices are separated into three groups. Group 1 contains acupuncture, group 2 tattooing, ear-piercing and electrolysis and group 3 consists of all four practices. A local authority may resolve that the provisions relating to one of these groups apply to their area, although in the case of group 2, one, two or all of the practices may be contained in the resolution with the possibility of each one coming into force on different days. The resolution must also state the day, (at least a month after the date of the resolution) on which it comes into force.

The public must be made aware of this by publication in a local newspaper for two consecutive weeks and the first publication must not be later than 28 days before the resolution comes into force.[22]

Registration

Where a resolution is in force in a local authority area, a person wishing to practice any of the skin piercing activities mentioned must be registered, unless he is a registered medical practitioner or a dentist. The premises must also be registered but the Act does not prevent a registered practitioner from occasionally treating persons in his own home. **3.10**

If a person is operating from a stall then whether this can be regarded as premises that need to be registered depends on the degree of permanence. For example, if it is always erected in the same place then it should be registered, otherwise it would appear that the operator will be carrying on the business from his home as is the case if he uses a mobile vehicle. In these situations the operator's home must be registered.

Upon receiving an application, the local authority must register the applicant and premises but if he has been convicted of an offence under by-laws made by the local authority and the local magistrates' court has cancelled his registration, the consent of the court is necessary before he can be re-registered. A certificate of registration is issued to the applicant who must display it in a prominent position at his premises,

---

[21] For further information see "A Guide to Hygienic Skin Piercing" by Dr. Norman D. Noah, obtainable from the Public Health Laboratory Service, Communicable Disease Surveillance Centre, 61 Colindale Avenue, London NW9 SEQ.

[22] *R. v. Swansea City Council, ex p. Quietlynn Ltd.* (1985) 83 L.G.R. 308.

together with a copy of any by-laws made under the Act. Reasonable fees, as the local authority thinks suitable, may be charged.

The making of by-laws

3.11 By-laws may be made by the council to secure cleanliness of the practitioner and his premises and the sterilisation of instruments, etc., and model by-laws have been produced by the Department of the Environment and the Welsh Office, upon which council by-laws may be based. These are set out, in respect of each practice referred to, in Appendix 1.

In addition to by-laws, most local authorities draw up codes of practice, which should be followed in order to properly comply with the by-laws. The British Acupuncture Association, the Register of Oriental Medicine and the Traditional Acupuncture Society have, in combination, produced a code of practice for their members of hygienic acupuncture, and information on acupuncturists is available from the three organisations. Their addresses are listed in Appendix II. The codes of practice on ear-piercing, electrolysis and tattooing are usually based on the advice given in the very useful booklet, "A Guide to Hygienic Skin Piercing" by Dr. Norman D. Noah.

Skin piercing practitioners must also comply with the Health and Safety at Work etc. Act 1974. This places a duty on them to conduct their undertaking in such a way as to ensure, so far as is reasonably practicable, that persons who may be affected thereby are not exposed to risks to their health or safety. Customers as well as employees are covered by this Act but if the codes of practice and the by-laws are adhered to, the duty will be fulfilled in respect of the risks to health.

Offences and penalties[23]

3.12 A person carrying on any of the four skin piercing businesses/practices in an area where a resolution is in force without registration of himself and his premises, will be guilty of an offence and liable, on summary conviction, to a fine not exceeding level 3 on the standard scale.

Also, if a person contravenes a by-law he will be guilty of an offence and liable to the same fine. However, in addition or instead of the fine, the court may make an order suspending or cancelling his registration and the registration of his premises. The operation of the order may be suspended until the expiration of the period prescribed by Crown Court Rules for giving notice of appeal to the Crown Court.

A person not displaying his certificate of registration or copy of the by-laws is guilty of an offence and may be liable, on summary conviction, to a fine not exceeding level 2 on the standard scale.

In all these contraventions, it is open to the accused to prove that all reasonable precautions were taken and he exercised all due diligence to avoid committing the offence.[24]

---

[23] Local Government (Miscellaneous Provisions) Act 1982, s.16.
[24] *Ibid.* s.16(11).

CHAPTER 4

HOURS OF CLOSING AND SUNDAY TRADING

HOURS OF CLOSING

The law governing the hours of closing of shops is contained in Part I of **4.01**
the Shops Act 1950 and the Shops (Early Closing Days) Act 1965. Part
IV of the 1950 Act is still concerned with Sunday trading despite the well
published attempts to alter the law which many feel is out of step with
modern attitudes to shopping on a Sunday.

Parts I and IV of the Shops Act 1950 do not apply to any shop situated
in a designated airport or to the sale (otherwise than at a shop) of any
goods at a designated airport and the sale is effected by or on behalf of a
person carrying on a retail trade or business in the designated airport. In
order to be exempt the shop and sale referred to must be in the part of
the airport which is ordinarily used by persons travelling by air to or
from the airport. A "designated airport" means an airport designated
for the purposes of the Shops (Airports) Act 1962 by an order made by
the Board of Trade as being an airport at which there appears, to the
Board, to be a substantial amount of international passenger traffic.[1]

Definition of a "shop"

A "shop" is defined in section 74(1) of the 1950 Act as including any **4.02**
premises where any retail trade or business is carried on. There has to
be premises, which means some form of fixed structure. A mobile shop
would not come within the definition[2] and neither would a stall.[3]
Although a stall may be regarded as a place from which a retail trade or
business is carried on for the purposes of Part IV of the 1950 Act regarding Sunday trading.[4]

Where a statutory definition contains the word "includes," it may be
that the ordinary meaning of the term is extended or that it is restricted
to those terms contained in the definition.[5] Mann J. in *Lewis* v. *Rogers*,[6]
stated that he was of the opinion "includes" in this definition was a
deliberately chosen word of enlargement and as a result the meaning of
the phrase may be enlarged so as to encompass a meaning which it
would not ordinarily bear.

Under section 74(1) of the 1950 Act, the expression "retail trade or

---

[1] Shops (Airports) Act 1962, s.1.
[2] *Eldorado Ice Cream Co. Ltd.* v. *Keating* [1938] 1 K.B. 715; *Stone* v. *Boreham* [1959] 1
    Q.B. 1; *Cowlairs Co-operative Society* v. *Glasgow Corporation*, 1957 S.C. (J.) 51.
[3] *Greenwood* v. *Whelan* [1967] 1 Q.B. 396.
[4] *Maby* v. *Warwick Corporation* [1972] 2 Q.B. 242 (see also p. 182).
[5] *Dilworth* v. *Stamp Commissioners* [1899] A.C. 99 at 105, 106, P.C.
[6] (1984) 82 L.G.R. 670 at 678.

business" includes the business of a barber or hairdresser, the sale of refreshments or intoxicating liquors, the business of lending books or periodicals when carried on for the purpose of gain, and retail sales by auction, but does not include the sale of programmes and catalogues and other similar sales at theatres and places of amusement.

Retail sale means the business of selling to customers whereas the selling of goods by wholesale means selling to persons who buy to sell again,[7] and retail trade or business includes not only the sale of goods across the counter but also retail trade done by order.[8] A coin operated launderette with vending machines was held to be a shop where retail trade business was carried on in *Ilford Corporation* v. *Betterclean (Seven Kings) Ltd.*[9] and the selling of services as opposed to goods was considered in *Frawley (M. & F.)* v. *Ve-Re-Best Manufacturing Co.*[10] The court said in that case, the words "retail trade or business" primarily suggests the sale of goods rather than services and that although "business" was a slightly wider word than "trade," it could only cover analogous situations such as repairing shoes, or cleaning clothes or mending watches for customers resorting to the premises in circumstances comparable with those in which the business of selling goods by retail to similar customers might be carried on.

The aforementioned two cases were considered in *Lewis* v. *Rogers*[11] where video cassettes were hired from premises to whom the defendant contended were members of a video club. It was held that the extended meaning of the word "shop" in section 74 of the 1950 Act, included not only premises where articles were sold to members of the general public but also those premises which provided services. The premises were a shop if a retail service was provided, namely, a service in regard to an article which was given to members of the general public in return for payment which was provided on the premises; that hirers of articles carried on a retail business if they dealt directly with members of the public. In this case any member of the public could become a member of the club without restrictions and no benefit flowed from club membership other than the right to hire video cassettes. The court held that this was nothing more than a purely commercial enterprise run as such by the defendant.

It is important to note that the services are in respect of an article. This means that although, for example, estate agents, banks, building societies and brokers provide a service in the high street they are not regarded as carrying on a retail business. In *Erewash Borough Council* v. *Ilkeston Consumer Co-Operative Society Ltd.*,[12] the occupier was

[7] *per* Bacon V.C. in *Treacher and Co. Ltd.* v. *Treacher* (1874) W.N. 4.
[8] *Wallace Brothers* v. *Dixon* [1917] 2 I.R. 236.
[9] [1965] 2 Q.B. 222.
[10] [1953] 1 Q.B. 318; see also p. 112.
[11] (1984) 148 J.P. 481.
[12] *The Times*, June 30, 1988.

prosecuted for the offence of trading on a Sunday in respect of a travel agency. It was held, on appeal, that a travel agency did not constitute a shop for the offence of Sunday trading within the meaning of sections 47 and 74 of the Shops Act 1950. Bingham L.J. said:

" . . . the travel agency was not a shop for no thing was in any sense offered or sold . . . The travel agent's business of booking hotel accommodation and issuing travel tickets was not at all closely comparable with or analogous to the typical retail shopkeeper's activity of selling goods across the counter or off the supermarket shelf. . . . "

A department store or supermarket where there are a number of retail outlets each of which may be leased by different persons or companies and which constitute a single hereditament has been held to be one shop.[13]

General closing hours

The general closing hours for shops are the hours fixed by or under **4.03** section 2 of the Shops Act 1950 or the hours substituted therefor by or under any other provision of the 1950 Act.[14]

Section 2 of the 1950 Act states that every shop shall be closed for the serving of customers not later than 9 p.m. on the late day and 8 p.m. on any other day of the week. Under subsection 3, a customer may be served after the aforementioned times if it can be proved that he was in the shop before the closing hour, or that reasonable grounds existed for believing that the article supplied after the closing hour to a customer was required in the case of illness.

The late day is a Saturday but the local authority may fix by order some other day as a late day.[15] Under section 3 of the 1950 Act, the local authority may by the afore-mentioned order fix the same late day for all the shops, or may fix:

(a) different days for different classes of shops; or
(b) different days for different parts of their area; or
(c) different days for different periods of the year.

There are other exemptions and modifications to the general closing hours. First, subsection 3(b) of section 2 provides that any transaction mentioned in Schedule 2 to the 1950 Act is exempt[16] and the general

---

[13] *Fine Fare* v. *Brighton Corporation* [1959] 1 W.L.R. 223.
[14] Shops Act 1950, s.74(1).
[15] *Ibid.* s.3.
[16] The transactions contained in Sched. 2 are as follows:
1. (a) The sale of meats or refreshments (including table waters, sweets, chocolates, sugar confectionery and ice-cream) *for consumption on the premises*, or (in the case of meals or refreshments sold on railway premises) for consumption on the trains; but (i) in the case of canteens attached to and situated within or in the immediate vicinity of any works, if persons are employed at such works after the closing hour, and the canteen is kept open only for the use of those persons, meals or refreshments may be sold

closing hours do not apply to post office businesses, or to any premises in which post office business is transacted. However, where a post office is carried on in any shop in addition to any other business the general closing hours apply to the shop.[17]

Secondly, there is exemption in respect of fairs lawfully held and any bazaar or sale of work for charitable or other purposes for which no private profit is derived. Also, any library at which the business of lending books or periodicals is not carried out for the purpose of gain other than that of making profits for some philanthropic or charitable object (including any religious or educational object), or for any club or institution which is not itself carried on for purposes of gain.[18]

Thirdly, the following are modifications to certain businesses or instances where the local authority may modify the hours by order:

(a) Where the trade or business carried on is the sale of table waters, sweets, chocolates or other sugar confectionery, or ice-cream, the general closing hours are 10 p.m. on the late day and 9.30 p.m. on any other day although the local authority may by order substitute in its area or any part thereof an earlier hour, not earlier than 8 p.m. The local authority must, however, be satisfied that such an order is desired by the occupiers of a majority of the shops to be affected by the order.[19]

(b) Where the trade or business carried on is the sale of tobacco and smokers' requisites, the general closing hours are 9 p.m. on the late day and 8 p.m. on any other day, but the local authority may by order substitute in its area, or any part thereof,

---

after the closing hour for consumption anywhere within the works premises; and (ii) for the purposes of the foregoing provisions, tobacco supplied at a meal for immediate consumption is to be deemed to form part of the meal; (b) The sale of newly cooked provisions (which includes newly baked bread) *London County Council* v. *Davis* [1938] 2 All E.R. 764; (c) Intoxicating liquors to be consumed on or off the premises; (d) Tobacco, table waters or matches on licensed premises during the hours when intoxicating liquor is permitted by law to be sold on the premises; (e) Tobacco, matches, table waters, sweets, chocolates, or other sugar confectionery, or ice-cream at any time during the performance in any theatre, cinema, music hall, or other similar place of entertainment so long as the sale is to a bona fide member of the audience and in a part of the building to which no other members of the public have access; (f) Medicine or medical or surgical appliances, so long as the shop is kept open only for such time as is necessary for serving the customer; (g) Newspaper, periodicals and books from the bookstalls of such terminal and main line stations as may be approved by the Secretary of State; (h) Aircraft, motor or cycle supplies or accessories for immediate use, so long as the shop is kept open for such time as is necessary for serving the customer; (i) victuals, stores, or other necessaries required by any naval, military or air force authority for Her Majesty's forces or required for any ship on her arrival at or immediately before her departure from a port, so long as the shop is kept open only for such time as is necessary for serving the customer.

2. The transaction of any post office business.

[17] Shops Act 1950, s.44(2).
[18] *Ibid.* s.45.
[19] *Ibid.* s.6.

later hours, not later than 10 p.m. on the late day and 9.30 p.m. on any other day. The local authority in this case must be satisfied that such an order is desired by the occupiers of at least two thirds in number of the shops to be affected by the order.[20]

(c) In holiday resorts and in places where sea fishing is principally carried on during certain seasons of the year, an application may be made to a local authority to substitute later hours of closing for the general closing hours. The local authority shall by order substitute later hours for such period specified in the order (as long as it does not exceed four months in any year) but only if they are satisfied that the majority of occupiers of shops that will be affected require such an order. The order may apply to the whole or any part of the area of the local authority and to all shops or to shops of any class as long as the order is made subject to such conditions as the local authority considers necessary for securing that shop assistants affected are not employed in or about the business of that shop for more than such number of hours as may be specified by the order. The order may also suspend any closing order which is for the time being in force in the area.[21]

(d) The local authority may, by order, substitute for the general closing hours later hours (not later than 10 p.m.) in respect of a retail trade or business carried on at any exhibition or show if satisfied that the retail trade or business carried on is subsidiary or ancillary only to the main purpose of the exhibition or show. The order must be made subject to such conditions as the local authority considers necessary for securing that shop assistants affected are not employed in or about the retail business for more than such number of hours as may be specified in the order.[22]

In *Havering London Borough Council* v. *Stone (L.F.) & Son*,[23] an evening of hi-fi equipment and stereo records was held in part of a department store between 7.30 p.m. and 9.30 p.m., the purpose being to advertise the equipment which was for sale. It was not the store's late day and admission was free to members of the public. There were no actual sales so one of the points at issue was whether the shop was open for the "serving of customers." It was held that it was open for the serving of customers and the decisions in *Betta Cars* v. *Ilford Corporation*[24]

---

[20] *Ibid.* s.4.
[21] *Ibid.* s.41.
[22] *Ibid.* s.42. Breach of a condition imposed by an order under this section makes the occupier of the shop liable to a fine not exceeding level 2 on the standard scale.
[23] (1973) 117 S.J. 893.
[24] (1959) 124 J.P. 19.

and *Monaco Garage* v. *Watford Borough Council*[25] were followed. Lord Parker of Waddington C.J's. comments in the course of giving judgment in the latter case was quoted by Bridge J. as follows:

" . . . in my judgment anything which can in a general sense come within the words 'serving a customer' is sufficient to bring a case within the serving of a customer for the purposes of sale; an answer by an employee to any inquiry, the handing over of a brochure, assistance in examining a car, acts of salesmanship, anything of that kind is sufficient to be the serving of a customer. . . . "

Bridge J. also mentioned the problem where a mixed shop is open primarily and legitimately for the sale of exempt goods and whether there is a casual serving of a customer by answering a query on non-exempt goods displayed in the shop but which were not for sale at the time the shop was open. An isolated act of serving a customer in this situation did not necessarily mean that the shop was open for a prohibited purpose, but where there was a degree of repetition, as was the circumstances in this case, it could be said that the shop was open as a matter of business to promote sales from the shop.

The meaning of "serving of customers" was also considered in *Bury Metropolitan Borough Council* v. *Courburn*.[26] A showroom was open on Sundays in contravention of section 47 of the 1950 Act whereby persons could view kitchen units. These were purpose built and all that customers could do at the respondent's premises was to look at samples and make an appointment for a home visit. The magistrates' court held that although on the evidence they were satisfied that the premises were open for viewing on Sundays they were unable to find that they were open for the serving of customers. On appeal by the local authority, Taylor J. referred to the unreported decision of the Queen's Bench Division in *Manchester City Council* v. *Camperlands Ltd.*[27] There Ormrod J. stated that section 47 of the 1950 Act did not require that shops be closed in all circumstances on Sundays. What that section did require was that shops be closed for the serving of customers on Sundays and if the object of Parliament had been that places like this should have been closed in all circumstances on Sundays they would have said so.

It is legitimate for a shop to be open for some purposes on a Sunday. For example it would appear that the occupier of a shop would not fall foul of section 47 of the 1950 Act if silent viewing only was allowed. The area of activity between the two extremes, *i.e.* silent viewing and sale of an article " . . . is an area which must be very much within the discretion of the justices taking into account all the circumstances of the case." Taylor J. concluded (at 176) that the justices were right in the cir-

---

[25] [1967] 1 W.L.R. 1069.
[26] (1984) 82 L.G.R. 170.
[27] Unreported March 22, 1982. See (1984) J.P. March 10, p. 154.

cumstances of this case that the shop was not open for the serving of customers and he dismissed the appeal.

In the case of contravention of any of the provisions relating to
general closing hours the occupier of the shop will be liable to a fine, not
exceeding level 2 on the standard scale in respect of a first or subsequent
offence.[28]

Early closing days

Section 1(1) of the Shops Act 1950 states that every shop shall be **4.04**
closed for the serving of customers not later than 1 p.m. on one week
day in every week. However, a customer can be served legitimately at
any time at which the shop is required to be closed if it is proved either
that the customer was in the shop before then or that there was reasonable ground for believing that the article supplied to the customer was
required in the case of illness.[29] There is also an exemption for the serving of customers with victuals, stores or other necessaries for a ship, on
her arrival at or immediately before her departure from a port.[30]

Certain classes of trade are exempt and these are contained in Schedule 1 to the 1950 Act.[31] Shops are exempt only if the trades or businesses
listed in the schedule are carried on.

Also exempt are:

- (a) fairs lawfully held or any bazaar or sale of work for charitable
  or other purposes from which no profit is derived;
- (b) any library at which the business of lending books or periodicals is not carried on for purposes of gain other than that of
  making profits for some philanthropic or charitable object
  (including any religious or educational object), or for any club
  or institution which is not itself carried on for purposes of
  gain[32];
- (c) a post office business or any premises in which post office business is transacted. Where, however, the Post Office business is
  carried on in any shop in addition to any other business, the
  early closing obligation applies except where the shop is a tele-
  graph office. In that case the early closing obligation does not

---

[28] Shops Act 1950, s.14(2). Criminal Justice Act 1982, ss.35, 46.
[29] Shops Act 1950, s.1(7).
[30] *Ibid.* s.1(8).
[31] Schedule 1 exempts the following businesses: the sale by retail of intoxicating liquors;
refreshments, including the business carried on at a railway refreshment room; motor,
cycle and aircraft supplies and accessories to travellers; newspapers and periodicals;
meat, fish, cream, bread, confectionery, fruit, vegetables, flowers and other articles of a
perishable nature; tobacco and smokers' requisites; medicines and medical and surgical
appliances; the business carried on at a railway bookstall on or adjoining a railway platform; and any retail trade carried on at an exhibition or show, if the local authority certifies that such retail trade is subsidiary only to the main purpose of the exhibition or
show.
[32] Shops Act 1950, s.45.

apply to the shop so far as it relates to the transaction of Post Office business.[33]

As regards holiday resorts, a local authority may by order suspend for a period not exceeding in the aggregate four months in any year the early closing day obligation. The order may apply to the whole or to any part of the area of a local authority, and to all shops, or to shops of any class, within that area or part.[34]

The occupier of a shop affected by section 1 of the 1950 Act now selects which week day his shop is to be closed for the serving of customers by one o'clock in the afternoon[35] and he must keep a notice displayed conspicuously in the shop specifying the day he has selected as an early closing day. The notice must be at the entrance used by customers and visible from the outside.[36] Prior to 1965 and the passing of the Shops (Early Closing Days) Act the local authority fixed the early closing day.

The occupier of a shop may alter the early closing day by specifying a different day on the notice as long as a three month period has lapsed between changing dates. He may also change the day back again to the original day as long as one month has not expired from the date of change. He can do this by specifying the original day on the notice but he cannot do this again until three months has lapsed.[37]

Where a local authority have reason to believe that a majority of the occupiers of shops of any particular class in any area are in favour of being exempted from the provisions of section 1 of the 1950 Act, the local authority, unless they consider that the area in question is unreasonably small, shall take steps to ascertain the wishes of such occupiers. If the local authority are satisfied that a majority of the occupiers of such shops are in favour of the exemption, or, in the case of a vote being taken, at least one-half of the votes recorded by the occupiers of shops within the area of the class in question are in favour of the exemption, the local authority shall make an order exempting the shops of that class within the area from the provisions of section 1 of the 1950 Act.[38]

Where a shop is closed during the whole day on the occasion of a bank holiday, and that day is not the day fixed for the early closing day, the occupier may keep the shop open to customers after the closing time on the early closing day either immediately before or immediately after the bank holiday.[39]

Any contravention of the provisions of section 1 of the 1950 Act will

---

[33] *Ibid.* s.44.
[34] *Ibid.* s.40.
[35] Shops (Early Closing Days) Act 1965, s.1(1).
[36] *Ibid.* s.1(2).
[37] *Ibid.* s.1(3).
[38] Shops Act 1950, s.1(4). See also *Redbridge London Borough Council* v. *Wests (Ilford)* [1968] 2 W.L.R. 145 in relation to application of this order to mixed shops at p. 64.
[39] Shops Act 1950, s.1(5).

make the occupier of the shop liable to a fine not exceeding level 1 on the standard scale.[40]

Power of local authority to make closing orders regulating hours of closing

A local authority may, under section 8 of the Shops Act 1950, make an order called a "closing order," fixing the hours on the several days of the week at which, either throughout the area of the local authority or in a specified part thereof, all shops or shops of any specified class are to be closed for the serving of customers.

4.05

The closing hour cannot be earlier than 7 p.m. on any day of the week. The order may define the shops and trades to which it applies, may authorise sales after the closing hour in cases of emergency and in such other circumstances as may be specified or indicated in the order, and may contain any supplemental provisions which may appear necessary or proper.

A closing order may fix the closing hours earlier than the general closing hours but shall not authorise sales after the general closing hours, fixed by the 1950 Act, and must not contain provisions inconsistent with the 1950 Act relating to closing hours.[41]

As with the early closing day and general closing hours provision in the 1950 Act, there is a saving in respect of customers being in the shop before the closing hour fixed by the order and where there are reasonable grounds for believing that the article supplied after that hour was required in the case of illness. There is also an exemption for all transactions mentioned in Schedule 2 to the 1950 Act.[42]

Post Office businesses are exempt[43] as are fairs, bazaars, etc., and libraries where the business of lending books or periodicals is not carried on for gain.[44]

Again, as with the general closing hours, a local authority may, by order, substitute for any closing hour fixed by a closing order, later hours, (not later than 10 p.m.) in respect of a retail trade or business carried on at any exhibition or show if satisfied that the retail trade or business carried on is subsidiary or ancillary only to the main purpose of the exhibition or show.[45]

The procedure for making closing orders is contained in section 9(1) of the 1950 Act. Before making a closing order the local authority must give public notice in the prescribed manner and form[46] of their intention

---

[40] *Ibid.* s.14(1). Criminal Justice Act 1982, ss.35, 46.
[41] Shops Act 1950, s.8(4).
[42] *Ibid.* s.8(5). (See the note to General Closing Hours for the transactions listed in Sched. 2).
[43] Shops Act 1950, s.44.
[44] *Ibid.* s.45. (See also that these businesses are exempt from the general closing hours, p. 58).
[45] Shops Act 1950, s.42.
[46] See Shops Regulations 1912, regs. 6 to 22.

to make the order, specifying a period (not being less than the prescribed period) within which objections can be made. The objections must be considered and the local authority must be satisfied that the occupiers of at least two thirds, in number of the shops to be affected, approve it. The order may be revoked at any time by a local authority if they are satisfied that a majority of any class of shop affected by the order are opposed to the continuance of the order, so far as it affects that class of shop. Any such revocation is without prejudice to the making of any new closing order.[47]

Mixed shops

4.06 Section 13 of the 1950 Act deals with shops where more than one trade or business is carried on, for example, the modern supermarket. Sub-section (1) refers to exemption. It states that where several trades or businesses are carried on in the same shop, and any of those trades or businesses is of such a nature that, if it were the only trade or business carried on in the shop, the shop would be exempt from the obligation to be closed on the early closing day, the exemption shall apply to the shop so far as the carrying on of that trade or business is concerned, subject however to such conditions as may be prescribed.

Non-exempt trades or businesses may be considered incidental to the exempt trade or business being carried on. For example, it was held that the proprietor of a confectioners and refreshment room had committed no offence when he sold pork sausages for consumption off the premises after one o'clock on an early closing day for pork butchers. This was incidental to his main business.[48] Also, in a Scottish case, a company was held to have committed no offence where it carried on a number of businesses in one premises including a hairdressing section that stayed open on a Wednesday afternoon, the day the local authority had fixed as an early closing day for hairdressers.[49]

In *Fine Fare* v. *Brighton Corporation*,[50] the local authority had fixed Wednesday for early closing day for certain businesses. The company was trading in a number of businesses on one premises, including those fixed by the local authority to close early on a Wednesday. The company closed the shop on a Thursday instead but it was held that they committed no offence. There was no need to close various parts of the shop on different days of the week.

A multiple store not affected by a class order made by a local authority exempting certain shops from early closing may remain open for the trades or businesses exempt from early closing by virtue of section 13(1) of the 1950 Act. In *Redbridge London Borough Council* v. *Wests*

---

[47] Shops Act 1950, s.11, which was substituted by the Local Government, Planning and Land Act 1980, s.1(4), Sched. 1(4).
[48] *Margerison* v. *Wilson* (1914) 79 J.P. 38.
[49] *Thomson* v. *Somerville*, 1917 S.C. (J) 3.
[50] [1959] 1 W.L.R. 223.

(Ilford),[51] the local authority made an order under section 1(4) of the 1950 Act exempting certain classes of shops from early closing. The shop was a multiple store and although those departments of the store selling commodities not mentioned in the exemption order closed early on one day in each week, the store was kept open for the sale of those included in the order. The local authority prosecuted the company for failing to close the store by 1 p.m. on one week day in accordance with section 1(1) of the Shops Act 1950. The company conceded that the exemption order did not apply directly to their store because it did not fall into any of the classes specified in it, but they contended that section 13(1) of the 1950 Act applied the order to those departments which they had kept open. It was thus held, that while the exemption order, being a class order under section 1(4) of the 1950 Act, did not apply directly to the multiple store, it applied by virtue of section 13(1) of the 1950 Act to the carrying on in the store of the trades or business of the nature to which it referred and therefore those parts of the store selling goods mentioned in the exemption order were allowed to remain open throughout the week.

Section 13(2) of the 1950 Act has the same provision as section 13(1), except that it relates to general closing hours instead of early closing days, and section 13(3) where the same provisions relate to closing hours fixed by a closing order.

In *Fine Fare Ltd.* v. *Aberdare Urban District Council*,[52] a supermarket sold a very large range of articles, including groceries and greengroceries. The local authority made a closing order and one of the trades specified in the closing order was that of a grocer. The trade of greengrocer was not specified. The order also contained a provision along the lines of section 13(3) of the 1950 Act in that it provided that if greengrocery was sold after the closing hours prescribed for other trades, then certain notices had to be exhibited in the shop. The company took the view that the closing order had no application to the supermarket and proceeded to sell groceries after the hour specified in the closing order and also proceeded to sell greengroceries without exhibiting the notice which the order required. The company was prosecuted but it was held, on appeal, that the order did not apply to a supermarket where a multitude of trades or businesses was carried on. As explained by Widgery J. in *Redbridge London Borough Council* v. *Wests (Ilford)*,[53] a closing order cannot operate in a piecemeal fashion. It cannot operate to close the grocery department without closing the greengrocery department. He stated that since the supermarket was not in any of the specified classes of shop, the closing order did not apply to the supermarket at all and since a prosecution based on section 8 must clearly establish that the closing order was effective for the particular shop, that prosecution was

[51] [1968] 2 W.L.R. 145.
[52] [1965] 2 Q.B. 39.
[53] [1968] 2 W.L.R. 145.

doomed to failure before any reference came to be made to section 13(3) of the 1950 Act at all.

It was also held in the *Fine Fare* case that section 13(3) of the 1950 Act operated only in regard to some ancillary business carried on in connection with a main business specified as a class under section 8(1) and not in respect of premises in which a multiplicity of main trades or business was carried on; and that the term in the closing order providing for a special notice to be exhibited was made under section 13(3) and had no application to the defendant's premises.

Section 13(4) of the 1950 Act states, that where several trades or businesses are carried on in the same shop, the local authority may require the occupier of the shop to specify which trade or business he considers to be his principal trade or business, and no trade or business other than that so specified shall (for the purpose of determining a majority, or any proportion or number of occupiers or of shops, for the purposes of Part I of the 1950 Act) be considered as carried on in the shop, unless the occupier of the shop satisfies the local authority that it forms a substantial part of the business carried in the shop.

Takeaway food shops

4.07   Takeaway food shops are notorious for attracting persons who cause noise and unreasonable disturbance late at night to local residents. Unless the hours of closing are governed by conditions attached to the planning permission, or the premises come under the definition of a late night refreshment house under section 1 of the Late Night Refreshment Houses Act 1969,[54] the local authority has no control.

Where, however, residents in the neighbourhood of a takeaway food shop have complained to a local authority about being unreasonably disturbed either by persons resorting to the premises or by the use of the premises for the supply of meals or refreshments, the local authority, if satisfied of this, may make a "closing order."[55]

They may only make the closing order in respect of premises where meals or refreshments are supplied for consumption off the premises, other than: (a) premises coming under the definition of a late night refreshment house; and (b) any premises that are exempt licensed premises defined under section 1 of the Late Night Refreshment Houses Act 1969.[56]

The closing order will specify the premises and the hours that the premises may not be used for the supply of meals and refreshments to the public but, under section 4(3) of the 1982 Act, the closing order cannot prohibit the use of the premises for the above purposes earlier than midnight and later than 5 a.m. The closing order may prohibit the use of

---

[54] See p. 41.
[55] Local Government (Miscellaneous Provisions) Act 1982, s.4.
[56] See p. 41.

the premises for the above purposes between different hours on different days of the week.[57]

A closing order may be revoked or varied by a revocation and variation order respectively[58] and, without prejudice to the power of the district council to make a further closing order, a closing order shall cease to have effect three years from the date on which it was made.[59] A variation or revocation order may be made on the written application of the "keeper" of the premises, *i.e.* the person having the conduct or management of the premises.[60]

Procedure and appeals are contained in section 5 of the 1982 Act. The local authority must take all relevant circumstances into consideration but it can only act on a complaint from residents in the neighbourhood about unreasonable disturbance from the takeaway.

If the local authority propose to make a closing or variation order they must first serve a notice on the keeper of the premises giving their reasons for seeking to make the order and giving the keeper an opportunity to make representation to them concerning the matter. The name and address of the person who complained must not be divulged to the keeper without that person's consent.

After the order is made, a copy is served on the keeper of the premises, coming into force 21 days after the date of service. An appeal may be brought to the magistrates' court but it must be brought before the order comes into force. If there is to be an appeal then the order shall not come into force until the appeal has been determined or abandoned. An appeal may also be brought against the refusal by a district council to make a variation order or a revocation order, but in this case no appeal can be brought after the expiration of 21 days from the date on which the keeper was notified of the refusal. A further appeal against a decision of a magistrates' court may be brought to the Crown Court.

The keeper of premises to which a closing or variation order applies shall be guilty of an offence if there is a contravention of any of the provisions of the order, although there is a defence if it can be proven that the keeper took all reasonable precautions and exercised all due diligence to avoid commission of the offence by himself or by any person under his control.[61]

A person found guilty is liable on summary conviction to a fine not exceeding level 4 on the standard scale.

In the case of an offence committed by a body corporate, a director, manager, secretary or other similar officer of the body corporate will also be guilty of an offence if it is proved that it was committed with his

---

[57] Local Government (Miscellaneous Provisions) Act 1982, s.4(4).
[58] *Ibid.* s.4(5), (6).
[59] *Ibid.* s.4(8).
[60] *Ibid.* s.4(7).
[61] *Ibid.* s.6(1), (2).

consent or connivance or attributable to any neglect on that persons' part.[62]

SUNDAY TRADING

General

4.08   The restriction on Sunday trading is contained in Part IV of the 1950 Act. Section 47 states that every shop[63] shall, save as otherwise provided by this part of this Act, be closed for the serving of customers[64] on Sunday: provided that a shop may be open for the serving of customers on Sunday for the purposes of transactions mentioned in Schedule 5 to this Act.[65] Also, goods sold retail to a customer must not be delivered or despatched for delivery from a shop at any time when, under the provisions of Part IV of the 1950 Act, a customer could not be served with those goods in that shop. This particular prohibition does not apply to any Sunday which is also Christmas Day and any Sunday when the succeeding Monday is Christmas Day.[66]

There are many anomalies in the list of exempt transactions and this is one of the reasons for the pressure from lobbyists to rationalise the law. For example, the traditional fried fish and chip shop must close on a Sunday but other takeaway shops may remain open. With the substantial increase in the number of Chinese and Indian takeaway shops in recent years it could be argued that under the 1950 Act the occupier of a traditional fried fish and chip shop is placed at an unfair disadvantage. Dried fruit and vegetables may be sold but not tinned or bottled fruit and vegetables, clotted cream but not tinned cream and motor accessories but not household accessories. A loaf of bread is regarded as refreshment,[67] "newly cooked provisions" includes newly baked bread[68] and a raw kipper which can be eaten without any preparation is also regarded as refreshment, but articles of food such as packets of tea or flour are not because they require preparation before consumption.[69]

There are also exemptions and savings contained in section 56 of the 1950 Act. The prohibition on Sunday trading does not affect the sale, dispatch or delivery of victuals, stores or other necessaries required by any person for a ship or aircraft on her arrival at, or immediately before her departure from, a port or aerodrome; or the sale, dispatch or delivery of goods to a club for the purposes of the club; or to the cooking on Sunday, before 1.30 p.m., at any shop of any food brought to that shop by a customer and required by him for consumption on that day, or

---

[62] *Ibid.* s.6(4).
[63] For the meaning of "shop," see p. 55.
[64] For the meaning of serving customers, see p. 59.
[65] See Appendix III.
[66] Shops Act 1950, s.55.
[67] *Burns* v. *Wardale* [1946] K.B. 451, D.C.
[68] *London County Council* v. *Davis* [1938] 2 All E.R. 764.
[69] *Newberry* v. *Cohen's (Smoked Salmon)*; *Newberry* v. *Adelson* (1956) 54 L.G.R. 343.

the dispatch or delivery not later than 1.30 p.m. of any such food so cooked.

A person carrying on, or employed in, the business of a hairdresser or barber may, without contravening the 1950 Act, at any time for the purposes of that business attend another person in any place, if the attendance is necessary by reason of the bodily or mental infirmity of that person, or in any hotel or club, if the person attended is resident there.

There are two defences contained in section 56 of the 1950 Act. The first is where goods are supplied, etc., in the case of illness. A person has a good defence to a charge of keeping a shop open for the serving of customers, or with despatching or delivering goods in contravention of the restriction on Sunday trading, if he can prove that reasonable grounds existed for believing that the goods supplied, despatched or delivered were required in the case of illness.

The second defence relates to the serving of customers after the permitted hours of opening. Where a person is charged with keeping open after the permitted hours for the serving of customers of a shop which is permitted to be open until a certain hour, it is a good defence for him to prove that the customer was in the shop before that hour and left the shop not later than half-an-hour after that hour.

In addition, under section 56 of the 1950 Act, where a person is engaged at home in handicraft and he depends for his livelihood on the sale on Sunday of articles which he has produced in the course of his handicraft to such extent that the prohibition of such sale would involve substantial hardship, a local authority may, if satisfied of these facts, grant a certificate exempting said person from the restrictions for such period and subject to such conditions as it specifies.

Local authorities that have pursued an active role in enforcing the provisions of the 1950 Act in relation to Sunday trading have found that many of the large retail "out of town" trading companies tend to regard the relatively small maximum fine that can be imposed by local magistrates as a licence fee to continue trading.

Any person found guilty of a contravention of any provision of the 1950 Act in relation to Sunday trading is liable to a fine not exceeding level 4 on the standard scale in the case of the first, second or any subsequent offences.[70]

Where the penalties allowed under the 1950 Act fail to deter the occupier of the shop from committing the offence some local authorities have applied successfully to the High Court for an injunction under section 222 of the Local Government Act 1972. This section provides that where a local authority considers it expedient for the promotion or protection of the interests of the inhabitants of their area:

(a) they may prosecute or defend or appear in any legal proceed-

---

[70] Shops Act 1950, s.59, as amended by the Criminal Justice Act 1982, ss.38, 46.

ings and, in the case of civil proceedings, may institute them in
their own name; and

(b) they may, in their own name, make representations in the
interests of the inhabitants at any public inquiry held by or on
behalf of any Minister or public body under any enactment.

The power of the local authority to seek injunctions in their own
name, under section 222 of the Local Government Act 1972, to restrain
illegal Sunday trading rather than applying for the fiat of the Attorney-
General in a relator action was confirmed in the consolidated cases of
Stoke-on-Trent City Council v. *B. & Q. (Retail)*; *Barking & Dagenham
London Borough Council* v. *Home Charm Retail*[71]; Lawson L.J. stated
that a local authority's power, under section 222 of the 1972 Act, to
institute proceedings for injunctive relief was not limited to restraining
public nuisances as claimed by the defendants. All local authorities who
gave thought to the various factors and satisfied themselves on reasonable grounds and on adequate evidence that an injunction was the only
way of stopping anticipated offences amounting to deliberate and fla-
grant flouting of the law, might use their powers under section 222 of the
1972 Act to apply for injunctive relief. Ackner L.J. also stated that the
local authority would have to show that its complaints were unheeded
and that subsequent prosecutions resulting in convictions and fines had
failed to deter the defendant. The decision was unanimously upheld by
the House of Lords in *Stoke-on-Trent City Council* v. *B. & Q. (Retail)*.[72]

There have been many other defences tested in the courts by retailing
companies determined to trade on a Sunday.[73] The so-called "club
defence" under section 56(1)(*b*) of the 1950 Act which has been tried
without success is an example.[74] In *Stafford Borough Council* v. *Elken-
ford*[75] the court held that a club defence can only work where the club is
a members' club, not where it is a proprietary club. This is because the
proprietary club is owned by someone; those who join the club are his
licensees. The object of the proprietary club is that the proprietor makes
money: it is a business venture run for profit. A proprietary club cannot
provide a defence under the 1950 Act.

A novel argument for the defence was considered in *Hadley* v. *Texas
Homecare* and seven other appeals.[76] It was contended that items sold
on a Sunday in a D.I.Y. shop were capable of being motor accessories
which is an exempt transaction under Schedule 5. Most of them were

---

[71] [1984] A.C. 754.
[72] *Ibid.* The reasonableness or otherwise of a decision to institute civil proceedings under
section 222 of the 1972 Act is to be tested at the date of issue of the writ and not at the
date of the relevant resolution. *Waverley Borough Council* v. *Hilden* [1988] 1 W.L.R.
246.
[73] See the interpretation of "shop" on p. 55 and "serving of customers" on p. 59.
[74] See *Lewis* v. *Rogers* (1984) 148 J.P. 481, where the defence was used in the hiring of
videos. (See p. 56).
[75] [1977] 1 W.L.R. 324.
[76] *The Times*, December 31, 1987.

used in the furbishing and fitting out of motor caravans while a watering can was used for the filling of car radiators. It was stated by Mann J. that there was a difference between asserting that an object could be used as a motor accessory and that an object was a motor accessory. A woman's stocking could be used as a motor accessory, in that it could serve as a fan belt, but no one using language with its ordinary and natural meaning would regard a hosiery counter as selling motor accessories. Justices should ask themselves whether in the ordinary and natural use of language an item was capable of being described as a motor supply or accessory. In reaching their conclusion, justices did not need evidence as to capacity. It was irrelevant. They needed only a knowledge of the English language.

Faced with all these defeats a major D.I.Y. company (B. and Q. (Retail)) in April 1988 at Shrewsbury Crown Court successfully appealed for their case to be referred to the European Court. They argued that the Shops Act 1950 contravened Article 30 of the Treaty of Rome which applies where a provision of national law:

(a) discriminates against goods imported from other member states; and/or

(b) places goods at a competitive disadvantage compared to similar domestic products.

Most of the E.E.C. countries have some form of Sunday trading. A reference (No. 145/88) to the European Court by the Cwmbran magistrates' court in respect of a presentation by Torfaen Borough Council against B and Q plc was heard recently. In June 1989 the Advocate General gave an opinion that a national rule which prohibits Sunday trading is not covered by Article 30 if it does not discriminate against imported goods, place them at a disadvantage, screen off the domestic market of a member state or make access to that market more difficult. This is, however, an impartial and independent opinion which is given in order to assist the judges in their consideration of the case.

In response to a query from the Keep Sunday Special Campaign, the Attorney-General has stated that the fact that there is an appeal to the European Court on one case need not inhibit another court, when dealing with other proceedings, and that the courts may properly be asked by local authorities *not* to adjourn merely because one or more references are pending before the European Court.

Shops where several trades or business are carried on

Section 50 of the 1950 Act provides that where several trades or businesses are carried on in the same shop and any of them consist only of transactions to which an exemption from closing for the whole or part of Sunday applies, the shop may be kept open for the whole or part of Sunday for the purposes of those transactions alone, subject to such conditions as may be prescribed. **4.09**

The section creates no offence, but if the conditions are not observed, an offence is committed under section 47 of the 1950 Act.[77] The conditions are listed in the Shops Regulations 1937 (S.R. and O. 1937 No. 271) as follows:

(a) during any time on Sunday when the shop is open for the serving of customers there shall be exhibited in some conspicuous places on the exterior and in the interior of the shop notices in the form marked I in the Schedule to the 1937 Regulations and in letters of not less than one inch in height; and

(b) so far as is reasonably practicable, no goods in connection with any trade or business shall be exhibited either inside or outside the shop at any time on Sunday when the shop cannot lawfully be kept open for the serving of customers with these goods.

Local authority power to make partial exemption order

4.10   Under section 48 of the 1950 Act, a local authority has the power to make a "partial exemption order" providing that shops situated in their area, or in such part thereof as is specified in the order, may for the purposes of such of the transactions mentioned in Schedule 6 to the 1950 Act,[78] as may be specified in the order, be open for the serving of customers on Sunday. A partial exemption order may not, however, authorise a shop to be open for the serving of customers after 10 a.m. on Sunday except in cases of emergency, and in such other cases as may be specified in the order. A partial exemption order may contain such incidental, supplemental or consequential provisions as may appear to the local authority necessary or proper. The procedure for making such an order is contained in section 52.

Local Authority power to make an order restricting the opening on Sunday of "takeaway" food shops

4.11   In the case of shops that may lawfully be open on Sunday for the serving of customers, for the purposes of the sale of meals or refreshments for consumption elsewhere than at the shop, the local authority may by order provide that they shall cease to be entitled to be open on Sunday for that purpose. The order may apply to all such shops or any class thereof being shops situated in the area of the local authority or part thereof; but no such order may apply to shops in which the sale of meals or refreshments for consumption at the shop form a substantial part of the business or prevent the sale on Sunday of meals and refreshments

---

[77] *Tonkin* v. *Raven* [1959] 1 Q.B. 177.
[78] These are the sale of: (a) bread and flour confectionery, including rolls and fancy bread; (b) fish (including shell fish); and (c) groceries and other provisions commonly sold in grocers shops, in so far as such sales are not included amongst the transactions mentioned in Sched. 5 to the 1950 Act.

elsewhere than at a shop except to such extent and subject to such conditions as may be specified in the order.[79]

An order made for this purpose may apply during the whole year or during such periods as may be specified and may be subject to prescribed conditions.[80] Section 52 of the 1950 Act sets out the procedure for making such an order.

Power of local authority to make an order regarding Sunday trading at a holiday resort

There is a power, under section 51 of the Shops Act, to allow a local **4.12** authority to make an order specifying that shops or any class of shop can remain open for the serving of customers on a Sunday.[81] A "holiday" resort is not defined in the 1950 Act but it probably includes areas that are not seaside resorts.

The Sundays specified in the order must not be more than 18 in any year and the only transactions that may be carried out are any of those contained in Schedule 7 to the 1950 Act.[82] The order may lay down hours of opening and other conditions.

Notices relating to orders modifying Sunday trading restrictions

Where a shop is open on a Sunday for the serving of customers, a **4.13** notice must be conspicuously posted in the shop in the prescribed form stating the terms of any order applying to the shop.[83]

Persons observing the Jewish Sabbath

Section 53 of the 1950 Act provides for registration by the local auth- **4.14** ority of a shop occupied by a person of the Jewish religion, or by any person who is a member of any religious body regularly observing the Jewish Sabbath as it applies to a person of the Jewish religion. If a shop is so registered the shop must be closed on Saturday for all purposes connected with trade or business, the Sunday trading restrictions shall not apply to the shop until 2 p.m. and a notice must be conspicuously displayed in the shop. This notice must state that the shop will be closed on Saturday and if it is to be kept open after 2 p.m. for any permitted transaction under the 1950 Act the notice must state the hours of opening and purposes for which it is open. No other shop occupied by the same occupier may be kept open for any purpose connected with trade

---

[79] Shops Act 1950, s.49(1).
[80] *Ibid.* s.49(2).
[81] There was also power, under s.54 of the 1950 Act, for the common council of the City of London and the former London County Council to make orders authorising certain shops or classes of shops to be open for the serving of customers on Sunday. Orders cannot now be made apart from those revoking previous orders made under the Act (London Government Act 1963, s.51(3)).
[82] These are the sale of: (a) any articles required for the purposes of bathing or fishing; (b) photographic requisites; (c) toys, souvenirs and fancy goods; (d) books, stationery, photographs, reproductions and postcards; (e) any article of food.
[83] Shops Act 1950, s.57.

or business on Saturday. Also, no person by whom the necessary statutory declaration has been made in connection with the application or registration of the shop, shall be employed or engaged on the Jewish sabbath about the business of any shop or shall so employ, or be directly concerned in the control or management of any partnership or company which so employs, any person in such business.

A statutory declaration by the occupier of a shop must accompany an application on the prescribed form for registration.[84] This must declare that he conscientiously objects on religious grounds to carrying on trade or business on the Jewish Sabbath.

A shop occupied by a partnership or company is deemed to be occupied by a person of Jewish religion if the majority of partners or directors, as the case may be, are persons of that religion, but not otherwise. Such a shop may not be registered unless the statutory declaration is made by the majority of partners or directors and specifies the names and addresses of all the other partners or directors.

The local authority must refuse to register a shop if the registration of that shop has been revoked or cancelled while it was in the occupation of the applicant. Also, registration may be refused if the registration of that shop, or of any other shop occupied or formerly occupied by the applicant, or by any partnership or company of which he was a partner or director, has been revoked or cancelled.[85]

In *Thanet District Council* v. *Ninedrive*,[86] a company applied to the local authority for registration of land for Sunday trading. A market was held on the land with approximately 40 stalls occupied by independent stallholders. They were not employed by the company and not necessarily of the Jewish faith. The defendants contended, *inter alia*, that the land in question was a "shop" within the meaning of section 53 of the 1950 Act and that "shop" was defined widely enough to include a field and there was nothing in the Act to prevent a Jewish registered shop from including places where other traders, not necessarily of Jewish faith could carry on business. The court held that the land in question was a "place" and not a "shop" and, therefore, for the purposes of section 58 of the Act of 1950, if retail business was carried on at a number of stalls, each with a varying trade carried on by a varying proprietor, each such stall was to be treated for the purposes of section 53 as a separate shop and that nothing in the Act permitted a "blanket" registration.

If upon representations made to the local authority, it appears to the authority that there is reason to believe that the occupier of any registered shop is not a person of the Jewish religion (or other religion

---

[84] For the prescribed form of application and declaration see the Shops Regulations 1937 (S.I. 1937, No. 271).

[85] There is a right of appeal against refusal of registration in the second situation where the local authority has a discretion (Shops Act 1950, s.53(11)).

[86] (1977) 121 S.J. 706.

observing the Jewish sabbath), or that a conscientious objection on religious grounds to carrying on business on the Jewish sabbath is not genuinely held by the occupier, the local authority may furnish particulars of the case to the tribunal prescribed for the purpose.[87] If the tribunal reports to the authority that, in its opinion, the occupier of the shop is not such a person, or holds no such conscientious objection, the authority must revoke the registration. Upon revocation, the registration of all other shops occupied by the same occupier, whether in the area of the same local authority or not, is deemed also to be revoked.

Should occupation of a shop registered under section 53 change, then it is the duty of the person who occupies the shop to notify the local authority by service of a notice. Whether or not the notice is served, the registration is automatically cancelled after the lapse of a period of 14 days unless a fresh application is made within that period or any extended period allowed by the local authority. These provisions also apply where there is a change of partnership or among the directors of any company occupying a registered shop.

Registration of any shop is cancelled upon application of the occupier but it is not cancelled until the expiration of 12 months from the date on which an application for registration of the shop was last made.

Any person who knowingly or recklessly makes an untrue statement or untrue representation for the purpose of procuring the registration of any shop shall be liable on summary conviction to imprisonment for a term not exceeding three months or to a fine not exceeding level 3 on the standard scale,[88] or to both such imprisonment and fine.

Exemption as respects Jewish retail dealers in meat

A person of the Jewish religion may keep a shop open for the serving **4.15** of customers on Sunday if he is in the business of a retail dealer in Kosher meat.[89] He must, however, be licensed for the sale of Kosher meat by the local Board of Shechite, or in the absence of such Board, by a committee appointed for the purpose by the local Jewish congregation established in accordance with Jewish law. He must not carry on a business on a Saturday as a retail dealer in Kosher or butcher's meat.

Notice must previously have been given to the local authority of the person's intention to carry on the business of retail dealer in Kosher meat on Sunday, and if he carries on the business in any shop a notice must be conspicuously displayed in the shop stating that it is open on Sundays for the purposes of retail dealing in Kosher meat, but is not open on Saturday.[90]

[87] Shops (Procedure for Jewish Tribunals) Regulations 1937 (S.I. 1937 No. 1038) and Shops Regulations 1937 (S.I. 1937 No. 271).
[88] Criminal Justice Act 1982, ss.38, 46.
[89] "Kosher meat" means butchers' meat killed and prepared by the Jewish ritual method (Shops Act 1950, s.74(1)).
[90] *Ibid.* s.62.

Retail meat dealers

4.16   Section 60 of the 1950 Act states that all the previous provisions relating to Sunday trading do not apply to retail meat dealers as there are special provisions concerning this trade in sections 61 to 65.

Section 61 provides that it shall not be lawful to carry on the business of a retail dealer in butcher's meat[91] on Sunday and, where the business is carried on in a shop, the shop shall for the purposes of that business be closed for the serving of customers on that day.

Section 62 relates to the sale of Kosher meat by Jewish retail dealers (see previous paragraph), section 63 states that the dispatch or delivery of butcher's meat is prohibited, with exceptions, at any time when the shop may not be open for the serving of customers,[92] and section 65 of the 1950 Act provides that the Sunday trading restrictions do not apply to the sale, dispatch or delivery of butcher's meat required by any person for a ship or aircraft on her arrival at, or immediately before her departure from a port or aerodrome.

The offences related to dealing in butcher's meat on Sundays are contained in section 64. Any person who contravenes the provisions is liable to a penalty not exceeding level 4 on the standard scale[93] in the case of first, second or subsequent offences.

Retail trading elsewhere than in shops

4.17   Under section 58 of the 1950 Act, the restrictions on Sunday trading extend to any place where any retail trade or business is carried on[94] as if that place was a shop, and as if, in relation to that place, the person carrying on the retail trade or business was the occupier of a shop. Also included is registration in the case of occupation by persons of the Jewish religion or observing the Jewish sabbath. In addition to those transactions listed in Schedule 5 to the 1950 Act[95] that are allowed to take place in a shop on a Sunday in respect of retail trading elsewhere than in shops, the sale by fishermen of freshly caught fish (including shellfish) and the sale at a farm, smallholding, allotment or similar place, of produce produced thereon are also allowed.

The following requirements do not apply to retail trading elsewhere than in shops:

   (a) the approval of orders by occupiers of shops;

---

[91] "Butcher's meat" means beef, mutton, veal, lamb, or pork (including livers, heads, feet, hearts, lights, kidneys and sweetbreads) whether fresh chilled, frozen or salted, and includes Kosher meat, that is to say, butcher's meat killed and prepared by the Jewish ritual method (*ibid.* s.74(1)).

[92] See p. 59.

[93] Criminal Justice Act 1982, ss.38, 46.

[94] "Place where any retail trade or business is carried on." It is a matter of fact or degree whether any particular establishment has a sufficient degree or permanency to fall within these words. See *Maby* v. *Warwick Corporation* [1972] 2 Q.B. 242 and also p. 182.

[95] See Appendix III.

(b) the fixing of notices where the shop is registered as occupied by a person of the Jewish religion or observing the Jewish sabbath;

(c) stating the terms of any notice applying to a shop which is lawfully kept open on Sunday.[96]

---

[96] Shops Act 1950, s.58, paragraphs (a), (b) & (c).

CHAPTER 5

HEALTH AND SAFETY OF SHOP ASSISTANTS AND
MEMBERS OF THE PUBLIC

General

5.01   Legislation dealing with health and safety at work, enacted before the
Health and Safety at Work etc. Act 1974, tended to lay down specific
duties on employers in great detail to suit known hazards or circumstances. Examples are the Construction (Working Places) Regulations
1966[1] that, *inter alia*, lay down precise widths for scaffolds used for different purposes, the Woodworking Machines Regulations 1974[2] that
deal in detail with the nature, position and structure of guards on circular saws, and the Offices, Shops and Railway Premises Act 1963 that
contain particular duties in respect of provision of proper welfare and
safety facilities in offices and shops.

The fact that the legal requirements dealt in precise detail with known
hazards "bolted the stable door after the horse had fled" and they could
not be used to prevent new hazards occurring. Most of the legislation
particularly in such industries as mining resulted from disasters. An accident occurs, the reason for the accident is investigated and legislation is
enacted to prevent a re-occurrence.

This approach to safety legislation was criticised particularly by the
Robens Committee on "Safety and Health at Work."[3] It was stated that
the law had become too complicated and technical for the people
engaged in industry to be completely aware of their duties. There was,
in fact, "too much law" and in the wrong form. It is necessary to be
clear, precise and unambiguous, but the law must be capable of being
applied to new risks.

The Health and Safety at Work etc. Act 1974 was passed in order to
counteract these criticisms. The existing health and safety legislation
was retained but new requirements were added which set out in the
widest possible terms, duties that were not directed to any particular
hazard but intended to be capable of being applied in almost any situation, even if the risk had not been known to exist previously.

It is basically a criminal law statute and although it applies to all
employees in all employment situations the enforcement authorities dif-
fer according to the business being carried on. Enforcement duties,
under the Health and Safety (Enforcement Authority) Regulations
1977,[4] are split between the Health and Safety Executive and district

[1] S.I. 1966 No. 94.
[2] S.I. 1974 No. 903.
[3] H.M.S.O. 1972, Cmnd. 5034.
[4] S.I. 1977 No. 746.

councils. The enforcing authority for warehouses, catering premises, offices and shops is the district council and the department normally responsible for administration of this function is the Environmental Health Department. Other businesses not allocated to the district councils by the Health Regulations are the responsibility of the Health and Safety Executive.

Certain duties are contained in the Act itself (sections 2 to 8). These are catch-all offences that would apply in matters not covered by other "relevant statutory provisions," such as the Offices, Shops and Railway Premises Act 1963. The enforcement of the "relevant statutory provisions" is by means of the enforcement sections of the Health and Safety at Work Act and although breach of the duties as laid down may make the offender immediately liable to prosecution there are other powers available to an inspector, appointed under section 19 of the Act. These are the service of an Improvement or Prohibition Notice.

The Environment and Safety Information Act 1988 provides that from April 1, 1989 enforcing authorities must keep a register of certain improvement and prohibition notices *i.e.* those notices that have been served in order to protect members of the public rather than persons at work. Entries must be kept for at least three years and members of the public must be allowed access to information on the register. There is a duty to inform the recipient of the notice of the entry.

Improvement notice

In any case where an inspector "is of the opinion that any person: (a) **5.02** is contravening one or more of the relevant statutory provisions; or (b) has contravened one or more of those provisions in circumstances that make it likely that the contravention will continue or be repeated," under section 21, he has the power to serve an improvement notice. The notice must state that the inspector is of the above opinion, the relevant legislation upon which he bases his opinion and the reasons why he is of that opinion. The notice must require the person to remedy the contravention within the time stipulated in the notice. This time must not be less than 21 days. Under section 24, there is a right of appeal to an industrial tribunal and this must be made within 21 days of receipt of the notice.[5] The effect of the improvement notice is suspended until the appeal is disposed of or withdrawn.

McNeil J. in *West Bromwich Building Society* v. *Townsend*[6] said:

"A properly drafted improvement notice should not merely state that in the opinion of the inspector there had been a contravention of section 2 of the Health and Safety at Work Act, and the want of

[5] Industrial Tribunals (Improvement and Prohibition Notices Appeals) Regulations 1974 (S.I. 1974 No. 1925).
[6] [1983] I.C.R. 257.

particularity was not cured by the giving of reasons for the opinion. The notice should identify the contravention by reference to the particular paragraph in section 2(2) of the Act or, if the contravention was not so identifiable, particulars should be given of it."

For example, if there is a contravention of section 18 of the Offices, Shops and Railway Premises Act 1963 (young persons cleaning machines) it is necessary for the inspector when drafting the notice to state that there is a contravention of section 2(1) of the Health and Safety at Work etc. Act 1974 (which is the general duty of care) and also include the particular breach of duty of care, *i.e.* section 18 of the Offices, Shops and Railway Premises Act 1963.

The notice includes a schedule which may be filled in by the inspector specifying the works required to be carried out in order to comply with the notice.[7] He is not obliged to do this, but if he does and the specification is inprecise or vague it does not render the notice invalid. In *Chrysler United Kingdom* v. *McCarthy*,[8] the first appeal against an improvement notice to reach the Court of Appeal, the Court held that the power of an industrial tribunal under section 24(2) of the Health and Safety at Work Act to affirm an improvement notice, "with such modifications as the tribunal in the circumstances think fit," includes re-drafting a notice which is not sufficiently precise.

There are two situations to be distinguished when challenging the decision of an inspector that there is a breach of duty. The first, is where there is an absolute duty on the employer under a statutory provision. An example would be the statutory duty under section 17 of the Offices, Shops and Railway Premises Act to fence securely exposed parts of machinery. In the absence of expert contradictory evidence the tribunal will accept the expert evidence of the inspector and there can be no defence where there is a breach of this absolute duty.

The second situation is where the duty is qualified by the expression "so far as reasonably practicable." The test of what is reasonably practicable is contained in *Edwards* v. *National Coal Board*.[9] Many appeals to the tribunal have been successful where the appellant has proved that he has done everything possible given the nature and degree of risk complained of. For example, an improvement notice was cancelled by the tribunal in *Roadline (United Kingdom) Ltd.* v. *T. R. Mainwaring*[10] where the employer was required to provide heating in a transit shed. Under section 2 of the Health and Safety at Work Act 1974, the employer is under a duty to ensure so far as is reasonably practicable the health, safety and welfare at work of all his employees. The tribunal

---

[7] Health and Safety at Work Act 1974, s.24.
[8] [1978] I.C.R. 939.
[9] [1949] 1 K.B. 704, (and see p. 89).
[10] "The Inspector," Vol. 24, No. 2, March-April 1978.

considered that the cost of heating was excessive in relation to the improvement in the employee's welfare and cancelled the improvement notice.

The cost of compliance with the notice is obviously a factor to be taken into account by the tribunal in appeal, but the current financial position of the employer must *not* be considered. This was discussed in *Harrison (Newcastle-under-Lyme)* v. *Ramsey*,[11] where the appellant argued that he should not comply with the notice that required him to clean, prepare and paint walls because the company was involved in a major economy drive. The appeal was dismissed.

Also, where the duty is absolute the fact that the requirements of the notice appear trivial will not be a successful basis for appeal. An appeal was brought in *South Suburban Co-operative Society Ltd.* v. *D. B. Wilcox*[12] "by way of protest against time being spent by officials on small matters." The notice referred to a cracked washhand basin. The tribunal, in dismissing the appeal, was of the opinion that they could not interfere where there was a clear breach even if the matter was petty.

Where an employer is prosecuted for non-compliance with an improvement or prohibition notice an interesting question is whether or not he can raise at that time the validity of the notice, even though he has not appealed to the industrial tribunal within the 21 days from the service of the notice. In *Deary* v. *Mansion Hide Upholsteries*,[13] the High Court stated that where a person who has been served with a notice does not appeal against its validity to the industrial tribunal within 21 days of service, he has no right to bring this matter up at the hearing of a prosecution under section 33(1) of the Act for failure to comply with the notice. The only question that the magistrates can deal with is whether or not the person is guilty of the offence of non-compliance.

The penalty which a person will face if found guilty of contravening a requirement of an improvement notice is on summary conviction £2,000 and up to £100 per day in respect of continuing offences, unless the court has given time to remedy under section 42(3), and on indictment an unlimited fine. It is the policy of most Environmental Health Departments to use persuasion and informal notification before using the penal sanctions as the last resort.

Prohibition notice

An inspector has the power to serve a prohibition notice in any case   **5.03** where activities "are being or are about to be carried on" by the person served, "being activities to or in relation to which any of the relevant statutory provisions apply or will, if the activities are so carried on,

[11] *Ibid.* No. 4, July-August 1978.
[12] *Ibid.*
[13] [1983] I.C.R. 610.

apply" and in respect of which the inspector is of the opinion that the activities involve or, as the case may be, *will involve a risk of serious personal injury.*[14]

The inspector must state in the notice that he is of the above opinion, specify the grounds for his opinion and, if there is a contravention of a relevant statutory provision, state what legislation is contravened. Also, he must direct that the activities concerned shall cease until the matters specified in the notice have been remedied.[15]

If the risk of serious personal injury is imminent then the activities must cease at once (an immediate prohibition notice). Otherwise the notice will take effect at the end of the period specified in the notice (a deferred prohibition notice). There is no need for the inspector to be satisfied that a contravention exists of a relevant statutory provision, only that the activities give rise to a risk of serious injury. Although, because of the very wide terms of the Act, this duplication between improvement and prohibition notices is purely academic.[16]

The right of appeal is the same as for an improvement notice, *i.e.* appeal on a point of law or fact to an industrial tribunal within 21 days of receipt of the notice. The bringing of an appeal suspends the operation of an improvement notice, but a prohibition notice, once issued, can be suspended only by special order of the tribunal in a preliminary hearing.[17]

The prohibition notice must be served on the person who has control of the activities. The appellants in *Stephensons (Crane Hire)* v. *Gorden*[18] merely hired out equipment and were thereafter not involved in the activities of the hirer. The notice was cancelled because it was not served on the person who controlled the activities, *i.e.* the person who hired the equipment.

A person found guilty of contravening a requirement of prohibition imposed by a prohibition order is liable on summary conviction to a fine not exceeding £2,000 and up to £100 per day in respect of continuing offences, unless the court has given time to remedy under section 42(3), and on indictment of an unlimited fine and/or two years imprisonment.[19]

INFORMATION AND NOTICES TO BE DISPLAYED FOR SHOP ASSISTANTS

Certain information must by law be displayed on the premises so that employees are fully aware of their rights.

---

[14] Health and Safety at Work Act 1974, s.22.
[15] *Ibid.*
[16] *Ibid.*
[17] Health and Safety at Work Act 1974, s.24. Industrial Tribunals (Improvement and Prohibition Notices Appeals) Regulations 1974 (S.I. 1974 No. 1925).
[18] "The Inspector," Vol. 24, No. 4, July–August 1978.
[19] Health and Safety at Work Act 1974, s.33.

Employers liability insurance

This is the most important information that employees must be aware **5.04**
of, and an environmental health officer in carrying out his duties must
ascertain whether or not a current insurance certificate is displayed.
Employees must be assured that any accident occurring on the premises
by the negligence or breach of statutory duty by the employer is covered
by insurance.

The Employer's Liability (Compulsory Insurance) Act 1969 section
1(1) lays down that every employer carrying on a business in Great
Britain shall insure and maintain an insurance against liability for bodily
injury or disease sustained by his employees arising out of and in the
course of their employment. The Act is enforced by the Health and
Safety Executive but probably because environmental health officers
are "thicker on the ground" than health and safety inspectors, the
Health and Safety Executive has requested that environmental health
officers check during routine inspections to see whether the Act has
been complied with and to report any contraventions to the Health and
Safety Executive for enforcement.

As long as a person is an employer within the legal definition he must
provide an insurance and it applies to any sort of trade or business,
including social clubs. It may be that the trade of a pub is carried on by a
husband and wife team but usually they will employ part time bar staff
or cleaners. In that situation they will have to have an insurance policy
but the Act does not apply if a person engages independent contractors,
close relations, domestic servants or persons who are not normally resident in Great Britain.[20]

The certificate of insurance must be displayed at each place of business and an inspector can request to see the certificate and on reasonable notice being given he can require the policy to be produced.[21]

It is an offence for an employer not to be insured in accordance with
the 1969 Act and where the offence of this nature is committed by a corporation the director, manager, secretary or other officer of the corporation will be deemed guilty of the offence if it is committed with his
consent or connivance or if it is facilitated by his neglect.[22] Also, it is an
offence if the employer fails to:

(a) display the certificate or copy of the insurance certificate;
(b) send the certificate or a copy to the inspector when so
required;
(c) produce the certificate or a copy on demand by an inspector;
and
(d) allow the inspector to inspect the actual policy document.[23]

[20] Employer's Liability (Compulsory Insurance) Act 1969, s.2.
[21] *Ibid.* s.4.
[22] *Ibid.* s.5.
[23] *Ibid.* s.4.

Safety policies

5.05   Every person or company who employs five or more persons[24] must
have a written policy on safety and health. This document must be
brought to the attention of all employees and should be revised from
time to time, as and when necessary, and the employees must also be
made aware of any revision.[25]

There is no set policy and the employer must give due consideration
to safety practices in the premises and compile the policy to suit the particular circumstances. It is important to produce well thought out policies which indicate to the employees that the employers have addressed
their minds properly to this problem. Although it would be difficult for
enforcing authorities to set a very high standard, it is possible for
improvement notices to be validly served on employers who produce
legally inadequate statements. For example, an improvement notice was
served on K Shoe Shops Ltd. by an officer of Ipswich Borough Council
in respect of failure by them to bring to the notice of their employees a
proper written statement of policy. The company had produced and
brought to their attention a very short statement comprising of ten lines
of words, together with some instructions on the safe use of ladders, the
procedure to be followed in the event of fire and a leaflet giving advice
on first aid treatment. According to the inspector, the notice was not
complied with, and proceedings were instituted at the magistrates' court
and the company was found guilty and fined.[26–27]

It is not necessary for the policy to be long and elaborate to be legally
effective but it must be appropriate to the circumstances. If the business
is low risk as to the possibility of accidents then the policy could consist
of simple and brief statements.

There should be three main elements of the policy:

    (a) the general statement;
    (b) the organisation for carrying it out; and
    (c) the arrangements for ensuring health and safety at the work-
        place.

The general statement should be a declaration of the employer's
intent to seek to provide the safest and healthiest working conditions
possible and to involve employers to attain that end. It must be signed
by the employer or chief executive.

The organisation section should give the names of persons responsible
for the various aspects of health and safety within the organisation from
the highest to the lowest. Someone will obviously be in overall charge of
ensuring fulfilment of the policy. That person's name must be given and

---

[24] The numbers are limited by the Employers Health and Safety Policy Statements
(Exceptions) Regulations 1975 (S.I. 1975 No. 1584).
[25] Health and Safety at Work Act 1974, s.2(3).
[26–27] *Ipswich Borough Council* v. *K Shoe Shops Ltd.*; "The Inspector," Vol. 29, No. 5,
September–October 1983.

also those with responsibilities down the line of management. These must be spelt out in some detail so that there is no confusion and each person listed must know what they are supposed to be doing. Any safety committees or safety representatives must be stated and methods of dealing with grievances with regard to health and safety.

The arrangements part will need to cover the full range of the employer's work activities and should include:

(a) the procedures for dealing with common hazards (for example, fire prevention, good housekeeping, precautions in the use of portable ladders, protection of machinery, effective inspection and maintenance of plant and equipment);

(b) the identification of and precautionary procedures for dealing with any special hazards relating to the premises, processes and work activities;

(c) safe systems and methods of work (for example, for maintenance activities and cleaning machinery and plant);

(d) accident reporting and investigation procedures;

(e) provision and use of protective clothing and equipment;

(f) procedure for introducing new machinery, substances or processes;

(g) emergency procedure (for example, in the event of fire or explosion);

(h) arrangements for obtaining and communicating to employees, information about health and safety matters, including articles and substances for use at work, especially on their first introduction, or when persons work with them for the first time;

(i) health and safety inspection, audits, or other systems for checking the effectiveness of the other arrangements for health and safety;

(j) an appropriate health and safety training programme for all levels of employees.

Where the arrangements necessarily take the form of detailed rules and procedures (possibly in the form of manuals) these need only be briefly outlined in the policy statement, together with a reference to where the detailed rules are set out and kept available for reference and inspection.

Arrangements must be made to bring the safety policy to the notice of employees. In a small company this could simply be the issuing of a copy to each individual and in the case of a large company the displaying of a copy on the notice board.

Some undertakings are of low risk and because of this employers often feel that it is a waste of time and effort drawing up a policy. However, even in low risk occupations there are many areas that need to be considered, for example, fire hazards, staircases and office machinery such as guillotines.

Approved poster and approved leaflet[27]

5.06   The Health and Safety Information for Employees Regulations 1989 entered force on October 18, 1989. The Regulations, made under section 15 and paragraph 15(1) of Schedule 3 to the Health and Safety at Work etc. Act 1974, provides that an employer shall ensure that an approved poster is displayed in a readible condition at a place reasonably accessible to employees at work and in a position where it can be easily seen and read by employees. Alternatively, the employer may hand out to each employee the approved leaflet but in order to comply with the Regulations he must hand out the leaflet as soon as reasonably practicable from either October 18, 1989 or the date the employee commences employment with him (if later).[27a]

In addition, the employer must provide further information; the name and address of both the enforcing authority for the premises and the office of the employment medical advisory service for the area must be written clearly and indelibly in the appropriate space on the poster. Where a leaflet is distributed the afore-mentioned names and addresses must be contained in a written notice and handed out with the leaflet. Where there is a change in this information the poster must be amended within 6 months of the date of change and in the case of the leaflet a written notice specifying the change must be given to each employee within the 6 month period.[27b]

A revision (in whole or in part) to the form of the poster or leaflet may be approved by the Health and Safety Executive and where it does so the Health and Safety Executive shall publish the revised form of poster or leaflet and issue a notice in writing specifying the date the revision was approved.[27c] In such a case the employer shall ensure, on or before the date the revision takes effect, that the revised poster is displayed or, in the case of a leaflet, give each employee a revised leaflet or bring the revision to their notice in writing.[27d]

Any person accused of contravening the 1989 Regulations may avail himself of the defence under regulation 7 in that he took all reasonable precautions and exercised all due diligence to avoid contravening the Regulations.

RECORDS TO BE KEPT AND SHOWN WHEN REQUIRED

Certain records must be kept in respect of health and safety and welfare of employees for a certain length of time and shown, if demanded, to an

---

[27] The "approved poster" or "approved leaflet" means, respectively, a poster or leaflet in the form approved and published for the purposes of these Regulations by the Health and Safety Executive, as revised from time to time in accordance with para. (2) (the Health and Safety Information for Employees Regulations 1989, reg. 3(1) (S.I. 1989 No. 682)).

[27a] *Ibid.* reg. 4.

[27b] *Ibid.* reg. 5.

[27c] *Ibid.* reg. 3(2).

[27d] *Ibid.* reg. 4(3).

authorised officer of the local authority, who will usually be an environmental health officer.

Notifiable accidents, diseases and dangerous occurrences

Regulation 7 of the Reporting of Injuries, Diseases and Dangerous   **5.07** Occurrences Regulations 1985[28] provides that records must be kept, by the responsible person,[29] of all reportable accidents, diseases and dangerous occurrences[30] for a period of three years. The records must be kept at the place where the work to which they relate is carried on or, if this is not reasonably practicable, at the usual place of business of the responsible person.

The records must state, in the case of accidents or dangerous occurrences:

    (a) the date and time of the accident or dangerous occurrence;
    (b) the following particulars of the person affected;
        (i) full name,
        (ii) occupation,
        (iii) nature of injury or condition;
    (c) the place where the accident or dangerous occurrence happened; and
    (d) a brief description of the circumstances.[31]

In the case of incidents of reportable diseases:

    (a) date of diagnosis of the disease;
    (b) occupation of the person affected;
    (c) name of nature of the disease.[32]

No particular way or method of keeping these records is stipulated in the Act. A register may be used or indeed a file containing a copy of the completed Form F.2508[33] appears to be adequate.

Inspection of hoists and lifts

Requirements as to the construction, maintenance and examination   **5.08** of hoists and lifts in shops are contained in the Offices, Shops and Railway Premises (Hoists and Lifts) Regulations 1968.[33a] Regulation 6 specifies that every lift must be thoroughly examined by a competent person at least once in every period of six months (12 months if non-mechanical) and a report sent within 28 days to the person responsible for complying with the Regulations. If the examination shows that the lift cannot continue to be used with safety unless certain repairs are car-

---

[28] S.I. 1985 No. 2023.
[29] See Appendix IV.
[30] See Appendices V and VI.
[31] R.I.D.D.O. Regulations 1985, Sched. 3, Part I.
[32] *Ibid.* Part II.
[33] See p. 88.
[33a] S.I. 1968 No. 849.

ried out immediately or within a specified time, a copy of this report must be sent to the local authority within 28 days. This is to ensure that major defects are brought to the attention of the local authority.

The report, which must be on a form prescribed by the Offices, Shops and Railway Premises (Hoists and Lifts) Regulations 1968, must be readily available for inspection by a local authority inspector for two years to enable an inspector to check that the periodic examinations are being carried out and that any minor defects are remedied.

The competent person referred to in the Regulations will usually be an insurance company surveyor who specialises in this type of work.

REPORTING AND NOTIFICATION OF ACCIDENTS AND DANGEROUS OCCURRENCES

5.09 The Reporting of Injuries, Diseases and Dangerous Occurrences Regulations 1985 impose duties on persons responsible for the activities of persons at work and on self-employed persons to report accidents resulting in death or major injury arising out of or in connection with work, and to report specified dangerous occurrences.

Where any of the following events occur the responsible person[34] must report it in writing (Form F.2508), to the local authority and in the case of events (a), (b) or (c) (below) must notify the local authority immediately, followed up within seven days by a written report on Form F.2508.

    (a) the death of any person—whether or not he or she is at work—as a result of an accident arising out of or in connection with work;

    (b) any person suffering a specified major injury or condition[35] as a result of an accident arising out of or in connection with work;

    (c) one of a list of specified dangerous occurrences arising out of or in connection with work[36];

    (d) a person at work incapacitated from his or her normal work for more than three days as a result of an injury caused by an accident at work;

    (e) the death of an employee if this occurs some time after a reportable injury which lead to that employee's death, but not more than one year afterwards; or

    (f) a person at work being affected by one of a number of specified diseases, provided that a doctor diagnoses the disease and that the person's job involves a specified work activity.

Other events which must be reported are in relation to gas. If a sup-

---

[34] "Responsible person" depends upon the circumstances and upon the type of event to be reported. (See Appendix IV.)
[35] See Appendix V.
[36] See Appendix VI.

plier of flammable gas through a fixed pipe distribution system or the filler, importer or supplier of liquefied petroleum gas (L.P.G.) in a refillable container, is notified (by anyone) that someone has died or suffered a specified major injury or condition[37] arising out of, or in connection with that gas, he must report the matter to the local authority. Also to be reported is where a supplier of flammable gas through a fixed pipe distribution system finds that there is, in any premises, a flammable gas fitting or associated flue or ventilation arrangement which could be dangerous in a specified way.[38]

There are two free explanatory leaflets obtainable from the Health and Safety Executive. These are entitled Reporting an Injury or Dangerous Occurrence (HSE.11 Revised) and Reporting a Case of Disease (HSE.17). Also guidance on the Regulations is contained in booklet (HSR.23) (ISBN 0 11 883413 4) obtainable from H.M.S.O. or booksellers.

GENERAL DUTY OF RETAILERS

General duty to employees

The general duty that a retailer has to his employees is contained in **5.10** section 2(1) of the Health and Safety at Work Act 1974. It spells out in general terms that he must ensure "as far as is reasonably practicable" their health, safety and welfare at work. He has no duty towards them when they are not at work.[39]

Although what is meant by "welfare" is not described in the Act, it is assumed that this refers to facilities that the employer must legally provide such as adequate toilet accommodation, washing and cloakroom facilities, etc.

This is a "catch all" subsection in that any obvious breach of duty by the employer which cannot be brought under a specified particular duty, whether it be contained in the Health and Safety at Work Act 1974 or Offices, Shops and Railway Premises Act 1963, will be caught by this subsection. It is always the right policy for a health and safety inspector when serving an improvement notice to quote breach of this section as well as any contravention if it has occurred, of a specific duty under the afore-mentioned Acts.

When considering what is "reasonably practicable," a retailer must not only take into account whether or not it is physically possible but indeed whether it is financially viable. The risk of injury must be balanced against the cost of removing that risk. If the risk is slight and the "cost of removing it" is disproportionately heavy then it is not reasonably practicable to take such action.[40]

---

[37] See Appendix V.
[38] See Appendix VI.
[39] "At work" is defined in s.52.
[40] *West Bromwich Building Society* v. *Townsend* [1983] I.C.R. 257, D.C., applying *Edwards* v. *National Coal Board* [1949] 1 K.B. 704.

The fact that there is an accepted practice with regard to a given situation does not mean that if the employer carries out that practice he automatically discharges his duty under the section. The onus of proof is still on the employer to prove that what he did was reasonably practicable, although the fact that an accepted method of carrying out a function is strong evidence on his behalf.[41]

Much good practice is contained in guidance documents[41a] issued by the Health and Safety Commission. These may be *approved* codes of practice and although they are not statutory requirements they may be used as evidence against persons alleged to be in breach of a duty.[42] If a defendant introduced evidence that he complied in all respects with an approved code of practice it is unlikely that he could be successfully prosecuted for an offence.

The status of other guidance documents[42a] is in some doubt. They could be classified as hearsay evidence, merely the expression of a person or persons opinions and unless these persons can be brought into the witness box to testify they could be inadmissable.

However, in *R. v. Somers*,[43] an expert witness, a medical practitioner, was called to give evidence on the rates at which blood destroys alcohol and this evidence was accepted although he did not carry out the experiments himself but merely quoted the results of experiments carried out by scientists many years ago. Therefore, it seems that an expert witness may quote from a code of practice even though he was not involved in its compilation and, in practice, courts do accept guidance notes and other publications as definitive of good practice.

One particular area of work that may require consideration by an employer under this section is where employees handle large sums of money. Adequate protection (so far as is reasonably practicable) from criminal assault where this can be anticipated will be necessary. This may also be classified as a particular duty to provide a safe system of work, and may entail the obtaining of advice from a crime prevention officer or specialist security firm.

It must be mentioned that employees also have a general duty under section 7 of the Health and Safety at Work Act 1974. The section stipulates that while at work the employee must take reasonable care for the health and safety of himself and of other persons who may be affected by his acts or omissions at work and to co-operate with the employer with regard to any duty imposed on him by the 1974 Act or any other relevant statutory provisions.

---

[41] *Martin v. Boulton and Paul (Steel Construction) Ltd.* [1982] I.C.R. 366, D.C.
[41a] See p. 90.
[42] Health and Safety at Work etc. Act 1974, s.17.
[42a] E.g. Guidance Note C58 (Appendix VIII), booklet; *Seats for Workers in Factories, Offices and Shops* (see p. 126).
[43] [1963] 1 W.L.R. 1306.

General duty to members of the public

There is also a general duty of employers and self-employed persons **5.11** under section 3 of the 1974 Act to members of the public. They must conduct their undertaking in such a way so as not to expose the public to risks to their health and safety. This is, of course, again qualified by the phrase, "so far as is reasonably practicable." The self-employed person also has a duty under this section to himself as well as other persons who may be affected by his undertaking. In appropriate cases this general duty also includes a duty to give information regarding safety to members of the public.[44]

An example of a breach of duty under this section is the improper disposal of potentially hazardous or clinical waste. A successful prosecution was brought against two doctors in the Bradford area by the Health and Safety Executive for depositing syringes, tablets and other potentially hazardous waste in an ordinary plastic refuse bag and placing this bag outside the surgery ready for collection by the local authority. Children ripped open the bag, were seen playing with the syringes and in possession of some of the tablets. Contaminated waste and tablets, etc., were scattered all over the area.[44a]

Chemist shops and other retail outlets, where waste is likely to cause damage to health or property, must be aware of their duty to dispose of the waste properly and advice should be sought from the local environmental health department on local facilities available for incineration or on specialist waste disposal contractors.

Another example is an accident which occurred to a six year old boy who was struck by trolleys that were being pushed along a car park by an employee of Tesco's Ltd. It was common practice for employees to push along lines of trolleys and control their direction by bumping them into concrete posts. The boy had been holding onto one of these posts and his arm became trapped by the trolleys and his wrist fractured in two places. Instructions had been given that up to six trolleys only should be pushed at one time but this had been ignored by the employee. The company was prosecuted under section 3(1) by Wrexham Maelor District Council and were found guilty by the magistrates, fined and awarded costs to the council.[45]

Persons who have control over non-domestic premises or means of access to or egress from those premises or use any plant or machinery in those premises also has the afore-mentioned duty to members of the public. This would apply to such persons as maintenance contractors or builders who have taken control over perhaps part of a business premises to carry out repairs. This criminal liability is separate from and in addition to any civil liability.

The question of what was an "undertaking" under section 3(1) was

[44] R. v. *Swan Hunter Shipbuilders* [1981] I.C.R. 831.
[44a] Wastes Management, Vol. LXXVIII, No. 11, November 1988, p. 758.
[45] Environmental Health News, October 30, 1987.

considered in *R. v. Mara*.[46] Mr. Mara was the managing director of a cleaning company that had a contract with International Stores Ltd. Cleaning equipment owned by the company was left at the stores for use by the staff and one piece of equipment, (a polisher/scrubber), had a faulty cable. A young "casual" employee used this, was electrocuted and subsequently died. Mr. Mara maintained that the arrangement his company had with International Stores did not amount to him conducting an undertaking. Counsel for the respondent submitted that the word "undertaking" was wide and vague in these terms and that the authors of the Act intended it to be interpreted that way. The court found for the respondents. The circumstances which existed at the time of the accident was part of an undertaking carried on by Mr. Mara's company.

PARTICULAR DUTIES OF RETAILERS

There are particular duties listed in section 2 of the 1974 Act and these include such duties as the provision of a written safety policy as described on page 84. Also some of the duties are contained in the Offices, Shops and Railway Premises Act 1963 and Regulations made thereunder. All these particular duties are without prejudice to the generality of the employer's duty under section 2(1) of the 1974 Act.

Plant and systems of work

5.12   Section 2(2)(*a*) of the 1974 Act provides that the employer's duty extends to the provision and maintenance of plant and systems of work that are, so far as is reasonably practicable, safe and without risks to health.

Although there is a requirement under section 7 of the 1974 Act that every employee while at work must take all reasonable care for the health and safety of himself and of other persons who may be affected by his acts or omissions, the responsibility for providing safe plant and systems of work rests solely with the employer. He must consider what work is to be done, and how it is to be done, and issue appropriate instructions.

The relationship between all the elements of the work process must be safe, *i.e.* all the plant, the employees, the material to be used, tools and work environment. For example, in *Peace v. Cedar Glades Ltd.*,[47] an employee was driving a fork lift truck when the throttle stuck and the truck overturned. He was injured and taken to hospital. Cedar Gables Ltd. denied failing to ensure the health and safety of their employees by not maintaining the truck.

An environmental health officer had examined the truck and found that it did not appear to have received sufficient routine maintenance. He stated that the accelerator pedal stuck and the tyre pressures were

[46] [1987] 1 W.L.R. 87.
[47] "The Inspector," Vol. 24, No. 6, November–December 1978.

much lower than the manufacturer's recommended minimum. The company was convicted and ordered to pay costs.

The process of the work must be safe from start to finish and there must be a proper system of monitoring the safety of the process and provision to take the appropriate action in the event of an emergency.

Use, storage and transport of articles and substances

The employer's duty also includes arranging and ensuring, so far as is **5.13** reasonably practicable, safety and absence of risks to health in connection with the use, handling, storage and transport of articles and substances.[48]

This may include such diverse obligations as providing protective clothing, making sure that racking is safe, that fork lift truck drivers are properly trained and instructed in stacking timber pallets, and that shop assistants and other employees do not carry excessive weights which may result in back injury; although this latter matter is also dealt with under section 23 of the Offices, Shops and Railway Premises Act 1963.

In *Associated Dairies* v. *Hartley*,[49] an improvement notice was served on the company which stated that:

> "arrangements have not been made for ensuring the safety of all employees whose employment causes them to be involved in operating the hydraulic trolley jacks for the handling and transport of articles and substances."

The schedule to the notice required the company, which was trading as ASDA Discount Centre, to:

> "ensure that all employees at the Grimsby branch whose employment causes them to be involved in the operation of the hydraulic trolley jacks should have available for wear, free of charge, safety shoes with a reinforced toe cap to BS.1870 and BS.953 as a minimum specification."

The notice was served following an accident when an operator broke a toe and on appeal the industrial tribunal accepted that there was a risk to employees using the trolleys. However, the appeal was allowed, the notice quashed and £300 costs were awarded against the inspector. These costs were subsequently indemnified by the council.

The company had pleaded at the appeal that up to 16 employees at the Grimsby store could be called upon to use the trolleys and that, owing to the "turnover" in warehouse staff, the cost in the first year to the Grimsby store would be £300 and £150 per annum thereafter. This would seem to be reasonable on its own but the company claimed that they owned 66 other stores and the same policy adopted at these stores would cost £20,000 in the first year and £10,000 per annum thereafter.

---

[48] 1974 Act, s.2(2)(*b*).
[49] [1979] I.R.L.R. 171.

The tribunal decided by a majority decision, that the inspector's requirement was practical but because the Grimsby store could not be considered in isolation it was not "reasonably practical."[50]

It is suggested that the Grimsby store should have been considered in isolation because no two stores are the same. In any case it seems that there were circumstances existing at the Grimsby store which made an accident more likely to happen than in the other stores.

Every year persons are seriously injured or killed as the result of the collapse of stacks and through the failure to ensure safe systems of storage. Guidance notes have been issued by the Health and Safety Executive on safety in the use of timber pallets[51] and they have also issued a booklet on the safety in the stacking of materials.[52] Where storage space is in short supply, goods are often seen stored in passageways and in front of fire exits. This is also obviously in contravention of the 1974 Act, section 2(2)(b).

Instruction, training and supervision

5.14   There is a particular duty laid down under section 2(2)(c) to provide such information, instruction, training and supervision as is necessary to ensure, so far as is reasonably practicable, the health and safety at work of employees. This is, of course, without prejudice to the general duty under section 2(1) and in addition to the duty contained in sections 18 and 19 of the Offices, Shops and Railway Premises Act 1963 which relate to young persons cleaning machinery and persons working at prescribed dangerous machines respectively. These are dealt with in more detail below.

The employer must give as much information as possible about any hazards associated with the employee's work and any precautions that he must take to avoid the danger of becoming involved in or creating an accident. Adequate training and instruction must be given where necessary. Magistrates fined Tesco Ltd. £1,700 after they had heard how a shelf-filler fell off a 10 foot high ladder and fractured his skull. They found the company guilty of failing to provide proper ladders for shelf-fillers and adequate training and instruction on how to use the ladders. The court was told that the employee's job was to restock shelves by taking goods from the warehouse. He often had to climb ladders to get to the goods in the warehouse but he was never told how to use the equipment. The employee said that he used his own initiative to get things out of the warehouse. It seems that on the day in question he had gone to the warehouse to fetch boxes of cake mix or packets of rice. He could remember going to get a ladder but nothing after that. It appears he had not climbed a proper ladder but the top of a maintenance scaf-

---

[50] See p. 89.
[51] Guidance Note PM.15, obtainable from H.M.S.O.
[52] Health and Safety at Work Booklet No. 47, obtainable from H.M.S.O.

folding tower. The inspector had maintained that training was not given or if it was it was so ineffective the employees could not remember anything about it. Supervision was inadequate in that staff were using a metal extension ladder against metal racking, without the ladder being footed or tied, even while the inspector was talking to the warehouse manager after the accident.[53]

An area of work where training is essential is in the operation of fork lift trucks. Many accidents have occurred over the years in warehouses and supermarkets because of insufficient training and supervision.

Bristol Magistrates Court were told of an injury to a woman employed by U.K.D. Ltd. of Flowers Hill, Brislington, Bristol. Her ankle was damaged when a fork lift truck jammed in between a pallet and a rack. The truck was being driven through a curtain which divided the assembly section from the rest of the depot and the forks were extended some 12 feet in front of the truck. The company denied failing to provide proper information, instruction, training or supervision.

The driver of the truck said that he had never driven a car or anything else before joining the firm in 1974 and three or four days after he started work within the company he was told to drive a fork lift truck. The only tuition made available to him was a half hour period from a youth aged 17, although he did agree that he had been told not to drive the truck through the curtain with the forks pointing forward but to reverse through the curtain.

The defence submitted that the employee had broken the rule and was the cause of the unfortunate accident. This was accepted by the court and the employee was convicted and fined £100 with £57.50 costs.[54]

Training in safety matters should be undertaken on a regular basis. This can be done "in house," but is not always possible as specialist advice may only be available on specially arranged courses. Employees must co-operate with the employer in these matters as non-co-operation is an offence under the 1974 Act[55] and may well be grounds for fair dismissal.

An *approved* code[55a] of practice was published in 1988 on the basic training of operators of rider-operated lift trucks and included within the code, but not part of it, is supplementary guidance on the general aspects of training. There is also a Health and Safety series booklet (HS(G)6) on lift trucks. This gives guidance on the operation of lift trucks, protection of personnel, etc. Both publications are available from H.M.S.O.

---

[53] *Worthing Borough Council* v. *Tesco Ltd.* "The Inspector," Vol. 29, No. 3, May–June 1983.
[54] *Bristol City Council* v. *U.K.D.* "The Inspector," Vol. 27, No. 4, July–August 1981.
[55] s.7(*b*).
[55a] See p. 89 for legal status of approved code of practice.

Place of work and access thereto and exit therefrom

5.15   Under section 2(2)(*d*) of the 1974 Act as regards any place of work
under his control, the employer must, so far as is reasonably practicable,
maintain it in a condition that is safe and without risks to health and provide and maintain that the means of access to and egress from it are safe
and without such risks. Again, there is a similar duty contained in section 16 of the Offices, Shops and Railway Premises Act 1963 which is
restricted in application, of course, to the category of premises mentioned in paragraph 6.02.

One issue which has been considered by the courts is the question of
whether an employer is in breach of duty if he provides and maintains a
safe access to the place of work and some temporary event or obstruction renders the access unsafe.

In *Higgins* v. *J. Lyons and Co.*,[56] the means of access to an office was
through a yard which was quite safe. Unfortunately, two employees
were pushing a truck carrying flour in a negligent manner and injured a
girl returning to the office. The Court of Appeal held that this incident
in itself did not amount to making the access unsafe.

Another example is *Levesley* v. *Firth (Thomas) and John Brown*[57]
where, for a short period, various articles had been allowed to stand
upon a means of access in such a way as might give rise to danger to
those who were using it. The court found that once a safe means of
access was provided the occupier was not responsible for every temporary obstruction which might, through some accident or mischance,
occur in it.

These two cases were considered by the Divisional Court of the
Queen's Bench Division in *Evans* v. *Sant*.[58] Regulation 6 of the Construction (Working Places) Regulations 1966[58a] provides that every
place at which any person at any time works shall, so far as is reasonably
practicable, be made and kept safe for any person working there. In the
Levesley Case the obligation was that the safe place of work should be
"maintained" but Widgery L.C.J. found it very difficult to believe that
"kept safe" in regulation 6 had any significant difference from "maintained."

The facts of the case were that a civil engineering contractor had
undertaken to lay a water main and after completion it had to be tested
by applying a water pressure test. The process of building up the
required pressure for the test lasted some hours and when it was nearing
200 p.s.i. the foreman noticed that the test head, which was wedged
against a solid object, was about to blow off. One of the men ran
towards the pump in order to stop it but before he could reach it the test
head blew out of the end of the pipeline. The foreman in trying to

---

[56] (1941) 85 S.J. 93.
[57] [1953] 1 W.L.R. 1206.
[58] [1975] 2 W.L.R. 95.
[58a] S.I. 1966 No. 94.

escape from this ran into the adjacent road and was knocked down and killed by a passing car.

The Factory Inspectorate brought a prosecution against the firm. The magistrates convicted them and the firm appealed on the basis that there is a distinction between a danger which is a danger arising from the place as a place, and a danger arising from the particular operation which at the moment in question is being carried on in the place.

Widgery L.C.J. said that he thought the guiding light in the court's approach to the problem was to say that in deciding whether the place of work was made safe, it is the place as a place that should be looked at, and not the place in relation to the operation being carried on at it. This did not mean, of course, that in deciding whether the place is made safe one has total disregard for the activities which go on in the place itself. The safety of the place depends not simply on the construction of the floor or the solidity of the walls but it also depends to some degree upon the nature of the operations performed therein. In so far as there is permanent equipment in the place, then its safety can reflect on the safety of the place. In so far as the activities carried on in the place which are constant, regular and recurring, he could well see that they may have an impact on the question of whether the place is being made safe. But where, as in the present case, you start with a place safe in every degree, and the only thing which renders it unsafe is the fact that equipment brought upon it for a particular operation, and being used for a particular operation on a particular day, produces an element of danger, it seems that it is not enough to justify the allegation, certainly in criminal proceedings, that the place itself was not being made safe. The appeal was allowed and the conviction quashed.

The circumstances in this case would now, of course, be caught by the general duty under section 2(1) and the particular duty under section 2(2)(a) of the 1974 Act but the interpretation of the law is still relevant to the particular duty under section 2(2)(d).

Floors, passages and stairs

Section 16 of the Offices, Shops and Railway Premises Act 1963[59] **5.16** contains the duty that an employer must fulfill with regard to the safety for floors, passages and stairs. The section is largely based on section 28(1) of the Factories Act 1961. All floors, stairs, steps, passages and gangways shall be of sound construction and properly maintained, and shall, so far as is reasonably practicable, be kept free from obstruction and from any substance likely to cause persons to slip.

"Sound construction," based on cases brought under the Factories Act, means that the floor, etc., shall be fit for the purpose for which the premises are intended to be used, not that it should be fit to withstand

---

[59] As regards duty of owner of the building in respect of floors, passages and stairs in common parts see ss.42(4), (5) and 43(3).

some abnormal stress[60] and "properly maintained" imparts an absolute duty and means properly in relation to safety. The question whether stair treads are in good repair and properly maintained is one of degree, depending on whether they are safe or not. For example, when they are worn to a depth of one eighth of an inch they are still in good repair, but when they are worn away to a depth of four inches they are not in good repair, and once there is a breach of duty the liability of the employer is absolute.[61]

The duty in relation to obstructions and substances likely to cause persons to slip is qualified by the words, "as far as is reasonably practicable." If it was not for these words it would be necessary for the employer to ensure at all times the floor was free of a slippery substance or any obstruction. As long as the employer takes reasonable measures to ensure that the section is complied with in accordance with the test laid down in *Edwards* v. *National Coal Board*[62] he will have fulfilled his duty.

A substantial handrail or hand-hold must be provided on every staircase.[63] If there is an open side it must be provided on that side. The handrail does not have to be fixed or rigid as long as it is substantial. If the staircase has two open sides or which "owing to the nature of its construction or the condition of the surface of the steps or other special circumstances" is liable to cause accidents, a handrail or hand-hold must be provided on both sides.

"Special circumstances" has to be something which was being continually repeated or so often repeated as to be specially liable to cause accidents, so that a permanent protection was necessary.[64]

All openings in floors shall be securely fenced except in so far as the nature of the work renders such fencing impracticable.[65]

Section 16 does not apply to fuel storage premises. However, even in these premises the surface of the ground must be kept in good repair, all steps and platforms must be of sound construction and properly maintained and all openings in platforms shall be securely fenced, except in so far as the nature of the work renders such fencing impracticable.

Fencing and machinery

5.17   All machines must be "securely fenced" so that no employee can come into contact with any dangerous part while the machine is in motion. If the dangerous part is in such a position or so constructed that it is safe to every person working on the premises as if it were securely

---

[60] *Mayne* v. *Johnstone & Cumbers* [1947] 2 All E.R. 159.
[61] *Payne* v. *Weldless Steel Tube Co.* [1956] 1 Q.B. 196 applied in *Fisher* v. *D.L.A.* [1962] 1 All E.R. 458.
[62] [1949] 1 K.B. 704 (see p. 89).
[63] This does not, it seems, include steps from the floor to part of a machine; see, *Kempton* v. *Steel Co. of Wales Ltd.* [1960] 2 All E.R. 274.
[64] *Harris* v. *Rugby Portland Cement Co.* [1955] 1 W.L.R. 648.
[65] Offices, Shops and Railway Premises Act 1963, s.16(4).

fenced, then fencing is not required. The fencing may be a fixed guard, or, where because of the nature of the operation that is not possible, an automatic safety device which offers adequate protection.[66]

The obligation to fence is not qualified. Therefore, it must be discharged even though the result would be to make the machinery commercially impracticable or mechanically useless.[67] It follows that it is not enough that the method of fencing adopted is the best method known enabling the machinery to work at all.[68]

There are not many machines that cannot be fenced without making it useless and although the courts have laid down an absolute duty, Regulations have been made under the Factories Act 1961 that lay down a less absolute duty though a more detailed standard of guarding in respect of these machines. From a practical viewpoint, with regard to those few machines not covered by the Regulations, it is suggested that the highest standard of guarding which is compatible with the machine remaining in use should be applied. Examples are circular saws, band saws, planing machines and certain grinding machines.

Providing means of achieving security is no compliance (*i.e.* it is the duty of the employer not merely to provide guards, but to fence the machinery securely) with the 1963 Act[69] but in the words of Stable J. in *Carr* v. *Mercantile Produce Co.*[70]:

> "there must be some limit placed on the word 'securely,' and a fence does not necessarily cease to be secure because by some act of perverted and deliberate ingenuity the guard can be forced or circumvented and the safeguards provided thereby rendered nugatory."

Part of machinery is dangerous if "it is a reasonably foreseeable cause of injury to anybody acting in a way in which a human being may be reasonably expected to act in circumstances which may be reasonably expected to occur."[71] Something may be part of the machinery even if it is removable and interchangeable such as a drill. In *Close* v. *Steel Co. of Wales*,[72] the bit of an electric drilling machine shattered and a piece entered the workman's eye. Though bits often shattered no such accident had happened before because the pieces were light and did not fly

---

[66] *Ibid.* s.17(1), (2).

[67] *Summers (John) & Sons* v. *Frost* [1955] A.C. 740.

[68] *Dennistoun* v. *Charles E. Greenhill Ltd.* [1944] 2 All E.R. 434.

[69] *Thomas* v. *Bolton (Thomas) & Sons* (1928) 92 J.P. 147 and *Charles* v. *Smith (S.) & Sons (England)* [1954] 1 W.L.R. 451.

[70] [1949] 2 K.B. 601.

[71] Du Parcq J. in *Walker* v. *Bletchley Flettons Ltd.* [1937] 1 All E.R. 170 at 175 (with a modification suggested by Lord Reid in *Summers (John) and Sons Ltd.* v. *Frost* [1955] A.C. 740 at 7).

[72] [1961] A.C. 367. See the Employer's Liability (Defective Equipment) Act, 1969 regarding liability of employers for injury to employees which is attributable to any defect in equipment.

out with force. The House of Lords held that the danger was not reasonably foreseeable and the bit was not dangerous.

Section 17(3) of the 1963 Act provides that no account is to be taken of any person carrying out an examination, adjusting or lubricating the machine while it is in motion if that job cannot be done other than while the machine is running. Also, under section 17(4), the guards must be of substantial construction "and properly maintained and kept in position while the machine is in motion or use unless it is immediately necessary to expose parts for lubrication, adjustment or examination."

"Motion or use" means normal motion or use and does not include the situation where the machine is moved by hand or by an "inching" device for the purpose of cleaning and adjustment.[73]

A British Standard Code of Practice for Safety of Machinery (BS.5304:1988) has been drawn up under the direction of the Machinery and Components Standards Committee and with the participation of representatives of the Health and Safety Executive. The Health and Safety Executive commend the use of this British Standard to those who have duties under the Health and Safety at Work etc. Act 1974.

Young persons cleaning machines

5.18   Section 18 of the 1963 Act imposes an absolute duty on an employer, subject to any defence under section 67, to ensure that no young person, *i.e.* any person under the age of 18, cleans any machinery if this exposes him to risk of injury from a moving part on that or any adjacent machinery.

In *Dewhurst (J.H.)* v. *Coventry Corporation*,[74] a hand-operated bacon slicer was being cleaned by a 16 year old boy when he cut off the top of his finger. Although he was instructed to clean one half of the blade, rotate it and then clean the other side, he ignored these instructions and pressed a cleaning pad against the cutting edge and rotated the blade. The firm was found guilty under the section, even though the blade was not to be moved whilst cleaning, as it was still a moving part which exposed the boy to a risk of injury. The prohibition was absolute and the company failed to establish a defence under section 67.[75]

Training and supervision of persons working dangerous machines

5.19   The Minister of Labour in 1964 compiled a list of machines which, in his opinion, were of such a dangerous character that persons ought not to work at them unless the requirements of section 19(1) of the 1963 Act were complied with. These requirements are that before any person works on such a machine he must be fully instructed as to the dangers

---

[73] *Thomas (Richard) & Baldwins* v. *Cummings* [1955] A.C. 321; *Knight* v. *Leamington Spa Courier* [1961] 2 Q.B. 253.
[74] [1969] 3 W.L.R. 249.
[75] See p. 128.

arising in connection with it and the precautions to be observed, and either:

(a) has received sufficient training on work at the machine; or
(b) is under adequate supervision by a person who has a thorough knowledge and experience of the machine.

The machines which are contained in the Prescribed Dangerous Machines Order 1964,[76] are those found in some shops and offices and consist mainly of mincing, chopping and slicing machines.[77]

It will be noticed that although there is an absolute prohibition on persons under 18 years of age from cleaning machines where there is risk of injury from a moving part, a young person is allowed to operate a dangerous machine (as prescribed) under supervision or if that person has had sufficient training.

A leaflet entitled "The Offices, Shops and Railway Premises Act 1963—Precautions Needed on Dangerous Machines" is obtainable from H.M.S.O. It sets out the main dangers and precautions to be observed in relation to each of the prescribed machines. Also available and of interest to butchers is the booklet HS/G 45 called "Safety in Meat Preparations." It is a 1988 publication by the Health and Safety Executive and is obtainable from H.M.S.O. The booklet gives advice on the risks associated with the use of knives, machines and other equipment found in the meat industry.

Prohibition of heavy work

Many thousands of the adult population suffer agonising backache **5.20** every day. One of the most common causes of loss of work is the result of employees suffering from back pain and it has been estimated that at least 26 million working days are lost every year because of this complaint. People doing heavy physical work and in certain occupations are particularly prone.

Section 23 of the 1963 Act[78] lays down a general principle which employers have to abide by in order to try and prevent this type of injury occurring, but because various individuals have different weight-lifting capacities which will depend on their strength, training, age, experience and possibly susceptibility to back strain it is impossible to be specific in this matter.

The section states that no person shall, in the course of his work in premises to which the Act applies, be required to lift, carry or move a load so heavy as to be likely to cause him injury. The section is so worded as to include not only persons who work regularly in the shop or office but also to anyone who works on the premises, for example,

---

[76] S.I. 1964 No. 971.
[77] See Appendix VII.
[78] There are similar provisions in the Factories Act 1961, s.72.

delivery men. Section 23(2) allows the Minister to make Regulations but none have been made to date.

There are two questions to be asked to establish contravention of the section:

    (a) Was the person employed to carry the load?

    (b) Was the weight excessive?

Whether an employee is employed to move a heavy load may depend on whether or not there was any other way in which he could do the work. In *Brown* v. *Allied Ironfounders*,[79] an employee was informed that if she needed help to move a stilage she should ask for assistance. This was normal practice, but it was also known to the foreman that some women moved the stilages by themselves and *no express prohibition* was issued. It was held that the employers were liable for the injury. To leave it to her to decide whether or not to ask for assistance meant that the moving of the load was part of her job which she was employed to do.[80]

Whether a load is likely to cause injury is also a factual issue. In *Kinsella* v. *Harris Lebus*,[81] it was held that a load of 145 lbs. was not so heavy as to be likely to cause injury to a man of experience. Whereas in *Hamilton* v. *Western S.M.T. Co.*,[82] it was held that 85 lbs. carried between two female office workers was too heavy.

A sharing of load does not result in the equalisation of the weight to be carried. Four dockers were carrying a crate of tobacco which weighed 560 lbs. It may be assumed that the equal weight between them would mean that each carried 140 lbs. However, one of the dockers was injured and the employers were held liable.[83]

Protective measures that can be taken including training employees on proper lifting and handling techniques, the introduction of mechanical lifting and handling machinery and finding out by screening those employees who are susceptible to back injury. Advice can be obtained from the Back Pain Association, Grundy House, Teddington, Middlesex.

First aid

5.21   Section 24 of the Offices, Shops and Railway Premises Act 1963, which stipulated requirements as to first aid in premises to which the Act applies has been repealed by the Health and Safety (First-Aid) Regula-

---

[79] [1974] 1 W.L.R. 527.

[80] A different conclusion was reached in *Black* v. *Carricks (Caterers) Ltd.* [1980] I.R.L.R. 448, C.A. and also in *Peat* v. *Muschamp (N.J.) & Co.* (1969) 7 K.I.R. 469, C.A. where a one legged man was injured carrying a 65 lb. chain. It was held that he was not employed to carry the load because he was specifically told to get assistance when he needed it.

[81] (1964) 108 S.J. 14.

[82] [1977] I.R.L.R. 439.

[83] *Fricker* v. *Perry (Benjamin) & Sons* (1973) 16 K.I.R. 356.

tions 1981.[84] These Regulations apply to all premises where people work, including premises of the self employed, the idea being to extend to areas of employment not previously covered by first aid legislation and to bring the requirements up to date. There are some exceptions listed in the Regulations, for example, vessels, mines and military forces.

The Regulations are made under the power contained in section 15 of the Health and Safety at Work etc. Act 1974, and there is a code of practice *approved* and issued by the Health and Safety Commission under section 16 of the afore-mentioned Act. The code of practice gives practical guidance on how to comply with the Regulations and failure on the part of any person to observe any provision of the approved code may not in itself make the person liable to criminal proceedings but evidence of this is admissible in any proceedings.[85]

The Regulations impose a duty on an employer to make provision for first aid and it does this by stating:

(a) that he shall provide, or ensure that there is provided, such equipment and facilities as are adequate and appropriate in the circumstances for enabling first aid to be rendered to his employees if they are injured or become ill at work; and

(b) that he provides, or ensures that there is provided, such number of suitable persons as is adequate and appropriate in the circumstances for rendering first-aid to his employees if they are injured or become ill at work; and for this purpose a person shall not be suitable unless he has undergone:

    (i) such training and has such qualifications as the Health and Safety Executive may approve for the time being in respect of that case or class of case; and

    (ii) such additional training, if any, as may be appropriate in the circumstances of that case.

Where, however, there is a temporary absence of the trained person the employer will comply with the Regulations if he appoints a person to take charge of first aid during the period of absence. Also, where because of the nature of the undertaking, the number of employees at work, and the location of the establishment, it would be adequate and appropriate to appoint an untrained person then this may be done instead of complying with (b) above. Examples are contained in the *approved* code of practice. In establishments with relatively low hazards such as shops it would not be necessary to provide a trained person unless 150 or more employees were at work.

What is adequate and appropriate with regard to equipment, facilities and trained personnel will depend on:

---

[84] S.I. 1981 No. 917.
[85] Health and Safety at Work etc. Act 1974, s.17.

(a) the number of employees;

(b) the nature of the undertaking;

(c) the size of the establishment and distribution of employees;

(d) the location of the establishment and the locations to which employees go in the course of their work.

Guidance on this is contained in the *approved* code of practice and in the Health and Safety series booklet (HSR.11) "First Aid at Work" obtainable from H.M.S.O. An extract from the approved code of practice is contained in Appendix II. The employer must inform all his employees of the arrangements that have been made in connection with the provision of first aid including the location of equipment, facilities and personnel.

SAFETY REPRESENTATIVES AND SAFETY COMMITTEES

5.22 The need for employees to be involved with health and safety matters at their place of work is given statutory force by section 2(4), (6) and (7) of the Health and Safety at Work etc. Act 1974. Safety representatives and safety committees may be appointed in cases prescribed by Regulations made by the Secretary of State and it is the duty of every employer to consult with a safety representative (if appointed) in order to make and maintain arrangements with employees regarding health and safety.

The Regulations referred to are the Safety Representatives and Safety Committees Regulations 1977[86] and an *approved*[87] code of practice has been made. A booklet entitled "Safety Representatives and Safety Committees" which is published by H.M.S.O. contains a copy of the Regulations together with the *approved* code of practice.

A recognised trade union[88] may appoint safety representatives from among the employees in all cases where one or more employee are employed by an employer by whom it is recognised. The trade union must notify the employer of the name(s) of the person(s) appointed and the employees he/they represent and he/they then become responsible for the functions contained in regulation 4 of the 1977 Regulations.[89]

Where at least two safety representatives request an employer to establish a safety committee he must do so and must:

(a) consult with the safety representatives who made the request

---

[86] S.I. 1977 No. 500.

[87] See p. 89 for the legal status of approved codes of practice.

[88] A "recognised trade union" means an independent trade union as defined in the Trade Union and Labour Relations Act 1974, s.30(1), which the employer concerned recognises for the purpose of negotiations relating to or connected with one or more of the matters specified in s.29(1) of that Act in relation to persons employed by him or as to which the Advisory, Conciliation and Arbitration Service has made a recommendation for recognition under the Employment Protection Act 1975 which is operative within the meaning of s.15 of that Act and Safety Representatives and Safety Committees Regulations 1977, reg. 2(1).

[89] Safety Representatives and Safety Committees Regulation 1977, reg. 3.

and with the representatives of recognised trade unions whose members work in any work place in respect of which he proposes that the committee should function; and

(b) post a notice stating the composition of the committee and the workplace or workplaces to be covered by it in a place where it might be easily read by the employees.

The committee must be established not later than three months after the request for it.[90]

THE STORAGE OF LIQUEFIED PETROLEUM GAS

General

The term "liquefied petroleum gas" (L.P.G.) is usually used to des-   **5.23** cribe commercial butane and propane. It is a by-product of petroleum refining, and pressurisation of the gas transforms it into a liquid. This is discharged into conveniently sized cylinders for distribution and in this state takes up about one two-hundredths of the volume needed to store it as a gas.

L.P.G. is supplied to the consumer by two methods, either in bulk to static tanks on consumer's premises, or in portable containers. The retailer will be concerned with portable containers and these are of two types, cartridges or cylinders that vary in size from 0.2 kg to about 50 kg.

Cartridges are disposable and are constructed to a recognised standard. They are usually fitted to the base of a small appliance that has a bayonet connector. This pierces the cartridge when connected and once the appliance is fitted it cannot be removed until all the gas has been used.

Cylinders are returnable and are owned and filled by the L.P.G. distributing company. They are pressure vessels and are required to be tested before and during use. Most have shut off valves fitted and they should never be charged by dealers or stockists.

Hazards on storage

If L.P.G. is mixed with air in a proportion of between 2 and 10 per   **5.24** cent. it forms a flammable mixture which is easily ignited. As with all petroleum gas the density is greater than air. Therefore, if there is a leak in one of the cylinders and the air is still the gas will flow to the lowest part of the premises. It could enter the drainage system if there is an open drain nearby and travel quite a distance before being dispersed. Ignition at a point some distance from the source could "flash-back" to the leaking cylinder and cause serious injury to anyone in the vicinity as well as igniting any inflammable material in its path.

A gas/air mixture enclosed to some degree in a vessel or underground void could present a risk of explosion and, of course, a cylinder in a fire

---

[90] *Ibid.* reg. 9.

is a potential bomb. There have been many incidents where cylinders stored improperly have caused severe damage with fragments of burst cylinders found up to 550 metres away from the site of the fire.

Nominally empty cylinders will still contain L.P.G. vapour and should be regarded as dangerous as full cylinders. A leaking or open valve could allow air to enter and form the easily ignited air/gas mixture.

Retailer's legal obligations

5.25 It is usual for cylinders, cartridges and other small primary containers to be sold in retail shops as a minor part of the main business. There is a general duty of care of the retailer to his employees under section 2(1) of the Health and Safety at Work etc. Act 1974 to ensure "as far as is reasonably practicable" their health, safety and welfare at work and also "so far as is reasonably practicable" to conduct their undertaking in such a way not to expose members of the public to risks to their health and safety under section 3 of the 1974 Act. Also under this latter section, self-employed persons have this duty to themselves as well as other persons who may be affected by this undertaking.

The Health and Safety Executive has issued guidance notes on the safe storage of L.P.G. that retailers should adhere to in order to fulfil their general duties under the 1974 Act. Guidance Note CS8 relates to small scale storage and display of L.P.G. at retail premises and is set out in Appendix VIII. Also, in Appendix IX is a statement of advice produced by the British Retailers Association in conjunction with the Health and Safety Executive.

THE CONTROL OF SUBSTANCES HAZARDOUS TO HEALTH

5.26 The Control of Substances Hazardous to Health Regulations 1988[91] is operative from October 1, 1989 and places specific duties on employers, self-employed persons and employees where there is a health risk created by work involving substances hazardous to health. The Regulations apply to substances that have already been classified as being very toxic, toxic, harmful, corrosive or irritant under the Classification, Packaging and Labelling of Dangerous Substances Regulations 1984,[92] substances which have maximum exposure limits or occupational exposure standards, a micro-organism which creates a hazard to the health of any person, dust of any kind, when present at a substantial concentration in air and any other substance which creates a hazard to health of any person comparable with the hazards of the substances mentioned above.[93] Also covered by the Regulations are those substances that have a chronic or delayed effects, for example substances that are carcinogenic, mutagenic or teratogenic.

[91] S.I. 1988 No. 1657.
[92] S.I. 1984 No. 1244, amended by S.I. 1986 No. 1922 and S.I. 1988 No. 766.
[93] Control of Substances Hazardous to Health Regulations 1988, reg. 2(1).

An employer must make a suitable and sufficient assessment of the risks created by any work which is liable to expose any employees to substances hazardous to health.[94] He must evaluate the risks to health and then decide how he can comply with all other relevant parts of the Regulations such as the steps to be taken to achieve and maintain adequate prevention or control of the risks[95] and the need for monitoring exposure[96] and the need for health surveillance.[97]

Self-employed persons are under the same obligations and duties as other employers except that regulations 10 and 11 which relate to monitoring exposures at the workplace and health surveillance do not apply.[98] Employees are under a duty to make full and proper use of any control measures and to report defects to the employer[99] and attend for medical examination, where appropriate, and give the medical officer such information about their health as may be reasonably required.[1] Where any duty is placed by the Regulations on an employer in respect of his employees, he shall, *so far as is reasonably practicable* be under a like duty in respect of any other person whether at work or not who may be affected by his work. The duty of the employer in respect of health surveillance and regulations 10 and 12(1) and (2), which relate respectively to monitoring and information, training, etc., do not apply to persons who are not his employees unless the persons are on the premises where the work is being carried on.[2]

Some areas for concern for retailers when considering compliance with the Regulations are mixing of paints, use and storage of solvents, and the presence of dust or powders created by any ancillary process. Two *approved* codes of practice[3] have been issued so far, *i.e.* control of substances hazardous to health in fumigation operations (ISBN 011 885469 0) and control of carcinogenic substances (ISBN 011 885468 2). Both are obtainable from H.M.S.O.

THE BURDEN OF PROOF

The general rule is that in criminal cases the legal burden of proving   5.27 every element of the offence lies with the prosecution.[4] However, section 40 of the Health and Safety at Work etc. Act 1974 contains one of the exceptions to this rule. The section states that in any proceedings for an offence under any of the relevant statutory provisions consisting of a failure to comply with a duty or requirement to do something so far as is

[94] *Ibid.* reg. 6.
[95] *Ibid.* regs. 7, 9.
[96] *Ibid.* reg. 10.
[97] *Ibid.* reg. 11.
[98] *Ibid.* reg. 3(2).
[99] *Ibid.* reg. 8(2).
[1] *Ibid.* reg. 11(9).
[2] *Ibid.* reg. 3(1).
[3] See p. 89 regarding legal standing of approved codes of practice.
[4] *Woolmington* v. *D.P.P.* [1935] A.C. 462.

practicable or so far as is reasonably practicable, or to use the best practicable means to do something, *it shall be for the accused to prove* (as the
case may be) that it was not practicable or not reasonably practicable to
do more than was in fact done to satisfy the duty or requirement, or that
there was no better practicable means than was in fact used to satisfy the
duty or requirement.

The degree to which this burden of proof must be discharged is governed by the "Carr-Briant" Construction. Humphreys J. stated *R.* v.
Carr-Briant:

> "In any case where, either by statute or at common law, some
> matter is presumed 'unless the contrary is proved' the jury should
> be directed that it is for them to decide whether the contrary is
> proved, the burden of proof required is less than that required at
> the hands of the prosecution in proving a case beyond reasonable
> doubt, and that the burden may be discharged by evidence satisfy-
> ing the jury of the probability of that which the accused is called
> upon to establish."[5]

Therefore, wherever a criminal statute casts a burden of proof on the
defendant the standard of proof required of the defence is not higher
than the burden which rests upon a plaintiff or defendant in civil proceedings, *i.e.* to prove his case on the balance of probabilities.

OFFENCES DUE TO THE FAULT OF ANOTHER PERSON

5.28 Where an employer is in breach of a duty under the Health and Safety at
Work etc. Act 1974 and that breach has come about by the act or default
of a third party, then the enforcing authority may prosecute the third
party irrespective of whether or not proceedings are instituted against
the employer.[6] For example, section 36(1) would apply where a company employs a safety officer who is in control of establishing a safe system of work. If the safety officer has not carried out his duties properly
and a safe system of work in the premises does not exist the health and
safety inspector may prosecute the safety officer instead of or in addition
to the company.

Also, where the Crown has committed an offence and the offence is
due to the act or default of a person other than the Crown that person
shall be guilty of the offence and may be charged and convicted.[7]

The defence of "due diligence" under section 67 of the Offices, Shops
and Railway Premises Act 1963 will, of course, apply to all offences
charged under that Act.[8]

---

[5] [1943] K.B. 607 at 612.
[6] Health and Safety at Work etc. Act 1974, s.36(1).
[7] *Ibid.* s.36(2).
[8] See pp. 128 and 160.

OFFENCES BY DIRECTORS, MANAGERS, SECRETARIES, ETC.

The Health and Safety at Work etc. Act 1974 provides for the prosecu-   **5.29**
tion of directors, managers, secretaries and other similar officers. However, it seems that this type of employee is not often the subject of
prosecution. The majority of prosecutions that are brought against individuals are against persons of a much lower status in the company—
usually shopfloor, employees under section 7 for "skylarking" or persons whose act or default causes an employer to be in breach of duty
under section 36.

Probably one of the main reasons why directors, etc., are not prosecuted often in addition to the company is because evidence must be
adduced and produced of either their knowledge and consent to the
offence or the offence to be at least attributable to their negligence. Section 37 states that where an offence under any of the relevant statutory
provisions committed by a body corporate is proved to have been committed with the consent or connivance of, or to have been attributable to
any neglect on the part of any director, manager, secretary or other
similar officer of a body corporate or a person purporting to act in any
such capacity, he as well as the body corporate shall be guilty of that
offence and shall be liable to be proceeded against and punished accordingly.

In 1977, the Director of Roads of the Strathclyde Regional Council
was successfully prosecuted under this section even though he was not
strictly a director of a body corporate. The court decided that he came
within the class of persons mentioned, *i.e.* manager.[9]

In another case in 1978, the Chairman of Singer Co. (United Kingdom) Ltd. was fined £250 as a result of a prosecution brought by the
Health and Safety Executive in respect of the company's failure to guard
drilling machines as required under the Factories Act 1961. The wording
of the section seems to indicate that both the company and the Chairman should have been prosecuted but proceedings were only taken
against the Chairman and a fellow director and the defence did not take
up the point. The jury was undecided on the guilt of the other director
and as it was a Scottish trial they returned a verdict peculiar to Scottish
law, that of "not proven."[10]

A person can be subject to a prosecution under this section even
though he is not a director or holding similar office. If he *acts* as a director or manager then he is caught by the section as the section states that
persons who purport to act as directors, managers, secretaries or similar
officers are also liable.

[9] *Armour* v. *Skeen* [1977] I.R.L.R. 310.
[10] See "The Inspector," Vol. 24, No. 6, Nov–Dec 1978.

CHAPTER 6

WELFARE ARRANGEMENTS FOR SHOP EMPLOYEES

6.01 Section 2(1) of the Health and Safety at Work etc. Act 1974 lays down the general duty of the employer to ensure, so far as is reasonably practicable, the health, safety and welfare at work of all his employees, but the details of the welfare arrangements that he must provide in shops are contained in one of the "relevant statutory provisions," the Offices, Shops and Railway Premises Act 1963 and Regulations made thereunder.[1]

There are a number of Acts listed in Schedule 1 of the 1974 Act that are "relevant statutory provisions," The intention is that eventually the Acts will be revoked and replaced by Regulations. In the meantime, the enforcement of the Acts is by means of the enforcement sections of the 1974 Act and the enforcement authorities are as defined in the Health and Safety (Enforcing Authority) Regulations 1977.[1a]

There is a presumption in law that the legislature uses the same language in the same sense when dealing at different times with the same subject.[2] The wording of the Offices, Shops and Railway Premises Act 1963 follows the same pattern of the Factories Act 1961 and both statutes may be interpreted in *pari materia*.

SCOPE OF THE OFFICES, SHOPS AND RAILWAY PREMISES ACT 1963

6.02 Although the 1974 Act covers all situations where persons are employed including, in some respects, the self-employed, the scope of the 1963 Act is more restricted. It only applies to those shops where persons are employed under a contract of employment (including apprentices and persons on the Youth Training Scheme), for an aggregate of at least 21 hours. However, if the person employed is the husband, wife, parent, grandparent, son, daughter, grandchild, brother or sister of the person by whom they are employed, the premises are exempt.[3]

Anyone employing or intending to employ people in shops must, under section 49 of the 1963 Act, serve a notification of the fact in the prescribed form on the local authority. It is usual for local authorities to have a supply of these forms available in the Environmental Health Department. Two copies must be served.

---

[1] Sanitary Conveniences Regulations 1964 (S.I. 1964 No. 966); Washing Facilities Regulations 1964 (S.I. 1964 No. 965); Offices, Shops and Railways Premises (Hoists and Lifts) Regulations 1968 (S.I. 1968 No. 849).

[1a] S.I. 1977 No. 746.

[2] *Hamilton v. National Coal Board* [1960] A.C. 633.

[3] Offices, Shops and Railway Premises Act 1963, ss.2, 3.

Definition of "shop premises"

Section 1(3)(*a*) of the 1963 Act defines "shop premises" as meaning: **6.03**

(i) a shop;

(ii) a building or part of a building, being a building or part of which is not a shop but of which the sole or principal use is the carrying on there of retail trade or business;

(iii) a building occupied by a wholesale dealer or merchant where goods are kept for sale wholesale or a part of a building so occupied where goods are so kept, but not including a warehouse belonging to the owners, traders or conservators of a dock, wharf or quay;

(iv) a building to which members of the public are invited to resort for the purpose of delivering there goods for repair or other treatment or of themselves there carrying out repairs to, or other treatment of, goods, or a part of a building to which members of the public are invited to resort for that purpose;

(v) any premises occupied for the purpose of a trade or business which consists of, or includes, the sale of solid fuel,[4] being premises used for the storage of such fuel intended to be sold in the course of that trade or business, but not including dock storage premises[5] or colliery storage premises . . . [6]

. . . and for the purposes of this Act premises occupied together with a shop or with a building or part of a building falling within sub-paragraph (ii), (iii) or (iv) or paragraph (a) above for the purposes of the trade or business carried on in the shop or, as the case may be, the building or part of a building shall be treated as forming part of the shop or, as the case may be, of the building or part of the building, and premises occupied together with fuel storage premises for the purposes of the activities there carried on (not being office premises) shall be treated as forming part of the fuel storage premises, but for the purposes of this Act office premises comprised in fuel storage premises shall be deemed not to form part of the last-mentioned premises.

The term "shop" is not defined but there should not be any problem of interpretation because of the extended definition of "shop premises."

---

[4] "Solid fuel" means coal, coke and any solid fuel derived from coal or of which coal or coke is a constituent (Offices, Shops and Railway Premises Act 1963, s.1(3)(*c*)).

[5] "Dock storage premises" means fuel storage premises which constitute or are comprised in premises to which certain provision of the Factories Act 1961 apply by virtue of s.125(1) (docks, etc.) of that Act (Offices, Shops and Railway Premises Act 1963, s.1(3)(*d*)).

[6] "Colliery storage premises" means fuel storage premises which form part of the premises which, for the purposes of the Mines and Quarries Act 1954, form part of a mine or quarry, other than premises where persons are regularly employed to work by a person other than the owner (as defined by that Act) of the mine or quarry. (Offices, Shops and Railway Premises Act 1963, s.1(3)(*e*)).

It seems that it has been left undefined deliberately so that it may have a wide application in accordance with the common usage of the word. It would cover, for example, a pawn shop or a school tuck shop as well as such places as a butcher's shop or grocer's shop. The business of the shop must be conducted on "premises" because, under the definition, "shop" is a species of the genus "shop premises." Therefore, a mobile shop, stall or any structure that has not a sufficient degree of permanency to be regarded as premises does not come within the definition. The ordinary and natural sense of the word "shop" must be looked at, and in coming to a decision on this question the court will probably consider whether or not any retail trade or business is being carried on.

Under section 1(3)(*b*) of the 1963 Act, the expression "retail trade or business" includes the sale to members of the public of food or drink for immediate consumption, retail sales by auction and the business of lending books or periodicals for the purpose of gain. The definition is plainly not intended to be exhaustive.[7] It will obviously cover such premises (that might also come under the definition of shop) as barber's or hairdresser's business places where goods may be hired (such as television rental shops and video hire shops)[8]; mail order business (whether dealing with the final customer through the post or through agents) and a gift shop (in which goods are supplied against coupons).

A building includes a structure[9] but may be no more than a structure.[10]

A retail trade or business may be carried on in a building or part of a building which would not, in the ordinary sense of the word, be a shop, for example, the sale of services. The services, however, must be of a type normally provided on shop premises and would not include the business of a builder and decorator. In *Frawley (M. & F.)* v. *Ve-Ri-Best Manufacturing Co.*,[11] Somervell L.J. held that the word "retail" primarily suggested the selling of goods rather than the selling of services and whilst both he and Jenkins L.J. thought that the terms of the definition suggested that a business might be a retail business although it was concerned with matters other than the sale of goods, they also took the view that to satisfy the definition, where there was a sale of services the ser-

---

[7] For discussion on the meaning of the word "includes" in statutory definitions see *Dilworth* v. *Commissioner of Stamps* [1899] A.C. 99, P.C.

[8] *Lewis* v. *Rogers*; *Gardiner* v. *Duffield* (1984) 82 L.G.R. 670, where in considering video hire under the Shops Act 1950 Mann J. said, at 678; "Whether the subject is a shop will depend upon the physical characteristics and upon the activities conducted in it. Do they combine to present a shop? Where the physical characteristics are true of a shop and the activity conducted in the subject is that of retail sales to members of the public who are present, the answer must be 'yes.' What of the case where the physical characteristics are true of a shop and the activity is the provision of a service in regard to articles such as shoes, clothes, watches and photographic films for members of the public who are present to receive it? I think in such a case that the subject is a shop."

[9] Offices, Shops and Railway Premises Act 1963, s.90(1).

[10] There is no definition of structure but see para. 1.03.

[11] [1953] 1 Q.B. 318.

vices rendered must be performed in circumstances comparable with those in which a sale of goods is carried on in a retail shop.

The definition of "shop premises" also includes a building (or part of one) occupied by a wholesale dealer or merchant where goods are kept for sale wholesale. It does not matter if people do not purchase goods at the premises and covers most warehouses occupied by wholesale dealers or merchants but excludes warehouses and dock warehouses covered by the Factories Act 1961. However, to come under the definition the goods must be kept for sale and not simply stored, for example, furniture depositories.

The 1963 Act extends to those premises or parts of the premises occupied, together with shop premises for the purposes of the activities carried on there. Included under the definition would be stairs, cloakrooms and storerooms that are used in connection with the business. The premises must be physically part of or adjacent to the shop premises. If not, they are not covered by the Act unless, of course, they come under the definition in their own right, for example, "office premises" or canteens catering wholly or mainly for workers in the shop.

Application of the Offices, Shops and Railway Premises Act 1963 to certain types of premises and businesses

(a) *Clubs*

All offices forming part of a club will be covered by the 1963 Act but the Act will not apply to bars and restaurants etc. of members' clubs (for example working men's clubs) if the principle purpose is the serving of club members. There is a problem with "night clubs" where patrons become temporary members. A useful but not conclusive guide is to refer to the club rules to see if it stipulates a delay of two days between application for membership and the enjoyment of privileges. This is required by the Licensing Act 1964, section 41. It is suggested that if this delay is not stipulated the bars and restaurant of the clubs should be subject to the provisions of this Act.

6.04

(b) *Public houses*

Public houses are quite often run by a husband and wife team who are tenants of a brewery. The 1963 Act will apply to the premises if one or both of them are "employed" by the brewery. If bar assistants or cleaners are employed then there is no doubt that the Act applies to the premises.

(c) *Stalls in market places*

If the stall has some degree of permanency and can be regarded as a "structure" then it is covered by the 1963 Act.[12]

---

[12] See p. 4 on the meaning of structure.

(d) *One-Man businesses which are limited companies*

Where one person is employed by a limited company and that person is the majority shareholder, he should be regarded as being self-employed. In such a situation the 1963 Act would not apply to his premises.

ARRANGEMENTS AND FACILITIES TO BE PROVIDED UNDER THE OFFICES, SHOPS AND RAILWAY PREMISES ACT 1963

Cleanliness (section 4)

6.05   Under the provisions of this section every employer has a duty:

> (a) to keep his premises and contents, *i.e.* furniture, furnishings and fittings clean;
>
> (b) to not allow dirt or refuse to accumulate; and
>
> (c) to clean floors and steps at least once weekly by washing or, if it is effective and suitable, by sweeping or other method.

The section does not apply to fuel storage premises which are in the open and there are special obligations in other sections of the Act which are in addition to this general section. These are sections 42(1), (2), (5) and 43(1), (2) (cleanliness of common parts of buildings), section 8(3) (cleanliness of windows and sky lights), section 9(2) (cleanliness of sanitary conveniences), and section 10(2) (cleanliness of washing places). It must also be remembered that if food is being sold on the premises, the Food Hygiene (General) Regulations 1970 will also apply.[13] Refuse allowed to accumulate in passageways or near fire-doors may also contravene fire regulations.

The Minister (then Minister of Labour, now the Secretary of State for Employment) may make Regulations under sub-paragraph (5) of the section but no Regulations have been made to date.

The standard of cleanliness to be obtained will obviously depend on the type of premises. Offices at fuel store depots will not be expected to be as clean as offices at a bank. A commonsense attitude should be taken and, although a weekly sweeping of floors is stipulated, in some premises where work produces dirt which cannot otherwise be easily moved more frequent cleaning will be necessary.

Overcrowding (section 5)

6.06   Overcrowding in workplaces is inextricably tied up with ventilation and temperature and can produce, in some cases, injury to both physical and mental health. There are two standards for overcrowding in the 1963 Act.

The first is in section 5(1) which provides that no room in premises to which the Act applies shall, while work is going on there, be so overcrowded as to cause risk of injury to the health of persons working in it.

---

[13] S.I. 1970 No. 1172.

For the purposes of determining whether a room is overcrowded, the space occupied by furniture, furnishings, fittings, machinery, plant, equipment, etc. must be taken into account as well as the number of persons expected to be working in the room at any one time. The sub-section applies to all rooms contained within premises to which the Act applies, whether or not members of the public are allowed resort thereto.

It is extremely difficult to prove that circumstances exist that could cause risk of injury to health before the injury has actually occurred. The application of section 5(1) must be based on commonsense and the yardstick is provided by section 5(2). This is that the number of persons habitually employed at a time to work in a room shall be such that there is a minimum of 40 square feet per person. If, however, the height of the ceiling is less than 10 feet, each person must have at least 400 cubic feet. In working out this calculation the presence of furniture and fittings etc. can be ignored, but space occupied by a chimney breast or by continuous radiator or duct casings should be regarded as diminishing the size of the room.

The minimum standard in subsection (2) does not prejudice the operation of subsection (1) and it does not apply to rooms where members of the public resort. The word "resort" does not necessarily imply "enter," and subsection (2) would not apply, for example, to the following rooms:

    (a) shop rooms to which the public are admitted;
    (b) offices intended for public use;
    (c) kiosks, whether inside or outside buildings, from which goods are sold or at which money is taken, over a counter or through a grille or opening;
    (d) theatre and cinema box offices.

In the first standard (subsection (1)) the term "working" is used, which is wider than "employed to work" and includes all persons working whether under a contract of service or not. The second standard (subsection (2)) includes the phrase "the number of persons habitually employed at a time." This could reasonably be interpreted as being employed for more than half the normal working hours.

A problem could occur when a room is divided by a partition. There is no definition of a "room" and the partition may only rise to perhaps half the height, so that the air is common to both sides. It would be a question of fact in each case.

Temperature (section 6)

Where persons are employed to work in rooms (with certain exceptions) otherwise than for short periods, effective provision must be   **6.07** made to maintain a reasonable temperature. The form of heating, however, must not be such as to cause offensive fumes (which includes gas or vapour) or which is likely to be injurious to health. If the work is substantially of a sedentary nature or does not involve severe physical effort a temperature of less than 16°C (60.8°F) shall not be deemed, after the first hour, to be a reasonable temperature while work is going on. A suitable thermometer must be provided and placed in a conspicuous place on each floor where there is a room to which the above provisions apply.

There are certain rooms where it is not reasonably practicable to maintain a reasonable temperature and the 1963 Act recognises this. These are:

(a) any office room "to which the public are invited to resort and in which the maintenance of a reasonable temperature is not reasonably practicable."[14] The two conditions must be satisfied. Not only must the room be one that the public are invited to resort, but it must also be shown that a reasonable temperature cannot be maintained, for example, betting offices, theatre and railway booking offices;

(b) rooms in a shop . . . where "the maintenance of a reasonable temperature is not reasonably practicable or would cause deterioration of goods."

The conditions here are alternatives. The first condition would apply to open fronted shops or open fronted sales kiosks and the second condition to such shops as wet fish shops, certain parts of butcher's shops and chill rooms, where the maintenance of the stipulated temperature would cause spoilage of the food.

In a case heard at Watford Magistrates' Court,[15] greengrocers were prosecuted for allowing low temperatures to prevail at their premises, for example 49°F at 9.50 a.m. Expert witnesses for the defendants gave evidence concerning the shortening of the life of fruit and vegetables by an increase in temperature. They agreed with the prosecution's contention that higher temperatures than 60.8°F prevailed outside in the summer months without spoilage of goods, but said that there were then more home produced vegetables on the market and these were better able to withstand such temperatures than imported produce. This was accepted by the magistrates and the case was dismissed. They were satisfied that above 32°F the higher the temperature the greater would be the spread of deterioration.

[14] "Reasonably practicable" implies that the risk must be balanced on the one hand against the sacrifice involved (*i.e.* money, time or trouble) to remove the risk on the other. Where it can be shown that the sacrifice greatly exceeds the quantum of risk the defendants will have discharged the onus placed upon them. *Edwards* v. *National Coal Board* [1949] 1 K.B. 704. This construction was followed in *McCartney* v. *Coldair* (1951) 3 T.L.R. 1226, C.A. and approved in *Marshall* v. *Gotham Co.* [1954] A.C. 360; (1954) 1 All E.R. 937, H.L.: see also p. 89.
[15] *Rickmansworth Urban District Council* v. *Ward (P.)*, March 1966 (unreported). See Local Authority Circ. 9 (Supplement 2) September 8, 1966.

Magistrates also dismissed a prosecution brought at Havant Magistrates' Court[16] in respect of a temperature reading of 48°F in a butcher's shop where a certain quantity of meat was on show and also a large amount of refrigeration.

Careful consideration is needed by local authorities before prosecutions are brought under section 6(1) in situations where there is a possibility that a temperature of 60.8°F and above would cause deterioration of goods (not necessarily food). The occupier cannot be expected to alter his system of work to comply with the 1963 Act, for example, installation of a refrigeration system, but the onus of proof is on the defendant to prove that his goods would deteriorate if such a high temperature is maintained.

If the room is excluded by section 6(3) of the 1963 Act, employees must be provided with "conveniently accessible and effective means" of warming themselves, and the employer must afford them reasonable opportunities for using these means.[17] This could be, for example, in an open fronted shop or a butcher's shop simply "a room at the rear with a fire." There is no requirement to provide a thermometer in rooms covered by section 6(3).

Where a prosecution is taken in respect of non-compliance with sections 6(1) or (2) of the 1963 Act, in a shop where deterioration of goods may be possible at the 60.8°F, it is wise to include a charge that conveniently accessible and effective means of enabling the staff to warm themselves is not provided. If the first count fails the second will stand.

Section 6(1) of the 1963 Act states, *inter alia*, that "effective provision shall be made for securing and maintaining a reasonable temperature . . . " and a minimum temperature is specified in subsection (2). No maximum temperature is mentioned. In the summer months occasionally high outside temperatures may make it difficult for employers to secure a reasonable temperature and many complaints are received at local authority offices particularly from people working in modern office blocks with a high percentage of glass on the external walls.

A London industrial tribunal in dismissing an appeal against an improvement notice requiring temperatures in a dry cleaning shop to be lowered acknowledged that concessions have to be made (*i.e.* high temperatures tolerated) where outside temperatures are exceptionally high. But the tribunal considered that a temperature of 89°F (32°C), recorded on one occasion in the dry cleaning shop by the inspector when the outside temperature was only 52°F (11°C), was unreasonable and a breach of section 3(1) of the Factories Act 1961 (a similar provision to section 6(1) of the 1963 Act).

Regulations covering specific industries which do include maximum

---

[16] *Havant and Waterloo Urban District Council* v. *Cooper and Sons (Portsmouth) Ltd.* 1966 (unreported).
[17] Offices, Shops and Railway Premises Act 1963, s.6(6).

temperatures were quoted by the prosecuting inspector: 75°F (23.9°C) in the pottery regulation and 70°F (21.1°C) in those concerned with lead compound processing. It was noted that these Regulations allow the maxima to be exceeded as long as work place temperatures do not exceed the outside temperature by more than 10°F (5.5°C).[18]

Ventilation (section 7)

6.08   In every room comprised in, or constituting premises to which the Act applies, effective and suitable means of ventilation[19] must be provided and maintained by the circulation of adequate supplies of fresh or artificially purified air.

There are four reasons for supplying air to buildings in relation to the health and welfare of employees. These are:

(a) to satisfy the respiratory needs of the occupants;
(b) to remove body odours and tobacco smoke;
(c) to maintain the bodily heat balance; and
(d) to control airborne contamination (generally encountered in factory conditions or in kitchens and canteens and which is usually dealt with by local exhaust ventilation).

"Fresh air" means unpolluted air from outside the building: the position of the inlet is important because if it is too low it will collect dust and fumes from passing vehicles, whereas if it is too high and in the wrong position it is liable to let in fumes or grit from chimneys.

"Artificially purified air" is air which has been treated chemically or physically so that its composition is similar to that of ordinary outside air and may also include air that has been passed through an air-conditioning plant.

It is suggested that the installation of ozone producing equipment that circulates artificially produced air does not comply with the 1963 Act. The reason being that air purifiers or ozonizers by themselves do not provide fresh air, and although they may purify the air by reducing contamination they do not ensure the circulation of fresh or artificially purified air. Where an apparatus of this type is installed in a room, other means of ventilation must be provided in addition.

The adequate supply of fresh air for any occupied room varies with the purpose for which the room is used, whether smoking is allowed, personal hygiene of the occupants as well as the sensitivity of the observer. Many standards for fresh air supplies have been suggested over the last hundred years or so varying from 5 to 50 cubic feet of fresh air per person per minute (300–3,000 cubic feet of fresh air per person per hour). Guidance Note EH.22 from the Health and Safety Executive ("Ventilation of Buildings: Fresh Air Requirements") contains a

---

[18] "The Inspector," Vol. 29, No. 4, July-August 1983.
[19] The standard text book on the subject is Bedford, *Basic Principles of Ventilation and Heating* (3rd ed., 1974).

number of tables and graphs indicating recommended fresh air requirements in differing situations. Quite apart from the fresh air supplied, it
must be remembered that there is an infiltration of air which may double
the amount of fresh air available inside a building and which is not taken
into account in the calculation. Nevertheless it is suggested that the
quantity of fresh air supplied should never fall below 10 cubic feet (0.28
cubic metres) per person per minute in ordinary normal buildings.

Lighting (section 8)

Sufficient and suitable lighting, either natural or artificial, must be **6.09**
provided in every part of any premises to which the 1963 Act applies, in
which persons are working or passing.[20] All artificial lighting apparatus
must be properly maintained[21] and all glazed windows and skylights
used for lighting premises covered by the Act must be kept, so far as
reasonably practicable, clean inside and outside and free from obstruction; but it permits them to be whitewashed or shaded to mitigate heat
or glare.[22]

The provision of this section applies to areas where persons work or
pass. This means that all exits, corridors, stairs or passages where members of the public or employees pass or work must be properly lit in
order to prevent accidents.

In *Zetland Park Garage* v. *Douglas (M)*,[23] the industrial tribunal had
to decide whether the appellant had provided adequate artificial lighting
in a stock room and adequate ventilation to the main shop. It was
pointed out to the tribunal that although sections 7 and 8 of the 1963 Act
had allowed (subsection now repealed) the Minister to make Regulations prescribing standards of adequate ventilation and lighting, no such
Regulation had been passed. Given that there is no statutory standard,
the tribunal members visited the premises to see the position for themselves. The standard required by the inspector was 107 lux (*i.e.* 10
lumens per square foot) at all shelves, being fairly normal for such an
area.

The tribunal decided that the lighting was sufficient and suitable and

[20] Offices, Shops and Railway Premises Act 1963, s.8(1).
[21] "Properly maintained." These words impose an absolute obligation under the Factories
Act 1961, s.22, that requires lifts etc. to be "properly maintained" and it is submitted
that this interpretation also applies to the Offices, Shops and Railway Premises Act
1963. In *Galashiels Gas Co.* v. *O'Donnell (or Millar)* [1949] A.C. 275, a lift mechanism
worked perfectly before and after an accident. No fault was found after the whole
mechanism had been dismantled and carefully re-assembled. The brake that had failed
on the occasion of the accident had not been known to fail for nine years previously.
Nevertheless, the House of Lords held that there was imposed on the firm an absolute
and continuing obligation which was not discharged if at any time their lift mechanism
was not maintained in an efficient state, in efficient working order, and in good repair.
The words of the subsection were imperative and nothing in the context or in the
general intention of the Act, read as a whole, implied any qualification of that absolute
obligation.
[22] Offices, Shops and Railway Premises Act 1963, s.8(3), (4).
[23] Middlesbrough C.O.I.T. No. 2/19 Case No. HS 20716/78.

so far as ventilation to the shop was concerned "at most times the door of the shop was open, providing an adequate supply of fresh air." Both improvement notices were quashed.

An advisory booklet on lighting has been issued by the Health and Safety Executive. It is part of the HSG. series numbered HS(G)38 and entitled "Lighting at Work." The booklet, which was first published in 1987, is mainly concerned with artificial lighting and advises on how to comply with the statutory provisions relating to safety and lighting, and is obtainable from H.M.S.O.

Sanitary accommodation (section 9)

6.10   Employers are obliged under section 9 of the 1963 Act to provide sufficient and suitable sanitary conveniences for their employees in premises to which the Act applies. They must be situated in a position that is conveniently accessible, kept clean and properly maintained and effective provision must be made for lighting and ventilation. The responsibility normally lies on the occupier of the building to provide the facilities but in the case of buildings in single or plural ownership, parts of which are held under a lease or licence, the responsibility is on the owner.[24]

Arrangements can be made for employees to have use of conveniences provided for the use of others and thereby comply with the Act.[25] An example would be where an employee in a small lock-up shop would have use of the sanitary convenience situated in adjacent premises. The sanitary convenience must comply with all the statutory provisions regarding cleanliness and accessibility, etc., but a nearby public lavatory cannot be regarded as complying with the Act.[26] The employer could make an application to the local authority for an exemption certificate if he considers that the local authority would consider that compliance with section 9 is "not reasonably practicable."[27]

Under subsection (3) of section 9, the Minister was empowered to make Regulations regarding what is suitable and sufficient for the purposes of subsection (1). Subsection (3) has been repealed from January 1, 1975 by the Offices, Shops and Railway Premises Act 1963 (Repeals and Modifications) Regulations 1974,[28] but Regulations were made on June 25, 1964 called the Sanitary Convenience Regulations 1964[29] and came into operation on January 1, 1966.[30]

The afore-mentioned Regulations that repealed subsection (3) of sec-

---

[24] Offices, Shops and Railway Premises Act 1963, ss.42(6), 43(4).
[25] *Ibid.* s.9(5).
[26] Sanitary Convenience Regulations 1964 (S.I. 1964 No. 966), reg. 3(2). (See Appendix X).
[27] p. 116.
[28] S.I. 1974 No. 1943.
[29] S.I. 1964 No. 966.
[30] See Appendix X.

tion 9 of the 1963 Act contained a proviso that the Regulations shall not affect the validity of anything done under any provision repealed or modified by the Regulations before the coming into operation of the Regulations. The Sanitary Convenience Regulations 1964 are therefore still valid. Markets are excluded from the effect of these Regulations by regulation 2,

Whether or not sanitary conveniences are conveniently accessible is a question of fact in each case. For example, in *Davis (A.C.) & Sons* v. *The Environmental Health Department of Leeds City Council*,[31] a toilet in a flat above a shop was considered conveniently accessible to women working in the shop.

In *Aldis Travel Agency, Pauls Turf Accountants, Bloom (D.M.)* v. *Surtees (A.G.)*,[32] the appellants against an improvement notice served under section 21 of the 1974 Act were tenants of lock-up shops owned by the London Transport Executive and situated near the entrance to Hornchurch London Transport Station. None of the premises had its own sanitary convenience but it was submitted by the appellants that three sets of sanitary conveniences were available and conveniently accessible. They were:

(a) on the station platform approximately 200 yards away;
(b) in the hotel at the rear of the shops (attached to the saloon bar); and
(c) in the same hotel on the first floor;

and the distance from the hotel to the three shops varied from 120 yards to 144 yards.

The London Transport Executive had given keys to the lavatories on the station platform and a licence to use them at any time, and the licencee of the hotel had given a key and permission to use the sanitary convenience on the first floor. The facilities attached to the saloon bar could only be used during opening hours.

The tribunal decided that all facilities were too distant to be conveniently accessible. It was stated that regard must be had to the problems employees would encounter during inclement weather and with respect to the toilets in the saloon bar, these would not be available at time when people would be employed in the shops.

Washing facilities (section 10)

Suitable and sufficient washing facilities including: **6.11**

(a) a supply of clean running hot and cold or warm water;
(b) soap; and

[31] [1976] I.R.L.R. 282, Industrial Tribunal.
[32] "The Inspector," Vol. 24, No. 2, March-April 1978, Industrial Tribunal.

(c) clean towels or other suitable means of cleaning or drying,

must be provided by an employer at a place which is conveniently accessible to his staff. Also, the place where these washing facilities are situated must be kept clean and in an orderly condition and have an effective means of lighting and the hand basins and all other equipment must be kept clean and properly maintained.

As with sanitary conveniences, the section may be complied with if the employees have use of washing facilities provided for use of others, but of course they must be conveniently accessible[33] and comply in all other respects with the statutory obligations laid down in section 10.

Exemption from the obligation to provide hot and cold or warm running water may be granted by the local authority under section 46.[34]

The Washing Facilities Regulations 1964[35] were made under the powers granted to the Minister by subsection (3). This subsection has since been repealed but as is the case with the Sanitary Convenience Regulations there is a proviso that the validity of any Regulations made before the coming into effect of the repealing Regulations shall not be affected.

The Washing Facilities Regulations determine what provision is "suitable and sufficient" and there is a very useful booklet published by H.M.S.O. called "Cloakroom Accommodation and Washing Facilities" (HS(G)10) that gives guidance on the practical application of the regulations. Markets are excluded from the effect of the Regulations by regulation 2.

Supply of drinking water (section 11)

6.12   An adequate supply of wholesome drinking water conveniently accessible to the employees must be provided. It is not necessary for the water to be from a piped supply, but if not it must be contained in vessels that are suitable for the purpose and removed at least daily. All practical[36] steps must be taken to keep the water and vessels free from contamination.

Disposable cups must be made available or alternatively a sufficient number of washable drinking vessels (for example, glasses) together with facilities for rinsing in clean water. If the drinking water is delivered in a jet from which people can conveniently drink there is no

---

[33] See the section on sanitary conveniences as to what is considered "conveniently accessible."

[34] See p. 127.

[35] S.I. 1964 No. 965. (See Appendix XI).

[36] "Practicable"; the questions of cost should not be considered in determining what is practicable. Measures may be "practicable" which are not "reasonably practicable" but, nonetheless, "practicable" means something more than physically possible. The measures must be possible in the light of current knowledge and invention. *Assett* v. *K and L Steelfounders and Engineers* [1953] 2 All E.R. 320.

necessity to provide cups in any form.[37] There is no requirement, as in the Factories Act 1961, for the water to be marked "drinking water."

Again, as with sanitary conveniences and washing facilities, the statutory obligation can be fulfilled by employees having use of drinking water provided for use by others as long as all the requirements of section 11 are met, including that of being conveniently accessible.[38]

Accommodation for clothing (section 12)

Suitable and sufficient provision must be made at suitable places for   **6.13** clothing not worn during working hours to be hung up. Also such arrangements as are reasonably practicable must be made for drying the clothes. Similar arrangements must be made for working clothes.

No mention is made in the section of cloakroom or lockers. For example, it would be considered suitable and sufficient in a small shop if a sufficient number of pegs or stands are provided. However, because of the risks of contamination of food, it must be remembered that in a food shop the Food Hygiene (General) Regulations 1970[38a] require that clothes be kept in a locker or cupboard in certain circumstances.

Although the Minister has power to make Regulations under section 12(3) of the 1963 Act concerning the provision of these facilities, no Regulations have been made, therefore guidance must be taken from the booklet "Cloakroom Accommodation and Washing Facilities."[38b] The type of arrangements necessary will obviously depend on the size of the establishment and number of employees, but in deciding whether accommodation for clothing is suitable the risk of theft must be considered. This was decided by the Court of Appeal in a case under a corresponding provision of the Factories Act 1937 (now section 59 of the Factories Act 1961). Pegs had been provided by the company for employees. A worker had clothing stolen from the pegs and claimed for the loss of clothing. The Court of Appeal held that the obligation to provide "adequate and suitable accommodation for clothing not worn during working hours" did not include a duty to keep the clothing safe, but that nevertheless the risk of theft was an element to be taken into consideration in deciding whether the accommodation was suitable.[39]

Regard must be had to the type of premises when considering what are "reasonably practicable" arrangements for drying clothes. Hot water pipes or electric tubular heaters under clothes stands could be regarded as suitable but it may be unreasonable to expect an employer to provide special facilities when employees are working under normal conditions. A warm room or space where clothes could be hung without

---

[37] Offices, Shops and Railway Premises Act 1963, s.11(3).
[38] *Ibid.* s.11(4) (see p. 121 regarding "conveniently accessible.")
[38a] S.I. 1970 No. 1172.
[38b] p. 122.
[39] *McCarthy* v. *Daily Mirror Newspapers* (1949) 113 J.P. 229.

inconvenience could be suitable. The question of available space and cost in a small business would have to be borne in mind.

Sitting facilities (sections 13 and 14)

6.14   Employers must provide seats for their employees if the employees are able to use the seats without any detriment to their work, and in the case of a shop where customers are invited to resort, the number of seats must be the ratio of not less than one seat to three employees. These seats do not have to be actually situated in the sales area of the shop but where they are not provided in the sales area, seating facilities should be made available elsewhere and shop assistants must have the opportunity to use them from time to time during slack periods.

In the case of situations other than a sales area, the ratio of seats to employees is left to the judgment of the employer. They must be suitable and sufficient and what is sufficient is a question of fact which the court would in a dispute have to decide according to the circumstances of each case as it arises.

Section 14 refers to the suitability of seats for workers who have to spend a substantial part of their time sitting. In these circumstances the seat must be of a design and dimensions suitable for the employee together with a foot-rest, unless he can comfortly support his feet without one. The seat and foot-rest must be adequately supported while in use and where the seat is adjustable, the "dimensions" are taken as its dimensions when adjusted.

The section is based on section 60(2) of the Factories Act 1961, the purpose being to avoid undue strain and fatigue for those who have to carry out their work in a sedentary position. A useful booklet giving advice on good seating arrangements in different working situations is "Seats for Workers in Factories, Offices and Shops" (HSW.45) published by H.M.S.O. The advice draws on experience gained by the Factory Inspectorate, and is supplemented by information obtained from various sources including the Industrial Health Research Board, the Medical Research Council and the British Standards Institution.

In *Tesco Stores* v. *Edwards*,[40] the industrial tribunal affirmed improvement notices requiring the appellants to improve the seating for their operators at check-out points in their supermarkets. They found that the existing seats did not comply with section 14 because they did not have foot-rests, and were unsuitable in design because they were not adjustable in height, had no back rest, could not swivel, and were generally uncomfortable. The inspectors had not specifically mentioned that a swivelling chair was necessary in the improvement notices, although they had pointed it out to the appellants during negotiations prior to this case.

The tribunal accepted the evidence of the inspectors, backed up by a

---

[40] [1977] I.R.L.R. 120.

written statement from a doctor employed by the Dorset Area Health Authority, even though the statement was not made on oath and the doctor was not at the hearing to be cross-examined:

> " . . . Having listened to the evidence about the work of these operators on the check-outs the Tribunal is satisfied that a suitable chair for such an operator is one which has a back rest and a foot-rest, is adjustable in height and can swivel. These operators have to work at a counter with the till in front of them. In the Tribunal's view suitable seating should be adjustable in height so that whatever the physical size of the check-out operator, she can arrange her seating at a convenient height for herself to operate the till. We also find that there is a certain amount of waist movement, in that the operator has to turn from the till to the customer. The doctor has said he felt that 'in view of the nature of the work which involves a substantial amount of arm and waist movement a chair which will swivel is necessary to neutralise the frequent turning from the waist action which is inherent with this work' . . . "[40a]

A similar situation was considered by the Bournemouth Crown Court in *Paul v. Weymouth and Portland Borough Council*.[41] There had been no appeal to the industrial tribunal and the Council successfully prosecuted Mr. Paul, who was trading as Fairprice, for non-compliance with the notice under section 33(3) of the Health and Safety at Work Act 1974. Mr. Paul appealed to the Crown Court and the Recorder ruled that the Crown Court was not bound by any decision of the lower court or industrial tribunal and before Mr. Paul was required to answer the charge of non-compliance with the improvement notice it was necessary for the prosecution to prove beyond all reasonable doubt that the notice itself was good in law and that the requirements of the schedule conformed with the provisions of section 14.

The inspector, appointed by the council under the Health and Safety at Work etc. Act 1974, was the only witness for the prosecution and the following evidence was produced:

(a) a written decision of the industrial tribunal in *Tesco Stores v. Edwards*[42];
(b) Booklet "Seats for Workers in Factories, Offices and Shops (HSW.45); and
(c) British Standard 3893 (1965).

The Recorder refused to admit all three under the rules of evidence. He stated that as far as he was concerned the only person able to give evidence on correct seating would be an orthopoedic expert and unless such a person was in court so that he could be cross-examined as an

---

[40a] *Ibid.* at 121.
[41] "The Inspector," Vol. 25, No. 3, May-June 1979.
[42] [1977] I.R.L.R. 120.

expert witness then the prosecution would have failed to prove what was suitable seating as required by the Act. Evidence was produced by the appellant that the notice had been complied with by the expiry date and also it was claimed that because only four hours a day were spent at the till it was not work of a kind that a substantial part had to be done sitting. The appeal was allowed and the sentence quashed.

It is interesting to note that the industrial tribunal in the *Tesco* Case accepted written evidence not on oath from a doctor whereas the Crown Court in this case would only accept the expert testimony in the witness box of an orthopaedist.

The evidence adduced by the prosecution must be capable of weathering an appeal to the Crown Court. Therefore, the opinion of an expert in this field must be sought if a prosecution is contemplated.

There is also the problem of admission as evidence codes of practice and guidance notes not approved by the Health and Safety Commission. Unless the authors of the codes of practice etc., can be produced and placed in the witness box to be subject to cross-examination these codes are strictly hearsay evidence. That does not mean to say that an expert witness cannot give his opinion on experiments not carried out by himself. In *R. v. Somers*,[43] a medical practitioner was allowed to give evidence on the rate at which blood destroys alcohol even though he himself had not carried out the experiments. It follows, therefore, that the orthopaedist, or other experts, may testify and refer to the Health and Safety booklet No. 45 and the British Standard 3893 (1965) and any other relevant guidance notes.

Industrial tribunals are not governed strictly by the rules of evidence and the booklet and British Standard would probably be accepted as evidence. It seems also that magistrates and higher courts can, and often do, accept guidance notes and other publications as definitive of good practice, particularly if referred to by a witness giving expert testimony.

Eating facilities (section 15)

6.15   Where shop assistants have meals on the premises, suitable and sufficient facilities for eating them must be provided. The expression used in the section is, "persons employed to work in shop premises" and would cover an employee such as a van driver who delivers goods from the shop.

It is only compulsory to provide these facilities in a shop and then only if the persons employed there do in fact eat their meals on the premises. There is no necessity to provide a canteen although the facilities to be provided will of course depend largely on the size of the establishment. Normally, chairs and tables with equipment for making a hot drink and screened from the public part of the shop will be sufficient.

---

[43] [1963] 1 W.L.R. 1306. See also p. 89.

EXEMPTIONS

In order for local authorities to have some flexibility in their approach to   **6.16**
the 1963 Act, section 46 empowers them to grant certificates of exemptions from all or any of the requirements of:

(a) section 5(2) (room space for employees);
(b) section 6 (temperature);
(c) section 9 (provision of sanitary conveniences); and
(d) section 10(1) (hot and cold, or warm, water supplied for washing facilities must be running water);

if the local authority is satisfied that compliance is "not reasonably practicable."

An exemption from (a), (b) and (c) above may be granted only for a
period of two years but an exemption from (d) may be granted either
without a time limit or for a specified period. The two year period may
be reviewed for a further period or periods not exceeding two years if
the enforcing authority are satisfied that the applicant has not failed to
do anything that would make compliance reasonably practicable. If the
local authority is no longer satisfied that compliance is not reasonably
practicable the exemption may be withdrawn on three months notice.
There is a right of appeal to the magistrates' court against refusal to
grant or to extend an exemption or against a decision to withdraw an
exemption within 21 days of refusal or service of notice to withdraw an
exemption.

Under section 45, the Minister may make an order exempting classes
of premises from any or all of the above requirements. Many orders
have been made and revoked, and the only order of interest to local
authorities that is in force is the Offices, Shops and Railways Premises
Act 1963 (Exemption No. 7) Order 1968.[44] This Order, which continues
without limit of time, exempts certain small buildings, for example,
kiosks used for retail sales and situated in certain public open spaces or
on or near beaches from section 9, *i.e.* the provision of a sanitary convenience as long as other sanitary conveniences are available.

The person responsible for making application for an exemption certificate is the person who is responsible for complying with the various
requirements of the 1963 Act. They are as follows:

(a) section 5(2): room space for employees—the occupier;
(b) section 6: temperature—the occupier;
(c) section 9: sanitary conveniences—the occupier, if he occupies
the whole of the building covered by the Act; and
(d) section 10(1): washing facilities—the owner,[45] where the prem-

---

[44] S.I. 1968 No. 1947.
[45] For definition of "owner" see s.90(1). Also see *Kensington Borough Council* v. *Allen*
[1926] 1 K.B. 576; *Nalder* v. *Ilford Corporation* [1951] 1 K.B. 822; *London Corporation*
v. *Cusack-Smith* [1955] A.C. 337.

ises form part of a building in single ownership and are held under a lease, agreement for a lease, or a licence[46] and where the premises form part of a building of which different parts are owned by different persons.[47] For these purposes "building" would normally be regarded as that area surrounded by party walls with no doors (other than fire exit doors) through which there is internal communication with neighbouring buildings.

The procedure for making an application for an exemption certificate is contained in section 46 of the 1963 Act.

OFFENCES AND PENALTIES

6.17 Under section 63, the occupier of the premises is liable if the requirements of the 1963 Act are not met unless responsibility is expressly placed instead of, or in addition, on some other person. The expression "occupier" is not defined in the Act, nor is it defined in the Factories Act 1961, but in *Ramsay* v. *Mackie*,[48] in which contravention of the Factories Act was considered, it was said that the "occupier" is the person who runs the factory, who regulates and controls the work that is done there. Under normal circumstances he would be the employer.

The situation where an owner would be liable is described in paragraphs 6.10 and 6.11, *i.e.* the provision of Sanitary Conveniences and Washing Facilities where section 42 and 43 of the Act would apply.

Penalties for offences are contained in section 33(3) of the Health and Safety at Work etc. Act 1974.

DEFENCES AVAILABLE TO PERSONS CHARGED WITH OFFENCES

6.18 A defence is available to an occupier or owner, as the case may be, where, for example, the fault lies solely with an employee. Section 67 provides that it shall be a defence for a person charged with a contravention of a provision of the 1963 Act, or regulations thereunder, to prove that he used all due diligence to secure compliance with that provision. However, even if the employer has a defence under this section this will not shield him from civil proceedings brought by a plaintiff who has suffered damage from breach of statutory duty by one of his employees, but where the employee himself is injured by his own act or omission in breach of the statutory duty he cannot plead that his injury was caused by the breach of the statutory duty and not caused by his own act or omission.[49]

---

[46] Offices, Shops and Railway Premises Act 1963, s.42.
[47] *Ibid.* s.43.
[48] (1904) 7 F. (Ct. of Sess.) 106.
[49] *Gallagher* v. *Dorman, Long & Co.* [1947] 2 All E.R. 38, C.A.

CHAPTER 7

HOURS OF EMPLOYMENT OF SHOP ASSISTANTS

The hours that shop assistants[1] are allowed to work are governed by the **7.01** following restrictions under the Shops Act 1950, *i.e.* weekly half-holi-day, meal intervals, Sunday work and employment in premises where refreshments are sold. There are also special restrictions which apply to young persons. A "young person" does not include a child, whose employment is regulated by section 18 of the Children and Young Persons Act 1933, but save as aforesaid means a person who has not attained the age of 18 years.[2]

The hours of closing of a shop is a different consideration and is dealt with in Chapter 4.

WEEKLY HALF-HOLIDAY

Section 17 of the Shops Act 1950 provides that on at least one week day **7.02** in each week a shop assistant shall not be employed about the business of a shop after 1.30 p.m. However, in the week preceeding a bank holi-day, as long as the shop assistant has a half day holiday in the following week in addition to the bank holiday, the provision does not apply.

Being "employed about the business of a shop" does not only apply to serving behind the counter. In *George* v. *James*,[3] handbills were distri-buted by shop assistants in their spare time, which was their statutory half-day holiday. The handbills advertised the shop's margarine but without giving the address of the shop. The court held that the shop assistants were employed about the business of the shop by distributing the leaflets. Also, where a person owns more than one shop he may be guilty of an offence under this section if he allows an assistant from one shop to work in another on his half day holiday.[4]

The occupier of a shop must display a notice, in a prescribed form,

---

[1] "Shop assistant" means any person wholly or mainly employed in a shop in connection with the serving of customers or the receipt of orders or the despatch of goods (Shops Act 1950, s.74) In order to come within this definition a person must be employed in connection with the serving of customers. It has been held that there is no necessity for him to come in direct contact with the customers but there must be a direct connection with the serving of customers not a remote or indirect one, *e.g.* a kitchen maid in a kitchen to a restaurant was said to be employed in connection with the serving of cus-tomers (*Melluish* v. *London County Council* [1914] 3 K.B. 325). Also, a person employed for the collecting of empty glasses, sweeping up, cleaning knives and pewter in a public house was held to be employed in connection with the serving of customers (*Prance* v. *London County Council* [1915] 1 K.B. 688).
[2] Shops Act 1950, s.74(1).
[3] [1914] 1 K.B. 278.
[4] *London County Council* v. *Wettman* [1922] 1 K.B. 153.

indicating the day of the week which each assistant is entitled to take as a half-day holiday. Different days may be fixed for different assistants.

Any offence under this section may attract a penalty not exceeding level 1 on the standard scale,[5] but an occupier of a shop charged with an offence of allowing a shop assistant to work after 1.30 p.m. in contravention of the section may have a defence if he can prove:

(a) that the shop assistant was still serving the customer who he was serving at 1.30 p.m.; or

(b) where the time for closing the shop on that day was 1.30 p.m.;

(c) the shop assistant was in the shop merely for serving customers who were in the shop at 1.30 p.m.

Young persons

7.03　　　The effect of section 17 of the Shops Act on young persons is modified by section 18 of the Act. With regard to weekly half holidays a young person is regarded as a "shop assistant" if he is wholly or mainly employed about the business of a shop or in connection with any retail trade or business carried on in any place not being a shop. It does not apply, however, to any person employed in a residential hotel. A young person employed as a shop assistant is not entitled to the weekly half day holiday if:

(a) he works 25 hours or less in that week; or

(b) he is employed in a theatre and he does not commence his job before midday on any day in that week. This applies even though he may be employed as a shop assistant for more than 25 hours in that week.[6]

Where a young person is employed in connection with any retail trade or business in a place not being a shop, the provision regarding the fixing of a prescribed notice does not apply because this stipulation in section 17 specifically applies to a shop. A young person is regarded as employed even though he may not receive any reward for his labour.[7]

A warehouse comes under the definition of shop if retail trade is being carried on.[8] However, in the case of a wholesale shop or warehouse of this type the young person must be employed within the premises or collects or delivers goods, runs errands, carries messages or attends upon customers to be deemed to be employed about a business of a shop. If he does any work which is ancillary to the business carried on in the shop, whether inside or outside the shop, he shall be deemed to be employed about the business of a shop.[9]

---

[5] Criminal Justice Act 1982, ss.35, 46.
[6] Shops Act 1950, s.18(2).
[7] *Ibid.* s.18(6).
[8] A warehouse cannot be classified as a "shop" if it is only used to store goods (*Eldorado Ice Cream Co.* v. *Clarke*; *Eldorado Ice Cream Co.* v. *Keating* [1938] 1 K.B. 715.
[9] Shops Act 1950, s.18(8).

In the situation where proceedings are brought against a person and the young person in question was not employed by that person in that week in contravention of the Act, it is a defence to prove that he did not know, and could not with reasonable diligence have ascertained, that the young person was also employed in that week as a shop assistant by some other employer.[10]

MEAL INTERVALS

Shop assistants must be allowed intervals for the consumption of meals   **7.04** in accordance with Schedule 3 to the Shops Act 1950. Where, however, the only shop assistants employed are members of the family of the occupier of the shop, live with him and are maintained by him then these provisions do not apply.[11]

Schedule 3 states that intervals for meals shall be arranged so as to secure that no person shall be employed for more than six hours without an interval of at least 20 minutes being allowed for meals. There is a proviso that:

(1) where the hours of employment include the hours from 11.30 a.m. to 2.30 p.m. an interval of not less than 45 minutes shall be allowed between those hours for dinner; and

(2) where the hours of employment include the hours from 4 p.m. to 7 p.m. an interval of not less than half an hour shall be allowed between those hours for tea;

and the interval for dinner shall be increased to one hour in cases where that meal is not taken in the shop, or in a building of which the shop forms part or to which the shop is attached.

Therefore, for instance, if a shop assistant is working in a large department store where there is a restaurant and she/he uses that restaurant for her meals she is legally entitled to only 45 minutes break.

An assistant employed in the sale of refreshments or in the sale of intoxicating liquor need not be allowed the interval for dinner between 11.30 a.m. and 2.30 p.m. if he is allowed the same interval so arranged as either to end not earlier than 11.30 a.m. or to commence not later than 2.30 p.m., and the same exemption shall apply to assistants employed in any shop on the market day in any town in which a market is held not more often than once a week, or on a day on which an annual fair is held.

Therefore, an assistant working in a public house or a restaurant cannot demand his meal breaks between 11.30 a.m. and 2.30 p.m. but he must be allowed the break before or after those times. Also in these type of premises the occupier may elect that the provisions of section 21

[10] *Ibid.* s.18(3).
[11] *Ibid.* s.19(1).

of the Shops Act 1950 will apply instead.[12] If that is so these restrictions will not apply to any shop assistant employed wholly or mainly in connection with the sale of intoxicating liquors or refreshments for consumption on the premises.

In the case of a contravention the occupier of a shop is liable to a fine not exceeding level 1 on the standard scale.[13]

Young persons

7.05   Section 20 of the Shops Act 1950 extends the benefits of section 19 above as to meal times for shop assistants to certain young persons who would not otherwise come within the scope of the section. These young persons are those wholly or mainly employed about the business of a shop[14] or in connection with any retail trade or business carried on in any place not being a shop. Again the provisions do not apply to an assistant employed wholly or mainly in connection with the sale of intoxicating liquors or refreshments for consumption on the premises *if the occupier of those premises elects that section 21 of the Shops Act 1950 applies*. In addition, they do not apply to a person whose hours of employment are regulated under the Factories Act 1961 and to persons employed in a residential hotel who do not come within the general definition of a shop assistant under section 74 of the 1950 Act.[15]

Part II of Schedule 3 modifies the application of the Schedule to young persons in that instead of "6 hours" there is substituted "5 hours or, on the day of the week on which he is not to be employed after 1.30 p.m., $5\frac{1}{2}$ hours."

A young person is regarded as being employed under this section even though he receives no reward for his labours, and if he is employed in connection with a wholesale shop or warehouse occupied by a wholesale dealer or merchant he must either work within the premises or be employed in carrying messages, running errends, attending upon customers, or delivering or collecting goods to be deemed to be employed about the business of a shop. Also, if he does any work which is ancillary to the business carried on in the shop, whether inside or outside the shop, he shall be deemed to be employed about the business of a shop.[16]

HOURS OF EMPLOYMENT IN PREMISES FOR THE SALE OF REFRESHMENTS

7.06   An occupier of a shop may elect that the terms of section 21 of the Shops Act 1950 apply to shop assistants who are employed wholly or mainly in connection with the sale of intoxicating liquor or refreshments for con-

---

[12] See p. 133. A notice in the prescribed form must be fixed and constantly maintained in a conspicuous position.

[13] Criminal Justice Act 1982, ss.35, 46.

[14] This includes any wholesale shop and warehouse occupied for the purposes of his trade by any person carrying on any retail trade or business or by any wholesale dealer or merchant. (Shops Act 1950, s.20(7)).

[15] See p. 129.

[16] Shops Act 1950, s.20(9).

sumption on the premises. If he does this, the requirements contained in sections 17 to 20[17] referring to half-holidays and meal-times will not apply to those shop assistants. In selecting this course of action he must elect to adopt the extended definitions of "shop assistant" as respects sections 17 to 20 and he cannot afterwards be heard to say that any person so employed in connection with the business (for example, a waiter) is not a shop assistant.[18]

The occupier must fix and constantly maintain in a conspicuous position a notice in the prescribed form[19] referring to the provisions of section 21 and the steps taken to ensure their compliance. The provisions are:

(a) that no assistant to whom this section applies shall be employed for more than 65 hours in any week, exclusive of meal times;

(b) that provision shall be made for securing to every assistant to whom section 21 applies:

    (i) 32 whole holidays on a week day in every year of which at least two shall be given within the currency of each month and which shall comprise a holiday on full pay of not less than six consecutive days so, however, that two half holidays on a week day shall be deemed equivalent to one whole holiday on a week day;

    (ii) 26 whole holidays on Sunday in every year, so distributed that at least one out of every three consecutive Sundays shall be a whole holiday;

(c) that unless the only persons employed as shop assistants are members of the family of the occupier of the premises maintained by him and dwelling in his house:

    (i) intervals for meals shall be allowed to every assistant to whom this Section applies amounting on a half holiday to not less than 45 minutes, and on every other day to not less than two hours;

    (ii) no assistant shall be employed for more than six hours without being allowed an interval of at least 30 minutes.

A half-holiday under this section means a day on which the employment of an assistant ceases not later than 3 p.m. and on which he is not employed for more than six hours including meal times.

An occupier may withdraw a notice after the expiration of 12 months from the date on which it was given and thereafter at the expiration of any succeeding year. The effect of such withdrawal is that sections 17 to 20 will apply to the shop as they applied before the notice was given

---

[17] See paras. 7–01 to 7–05 inclusive.

[18] *Rutherford* v. *Trust Houses* [1926] 1 K.B. 321.

[19] For the prescribed form of notice, see the Shops Regulations 1913 (S.R. & O. 1913 No. 250).

(section 21(7)). Any contravention of section 21 makes the occupier liable to a fine of up to level 1 on the standard scale.[20]

SUNDAY EMPLOYMENT

7.07   Section 22 of the Shops Act 1950 requires that a compensatory holiday is given to shop assistants who have to work on a Sunday "about the business of a shop[21] which is open for the serving of customers on that day." The holiday is in addition to his statutory half-holiday under section 17 and he must receive it either in the week beginning with the Sunday on which he worked or in the previous week. Shop assistants are only entitled to compensatory holidays if the premises are open for the serving of customers. If the shop is closed and the assistants are employed on other work such as, for example, stock taking or filling the shelves with goods, the section does not apply.

The amount of holiday due depends on the number of hours worked on a Sunday, *i.e.* if he is employed for more than four hours he is entitled to a whole day and less than four hours a half-day. A half-day is within the period not worked either before or after 1.30 p.m. However, nobody may be employed for more than four hours on more than three Sundays in the same calendar month, but where a person is employed on a Sunday for less than four hours he may be employed every Sunday. A person is regarded as being employed even though he may not receive any reward for his labour and a record must be kept in the prescribed form and in the prescribed manner of the names of the shop assistants who have worked on Sundays and their holiday entitlement.

There are exceptions to the requirement of compensatory holidays. These are:

(a) persons employed wholly or mainly in connection with the sale of intoxicating liquor;

(b) shop assistants employed in premises for the sale of refreshments where the occupier has elected that section 21 applies;

(c) any persons employed wholly or mainly as a milk roundsman;

(d) any person wholly employed in the transaction of post office business; and

(e) registered pharmacists (with certain exceptions).

The section does not apply to the carrying on on Sunday of the business of a retail dealer in butcher's meat but the section does extend to any place where any retail trade or business is carried on as if that place were a shop and to the persons who are wholly or mainly employed in connection with the retail trade or business carried on in that place.[22]

An occupier found guilty of an offence under this section is liable to a

---

[20] Criminal Justice Act 1982, ss.35, 46.
[21] See p. 129.
[22] Shops Act 1950, s.23.

fine up to level 2 on the standard scale for the first and any subsequent offences.[23] An offence for unlawful trading on a Sunday will be treated as an offence under this section. Section 22 does not extend to Scotland.

OTHER SPECIAL PROVISIONS RELATING TO YOUNG PERSONS

Young persons employed partly in a factory and partly in a shop

Under section 28 of the Shops Act 1950 no young person who, to the knowledge of the occupier of the shop, works on the same day partly in a factory[24] and partly in a shop, must be allowed to work so that the combined hours exceed the daily maximum permitted by section 86 of the Factories Act 1961.   **7.08**

"Shop" under this section includes any wholesale shop and any warehouse occupied for the purposes of his trade by any person carrying on any retail trade or business or by any wholesale dealer or merchant. Also, under section 33 of the Act, section 28 is extended to the employment of young persons in connection with any retail trade or business carried on in any place not being a shop.

Any contravention of this provision makes the occupier of the shop or any other place where retail trade or business is carried on, liable to a fine not exceeding level 1 on the standard scale[25] for every person in respect of whom the contravention occurs.

Night employment

Young persons who are employed about the business of a shop or any other retail trade or business[26] in the evening, must be allowed an interval of 11 consecutive hours off work within the 24 hour period from midday on one day to mid-day on the next day. This period must include the hours from 10 p.m. to 6 a.m. An exception to this are *male* persons between the ages of 16 and 18 years who collect or deliver milk, bread or newspapers. In their case the 11 consecutive hours need not include the hour between 5 a.m. and 6 a.m.[27]   **7.09**

Where *male* persons between the ages of 16 and 18 years are employed wholly or mainly in connection with the business of serving meals to customers for consumption on the premises, the 11 hours mentioned need not include any time between 10 p.m. and midnight. Therefore, as an example, no young person may work after 10 p.m. in a takeaway shop and no young female person may work after 10 p.m. in a place where food is consumed on or off the premises.

In 1983, McDonalds, the company specialising in the sale of hamburgers, were found guilty of employing four teenagers after hours and for failing to keep proper time records. The prosecuting solicitor, for

---

[23] Criminal Justice Act 1982, ss.35, 46.
[24] For definition of "factory" see Factories Act 1961, s.175.
[25] Criminal Justice Act 1982, s.46.
[26] Extended by the Shops Act 1950, s.33.
[27] Shops Act 1950, s.31(1).

Luton Council, stated that girls had worked as late as 4 a.m.—six hours longer than permitted under section 31 of the Shops Acts 1950, and boys had been employed until 2 a.m.—two hours longer than the permitted hours.[28]

Young persons between the ages of 16 and 18 who are wholly or mainly employed in connection with any retail sale or business in a theatre[29] also come within an exemption. Where the performance starts before and ends after 10 p.m. the interval of 11 consecutive hours need not include any time between 10 p.m. and the time at which the performance ends. Contravention of the section renders the offender liable to a fine up to level 1 on the standard scale for every person in respect of whom the contravention occurs.[30]

General restriction on hours of work

7.10   Section 24 of the Shops Act 1950 provides that no young person between[31] the ages of 16 and 18 years shall work about the business of a shop[32] more than the normal maximum working hours which is 48 hours in any week. Where, however, pressure of work is such that he must work overtime, for example during the Christmas period, he may be allowed to work overtime as long as no young persons in the shop have been employed on overtime for more than six weeks in a year[33] and that overtime must not exceed:

(a) 12 working hours in a week; and
(b) 50 working hours in a year.

Section 33 of the 1950 Act extends the application of this section to the employment of young persons between the ages of 16 and 18 years in connection with any retail trade or business carried on in any place not being a shop.

Contravention of this section makes the occupier, in the case of a shop, or the person carrying on any retail trade or business, as the case may be, liable to a fine not exceeding level 1 on the standard scale[34] for every person in respect of whom the contravention occurs.

[28] See "The Inspector," Vol. 29 No. 2, March–April 1983.
[29] "Theatre" includes any place for the exhibition of pictures or other optical effects by means of a cinematograph or other suitable apparatus and any music hall or other similar place of entertainment (Shops Act 1950, s.74(1)).
[30] Criminal Justice Act 1982, s.46.
[31] A person shall be deemed to be between any two ages mentioned if he has attained the first-mentioned age but has not attained the second-mentioned age (Shops Act 1950, s.74(2)). A person attains a specified age at the beginning of the day previous to the corresponding anniversary of his birthday. *Re Shurey, Savory*, v. *Shurey* [1918] 1 Ch. 263.
[32] "Shop" includes any wholesale shop and any warehouse occupied for the purpose of his trade by any person carrying on any retail trade or business or by any wholesale dealer or merchant. (Shops Act 1950, s.24(4)).
[33] "Year" means the period between midnight on the last Saturday night in the month of December and midnight on the last Saturday night in the next month of December (Shops Act 1950, s.24(4)).
[34] Criminal Justice Act 1982, s.46.

Restriction on hours of work in the catering trade

The particular requirements of the catering trade are taken into **7.11** account in section 25 of the Shops Act 1950. The occupier of a shop where meals, intoxicating liquors or refreshments are served to customers for consumption on the premises may, by exhibiting a notice[35] to that effect, secure the application of the provision of the section to the shop. It will apply to young persons between the ages of 16 and 18 years who are wholly or mainly connected with the afore-mentioned business.

Although the maximum permitted hours under section 24(1) will still apply, *i.e.* 48 hours per week, the occupier shall have the advantage of meeting the requirements of special periods of pressure without the young person having to work overtime. He may average the hours worked over any period of two consecutive weeks on not more than 12 occasions in any calendar year. However,

(a) the hours worked in either week must not exceed 60;
(b) the total hours worked in the two consecutive weeks must not be more than 96; and
(c) no overtime can be worked above this fortnightly total.

The overtime that can be worked in any week in the year when the above system is not in operation and the occupier has not made an election under section 25(2) is not more than:

(a) eight working hours overtime in any period of two consecutive weeks; and
(b) fifty working hours overtime in any year.

Where another business is carried on in the shop in addition to the catering business the weeks worked in overtime by young persons wholly or mainly employed in the catering side of the business are not considered when calculating for the purpose of the six weeks limitation under section 24(2)(*a*) with regard to the non-catering part of the shop.

If the occupier elects, by giving notice,[36] that section 25(2) does not apply to the shop he will have the benefit of extra overtime. Section 24(2) will apply without modification, *i.e.* no overtime employment may be worked in any shop for more than six weeks (whether consecutive or not) in a year and that overtime must not exceed:

(a) twelve working hours in a week; and
(b) fifty working hours in a year.

---

[35] Notice to be in the form prescribed by the Shops Regulations 1939 (S.R. & O. 1939 No. 1841). It must be kept exhibited in such a manner that it may be readily seen and read by any person whom it affects and must be renewed whenever it becomes defaced or otherwise ceases to be clearly legible.

[36] This is done by sending the notice, in prescribed form, to the local authority not later than seven days before the commencement of any year, and takes effect on the first day of that year. A copy of the notice must be exhibited in the shop for at least seven clear days immediately preceeding that date, (Shops Regulations 1939) (S.R. & O. 1939 No. 1841).

This provision will not apply, however, to any fortnightly period where the averaging system is in operation as described above.

The notice may be withdrawn by sending a notice of withdrawal to a local authority and exhibiting a copy in the shop.[37]

Restriction on hours of work selling accessories for motor vehicles

7.12   Section 26 of the Shops Act 1950 takes into account the requirements of persons selling car accessories. The section includes the business of selling accessories to aircraft and cycles but for ease of explanation and because the sale of motor car parts is more relevant these days only this business is mentioned. However, whatever is applicable to selling accessories for motor vehicles is applicable to selling accessories to aircraft and cycles.

The purpose of the section is not to provide for the situation that occurs when there is seasonal pressure of work as with the catering trade. It is intended that the occupier of a shop selling motor accessories for immediate use (if he gives notice that subsection (1) of the section applies to his shop[38]) to adopt the "averaging system" of long and short weeks as a long standing arrangement.

The section applies to young persons between the ages 16 and 18 years employed in connection with a shop where the principal business is that of selling motor car spares for immediate use. If this is not the principal business of the shop then the section applies only to those young persons who are wholly or mainly employed in connection with selling parts of motor cars.

Instead of the normal maximum of 48 hours in any week, the hours of employment of the young persons may be averaged over periods of three consecutive weeks, but not more than 54 hours may be worked in any week (including overtime) nor more than 144 hours in any period of three consecutive weeks (excluding overtime).

Overtime may be worked in any week of the year, but where the occupier elects that subsection (2) of section 26 of the 1950 Act shall *not* apply to the shop, the employment overtime is as laid down in section 24(2) of the 1950 Act.[39] However, if subsection (1) applies to the shop, *i.e.* the "averaging system," in addition to the restriction laid down in section 24(2), no overtime must be worked by a young person in any week in which he has been employed about the business of the shop for 54 hours.

If the occupier has *not* elected or taken any steps under subsection (2) of section 26, *i.e.* he has not given notice that the section does not apply to the shop, the restriction on overtime laid down in section 24(2) is

---

[37] Shops Regulations 1939.

[38] The notice is to be, in prescribed form, sent to the local authority and a copy exhibited in the shop. Notice of withdrawal cannot be given within six months of the giving of the notice, (Shops Regulations 1939).

[39] See p. 137.

modified. Overtime can be worked in any week of the year but it must not exceed 12 working hours in any consecutive period of three weeks and 50 working hours in a year.

Persons under 16—general restriction on hours of work

Persons under 16 years of age are, under section 27 of the Shops Act **7.13** 1950, only allowed to be employed about the business of a shop or retail trade or business[40] up to the maximum of 44 hours in one week.

The occupier of a shop[41] may, as long as he follows the procedure laid down in the section, average out the hours worked over the Christmas period so that this maximum is extended. The period it applies to is two consecutive weeks where Christmas Day falls in either week. During these two weeks the maximum hours that can be worked by the person under 16 is 48 in either week and not more than 88 hours in total for the fortnight.

In order to take advantage of this averaging of hours over the Christmas period the occupier must exhibit a prescribed notice[42] in the shop. *No person under 16 years is allowed to work overtime.*

The occupier of the shop or the person who is carrying on a retail trade or business as the case may be will be liable to a fine not exceeding level 1 on the standard scale[43] if found guilty of contravening the provision of the section.

Other employment to be taken into account when computing hours of employment

Section 29 provides that when computing the number of hours that a **7.14** young person has been employed about the business of a shop,[44] the time spent in working in other specified employment[45] is also taken into

---

[40] Extended by the Shops Act 1950, s.33.

[41] In this section, "shop" includes any wholesale shop and any warehouse occupied for the purposes of his trade by any person carrying on any retail trade or business or by any wholesale dealer or merchant. (Shops Act 1950, s.27(5)).

[42] The notice shall be exhibited not later than noon on the Saturday preceding the date on which the period specified in the notice is to commence, and shall continue to be exhibited until the end of that period. (Shops Regulations 1939 (S.R. and O. 1939 No. 1841, reg. 1(2)).)

[43] Criminal Justice Act 1982, s.46.

[44] For the purpose of this section, "shop" includes any wholesale shop and any warehouse occupied for the purposes of his trade by any peron carrying on any retail trade or business or by any wholesale dealer or merchant. (Shops Act 1950, s.29(3)).

[45] The specified employment is as follows:
  (a) about the business of any other shop;
  (b) in a factory;
  (c) in the collection or delivery of goods, or in carrying, loading or unloading of goods incidental to the collection or delivery thereof;
  (d) in connection with a business carried on at any premises in carrying messages or running errands, being employment wholly or mainly outside the premises;
  (e) at a residential hotel or club in carrying messages or running errands, or in connection with the reception of guests or members thereat;
  (f) in connection with the business carried on at any premises where a newspaper is published, in carrying messages or running errands;

account. In proceedings taken against the occupier for allowing a young person to work above the limit imposed by the 1950 Act, the occupier has a defence if he can prove that he did not know, or could not with reasonable diligence have ascertained, that the young person was employed by another person in the work specified.[46]

Records to be kept

7.15   Records[47] of hours worked and intervals allowed for rest and meals must be kept and retained for a certain period by occupiers of shops in respect of every young person who is employed about the business of a shop and overtime must be separately entered on the record.[48] The occupier may, instead of keeping such records, exhibit a notice in the prescribed manner[49] in the shop specifying the above information. If he does this then the only other record he needs to keep is of those hours worked by young persons employed about the business of a shop in excess of those specified on the notice. These hours will be regarded as overtime unless they are in lieu of the hours not worked as specified in the notice.[50] The records for any particular year must be kept for at least six months from the end of that year.[51]

Also, where young persons are employed about the business of a shop the occupier must exhibit a notice indicating the number of hours in a week that young persons are allowed, under the Shops Act 1950, to work about the business of a shop. Although the requirements regarding the keeping of records is extended by section 33 of the Shops Act 1950 to any place in which retail trade or business is carried on, the provision regarding the afore-mentioned notice, indicating the number of hours in a week that a young person is allowed to work, does not apply to premises other than shops.[52]

Any occupier of a shop or person carrying on a retail trade or business who is found guilty of a contravention of the foregoing requirements may be liable to a fine not exceeding level 1 on the standard scale. If, with intent to deceive he makes, or causes or allows to be made, a false

    (g) at a place of public entertainment or amusement, or at a pubic swimming-bath, bathing place or turkish baths, for carrying messages or running errands, or in the reception of or attendance upon persons resorting thereto;

    (h) elsewhere than in a private dwelling-house, in the operation of a hoist or lift connected with mechanical power;

    (i) in or in connection with the operation of cinematograph apparatus;

    (j) at any premises occupied for the purposes of a laundry, dyeing or cleaning works or other factory, in receiving or despatching goods.

Also included are certain processes and docker's work carried on in any docks, etc.

[46] Shops Act 1950, s.29(2).

[47] Shops Regulations 1939, Form E.

[48] Shops Act 1950, s.32(1).

[49] The notice shall be exhibited not later than noon on the Saturday preceding the first week in which it is to take effect, and shall continue to be exhibited while it is in force. (Shops Regulations 1939 (S.R. and O. 1939 No. 1841), reg. 5(2)). See previous pages.

[50] Shops Act 1950, s.32(2).

[51] Shops Regulations 1939, reg. 5(5).

[52] Shops Act 1950, s.32(4).

entry in a record which he knows to be false or omits to make an entry on a record or notice which he is required to make, he shall be liable to imprisonment for a term not exceeding three months or to a fine not exceeding level 2 on the standard scale.[53]

Cases where foregoing provisions do not apply

Section 34 of the 1950 Act stipulates that all the foregoing provisions, **7.16** *i.e.* sections 24 to 33 of the 1950 Act, do not apply to the employment of young persons in:

(a) residential hotels where the young person is *not* a shop assistant,[54] or where that person is employed in premises to which the provisions of section 21 of the 1950 Act apply and is not wholly or mainly employed in connection with the business of selling intoxicating liquors or refreshments for consumption on the premises;

(b) in theatres (including cinemas) unless employed wholly or mainly in connection with retail trade or business in the theatre. The selling of programmes is not retail trade or business for the purposes of the 1950 Act; and[55]

(c) factories where the hours of employment are regulated by the Factories Act 1961, except sections 28 and 29, in so far as they relate to employment in a factory.

---

[53] *Ibid.* s.32(6). The maximum fines are increased by virtue of Criminal Justice Act 1982, s.46.
[54] As defined in the Shops Act 1950, s.74(1).
[55] *Ibid.*

CHAPTER 8

PREPARATION, STORAGE AND SALE OF FOOD

INTRODUCTION

8.01 This chapter outlines the legal obligations on retailers selling, preparing and storing food. It does not cover the statute law governing such areas as composition and labelling but concentrates on the sale of food which is either unfit to eat or is adulterated in some way. Also included are the requirements as to hygienic practices and premises for the preparation and storing of food. The law relating to licensing and registration of premises selling, storing or manufacturing certain susceptible foods such as milk, ice-cream,[1] etc., should also be considered.

The relevant statute law is the Food Act 1984 and the Food Hygiene (General) Regulations 1970[2] made under the Food and Drugs Act 1955, the predecessor to the 1984 Act but note should be made of the intention of the government to introduce a Bill as soon as possible to amend the food law as mentioned in the introduction to the book.

It is interesting to note at this stage the comments made in the House of Lords in *Smedleys* v. *Breed*[3] by Viscount Dilhorne with which Lord Kilbrandon and Lord Cross of Chelsea agreed. He stated:

> " . . . In deciding whether or not to prosecute are they (the food and drugs authority) not to have regard to the general interests of consumers? I do not find anything in the Act[4] imposing on them the duty to prosecute automatically whenever an offence is known or suspected and I cannot believe that they should not consider whether the general interests of consumers were likely to be affected when deciding whether or not to institute proceedings . . . "

All authorities should, therefore, before taking a prosecution under the Food Act 1984, consider the seriousness of the offence and whether the interests of the consumer are best served by entering the matter into court.

The common law has always recognised that the sale of unwholesome and unfit food constitutes an offence. For example, in *Shillito* v. *Thompson*,[5] an inspector of nuisances was walking down a street in Doncaster on market day when he was attracted by an offensive smell which he found was caused by cheese in the appellant's passage, which he alleged to be in a putrid state and in his opinion unfit for human consumption.

---

[1] See Chaps. 2 and 3.
[2] S.I. 1970 No. 1172.
[3] [1974] A.C. 839.
[4] Food and Drugs Act 1955.
[5] (1875) 1 Q.B.D. 12.

The cheese, which weighed 10 stone, was exposed for sale and the inspector seized it. The sale of this food contravened a by-law made for the suppression or prevention of nuisances but it was contended by the defence that the by-law was *ultra vires* because the sale of unfit food was not a nuisance. The court held that the sale of unfit food was a nuisance at common law.

In *R. v. Kempson*,[6] it was held that if a person sells food knowing it to be unfit for human consumption or being grossly negligent in the way his trade allowed it to be sold he may be indicted for manslaughter if any person eats that food and thereby dies.

The meaning of food

"Food" is defined in the dictionary as any substance which, taken into **8.02** the body, is capable of sustaining or nourishing, or which assists in sustaining or nourishing the living being. Under section 131 of the Food Act 1984, which is the interpretation section of the Act, food includes drink, chewing gum and other products of a like nature and use, and articles and substances used as ingredients in the preparation of food and drink or of such products, but does not include:

  (a) water, live animals or birds;
  (b) fodder or feeding stuffs for animals, birds or fish; or
  (c) articles or substances used only as drugs.

Certain substances are included and others excluded. Such substances that are not mentioned should be decided on their merits taking into account the dictionary definition. From the fact that preparation is defined in section 131 of the 1984 Act as including manufacture and any form of treatment, it is clear that not only specific things consumed alone by human beings to maintain life and growth come under the definition, but also ingredients or potential ingredients such as flavourings, flour and condiments.

There is also a similar definition, which excludes milk, contained in the Food Hygiene (General) Regulations 1970.[7] This is because there are special Regulations applicable to the hygiene of premises where milk is stored or processed.[8]

The question whether or not the expression "sells . . . any food" in sections 2(1) and 8(1)(*a*) of the Food and Drugs Act 1955 (now the Food Act 1984) could apply to the supply of something which was purporting to be food, but which in reality was something completely different, was considered in *Meah* v. *Roberts*; *Lansley* v. *Roberts*.[9] A family visited a restaurant and the husband ordered a meal and drinks including lemonade for his children. The waiter brought him caustic soda (which had

[6] (1893) 28 L.J.O. 477.
[7] S.I. 1970 No. 1172.
[8] Milk and Dairies (General) Regulations 1959 (S.I. 1959 No. 277). (See Chap. 2).
[9] [1977] 1 W.L.R. 1187.

been stored in a lemonade bottle) by mistake. Subsequent analysis of the contents of the lemonade bottle revealed that it was a 20 per cent. caustic soda solution, stronger than that needed to remove paint from woodwork. The children consumed part of their drinks and were rushed to hospital. One child became very ill.

Although the caustic soda supplied to the customer on his request for lemonade was not in itself "food" within the definition contained in the 1955 Act where food is defined as "includes drink," etc., it was held that a purported sale of lemonade is sufficient to constitute a sale of "food" although something quite different was in fact supplied entirely unknown to both waiter and customer.

The court referred to a case decided in 1885, *Knight* v. *Bowers*,[10] which involved the sale of a drug and concerned section 6 of the 1875 Act which became section 2 of the 1955 Act. The purchaser wished to buy saffron (a drug used for the treatment of measles at that time) but was supplied with savin, a drug improperly used for procuring an abortion. In the course of his judgment Mathew J. said:

> "Here saffron was demanded and the respondent supplied savin, a wholly different article. I think that the legislature intended to protect purchasers from impositions of this kind."

The taking of samples

8.03   Although under section 79 of the 1984 Act any person who has purchased any food, or any substance capable of being used in the preparation of food, may submit a sample of it to be analysed by the public analyst, the vast majority of samples are submitted by "authorised officers" who are called "sampling officers" in the Act. These are officers, normally environmental health officers, who have the duty to protect public health and are authorised in accordance with section 73 of the 1984 Act. He has to be an officer of a council, authorised by them in writing, either generally or specially, to act in matters of any specified kind or on any specified matter. A police constable by virtue of his office and with the approval of the police authority concerned is an authorised officer with regard to the taking of samples.

A sampling officer has two choices.[11] He may *purchase* or *take* a sample of any food or of any substance capable of being used in the preparation of food.[12] However, he may only *take* a sample if either:

(a) the food appears to him to be intended for sale, or to have been sold, for human consumption; or

(b) is found by him on or in any premises, stall, vehicle, ship, air-

---

[10] (1885) 14 Q.B.D. 845.

[11] Food Act 1984, s.78.

[12] "Preparation" in relation to food, includes manufacture and any form of treatment (Food Act 1984, s.132(1)).

craft or place which he is authorised to enter to enforce the provisions of the 1984 Act.

He may also act by an agent. For example, in *Garforth* v. *Esam*,[13] an inspector sent his servant into an inn to purchase some gin and some minutes later the inspector entered. It was held that the inspector had made the purchase through his agent. An agent may also be used for taking a sample[14] and delivering it to the public analyst.[15]

When purchasing a sample the sampling officer is not under a duty to show his written authority but, if requested to do so where, for example, the retailer did not know the officer, he must produce it, otherwise the retailer cannot be prosecuted for refusing to sell the food.[16]

The sampling officer may *take* a sample of milk while at any dairy, or while deposited for collection, or at any time before it is delivered to a consumer in pursuance of a sale by retail, and he may take a sample of any food, etc., in the course of delivery or at the place of delivery if requested to do so by the purchaser, otherwise if it appears to him to be sold by retail he cannot take a sample unless it is within the purchaser's consent either during or after delivery.[17]

If any food or substance is exposed for sale and a sampling officer offers to purchase a quantity sufficient for a sample and the retailer refuses to sell he will be regarded as wilfully obstructing the officer. A person will also be considered as wilfully obstructing the officer if he is a consignor or seller of any article or substance and refuses to allow the officer to *take* a sample, assuming that the officer is acting within his authority under the 1984 Act.[18] The master is liable for the refusal of his servant under this section.[19]

Milk in an open container on a counter in a restaurant or cafe which is used solely for addition to tea or coffee is regarded for this purpose as being exposed for sale.[20] Likewise are loaves of bread sent out in a vehicle for delivery or sale to customers.[21] Sausages made to order and in a shop are not, however, exposed for sale.[22]

The rules governing the taking of samples are contained in Part I of Schedule 7 to the 1984 Act. A sampling officer or any other person who purchases or takes a sample of any food or substance for analysis by the public analyst must divide the sample into three parts. Each part must

---

[13] (1892) 56 J.P. 521.
[14] *Tyler* v. *Dairy Supply Co.* (1908) 98 L.T. 867.
[15] *Horder* v. *Scott* (1880) 5 Q.B.D. 552.
[16] Kennedy J. in *Payne* v. *Hack* (1893) 58 J.P. 165.
[17] Food Act 1984, s.78. S.78(2) states that a sampling officer may purchase samples of any food or of any substance capable of being used in the preparation of food, so he may purchase or take the sample with the consent of original purchaser.
[18] *Ibid.* s.91(2).
[19] *Farley* v. *Higginbotham* (1898) 42 S.J. 309.
[20] *McNair* v. *Terroni* [1915] 1 K.B. 526.
[21] *Keating* v. *Horwood* (1926) 135 L.T. 29.
[22] *Clark* v. *Strachan* (1940) S.C.(J) 29.

be marked and sealed or fastened up in such manner as its nature will permit.

The parts need not be mathematically equal or identical but must be of sufficient quantity that a proper analysis can be made.[23] They must be sealed or fastened in a suitable receptacle and the lid or cover should not be capable of being removed and replaced without the breaking of a seal.[24] Where, however, the food or substance is in an unopened container and it is either not reasonably practical to make a division, or division may affect the composition or impede proper analysis, the statutory requirements will be fulfilled if the containers are divided into three lots.[25]

If the sample has been purchased, one part is given to the vendor; but if it purchased from a vending machine the part is given to the owner if his name and address is displayed on the machine. If not, it is given to the owner of the premises on which the machine stands or to which it is affixed. Where the sample is taken rather than purchased the person who that part is delivered to depends on the circumstances of the taking of the sample.[26]

If the sampling officer is of the opinion that the food or substance was manufactured or placed in the container or wrapped by any person other than the person from whom he procured the sample and that person's name and address in the United Kingdom is displayed on the container or wrapper, he must inform that person (unless he decides not to have the analysis made) within three days of processing the sample:

(a) that the sample had been processed; and
(b) where the sample was taken or, as the case may be, from whom it was purchased.[27]

The person to whom part of the sample has been delivered is entitled to receive a copy of the analyst's certificate from the local authority on the payment of a fee of five pence.[28]

Analysis of samples

8.04   The sampling officer must send the sample to the public analyst for the area where it was taken or purchased if he considers that it should be analysed. Any other person, not being a sampling officer may also submit a sample for analysis but the public analyst in this case may demand his fee in advance. The sample must be analysed as soon as practicable and a certificate in a prescribed form showing the result of the analysis and signed by the public analyst must be given to the person submitting

---

[23] *Lowery* v. *Hallard* [1906] 1 K.B. 527.
[24] *Suckling* v. *Parker* [1906] 1 K.B. 527.
[25] Food Act 1984, s.84.
[26] *Ibid.* Sched. 7, Pt. 1.
[27] *Ibid.* s.80(3).
[28] *Ibid.* s.80(4).

the sample. Although the public analyst must sign the form personally the analysis may be made by any person working under his direction.[29]

The analyst must be careful in that he should keep to the prescribed form and not be too vague when expressing the result. For example, in *Newby* v. *Sims*,[30] the certificate stated:

> "I find the sample contains an excess of water over and above what is allowed by Act of Parliament; I estimate the excess of water at 13 per cent. of the entire sample; I am of the opinion that the said sample is not a sample of genuine rum."

This was held to be bad for vagueness as the total amount of water found in the sample ought to have been stated. The certificate must contain all the necessary information in such precise detail that the magistrates may form a conclusion as to whether or not the food was adulterated.

Prosecutions in respect of samples taken

Section 95(2) of the Food Act 1984 states that where a sample has   **8.05** been procured under the Act no prosecution shall begin after the expiration of 28 days in the case of a sample of milk and two months in any other case. There is an exception under subsection (3) in that where a justice of the peace, before whom the information is laid, certifies that he is satisfied on oath that having regard to the circumstances of the particular case it was not practicable to lay the information at an earlier date the time-limit will not apply; but in the case of a sample of milk the proceedings cannot be commenced after 42 days have expired.

The case must be taken before the court having jurisdiction in the area where the sample was procured (with certain exceptions[31]) and the summons shall not be made returnable less than 14 days from the day on which it is served. A copy of the analyst's certificate must be served with the summons, together with a certificate of the justice if the information is laid out of time.[32]

In *Manson* v. *Louis C. Edwards and Sons (Manufacturing)*,[33] a housewife bought from a retail shop one-and-a-quarter ounce jar of beef spread which had been manufactured by the defendants. When she opened the jar she was not satisfied with the appearance of its contents. She took it to the local environmental health officer who in turn took it to the public analyst. The environmental health officer obtained a report from the analyst and, being satisfied that the retailer could establish a defence under section 113(1) of the Food and Drugs Act 1955,[34–35] preferred an information against the defendants charging them with an

[29] *Ibid.* s.79.
[30] [1894] 1 Q.B. 478.
[31] Food Act 1984, s.95(4).
[32] *Ibid.* s.95(5).
[33] (1976) 84 L.G.R. 545.
[34–35] Now the Food Act 1984, s.100.

offence contrary to section 2 of the 1984 Act of supplying an article of food which was not of the substance demanded by the purchaser in that iron compounds and mineral oil were present in the food. No certificate of analysis was sent to the defendants with the summons.

The issue which the court had to decide on an appeal by way of case stated was whether or not the jar of beef spread was regarded as a sample taken by a sampling officer under the Food and Drugs Act 1955. If it was then the proceedings failed *in limine* because the procedure laid down in section 108(3) of the Act[36] would not have been complied with.

It was held that the size of an article did not determine whether or not it was a sample. It was a sample where it had been picked indiscriminately from a group of similar products with a view to making a random test, and that since the jar of beef spread had been bought for consumption and not picked out for testing purposes it was not a sample. Lord Widgery C.J. stated:

" . . . in section 92[37] one has authority for submission for analysis either at the suit of the sampling officer or at the suit of an ordinary individual such as Mrs. Thornton in the present case . . . It will be remembered that in the present case the sampling officer did not go into the shop and pick the article for himself. Mrs. Thornton bought it in the ordinary way without making a specific selection of the particular pot and handed it over to the sampling officer when she had discovered that it was not to her liking."

Environmental health officers often take "informal" samples of food and submit them for analysis. If only one sample is taken then the procedures as laid down in Part I of Schedule 7 to the 1984 Act are not followed. The purpose of the 'informal" sampling is to cover as much ground as possible in checking the quality of food with the limited staff resources available. No prosecutions can be taken on the strength of the results of these samples but they will indicate where problems exist. If unsatisfactory results are obtained from certain foods the proper sampling procedures will have to be adopted in order to carry out a successful prosecution.

Power of food and drugs authority and local authority to prosecute

8.06　　There are certain powers of prosecution vested in the Minister of Agriculture, Fisheries and Food and the Secretary of State.[38] The other two public bodies responsible for enforcement of the provisions contained in the Food Act 1984 are the food and drugs authorities and local authorities.

Food and drugs authorities are defined under section 71 of the 1984 Act as:

---

[36] *Ibid.* s.95(5).
[37] Now the Food Act 1984, s.79(2).
[38] See the Food Act 1984, ss.74, 96 and Sched. 6, para. 1 and Sched. 8.

(a) in England, for each county and London borough, the council of that county or borough, and for the City of London and the Inner Temple and the Middle Temple, the Common Council of the City of London; and

(b) in Wales, the county council;

and local authorities are defined (except for sections 44 and 45) under section 72 of the 1984 Act:

(a) as respects the City of London, the Common Council;

(b) as respects the Inner Temple and the Middle Temple, the sub-treasurer and the under treasurer respectively; and

(c) as respects any district or London borough, the council of the district or borough.

Every local authority has a duty to enforce in their district those provisions of the Act which have not been specifically or by implication allocated to another authority.[39] Those duties specifically allocated to a food and drugs authority are contained in paragraph 2 of Schedule 6 to the 1984 Act. They are:

(a) sections 1, 2 and 6;

(b) section 36, and Regulations having effect as if made under section 33 of the Food and Drugs Act 1955;

(c) section 39(1) and (2) (except as regards any use of a special designation in relation to raw milk, and as regards the making of any reference to raw milk by such a description as is mentioned in subsection (2), by the producer of the milk); and

(d) sections 40, 41 and 48.

A local authority cannot institute any proceedings for offences if the food and drugs authority is responsible for its enforcement or vice versa: but where an offence is committed under section 2 of the 1984 Act and it relates to food which is alleged to contain some extraneous matter a local authority may institute proceedings.[40] A local authority may also act on an agency basis for a food and drugs authority and many agency agreements are in existence.

A private person who has purchased food and is aggrieved may take proceedings against any person who has allegedly committed an offence[41] as can a sampling officer as a private person without having the authority of his local authority.[42]

---

[39] *Ibid.* s.74.
[40] *Ibid.* s.96(2).
[41] *Snodgrass* v. *Topping* (1952) 116 J.P. 332; *Buckler* v. *Wilson* [1896] 1 Q.B. 83.
[42] *Snodgrass* v. *Topping*, above; *Giebler* v. *Manning* [1906] 1 K.B. 709; *Connor* v. *Butlin* (1902) 2 I.R. 569.

Evidence and presumptions

8.07   The production of a document purporting to be an analyst's certificate or a document supplied by the opposing party as being a copy of such a certificate is sufficient evidence of the fact stated in the document unless in the first-mentioned case the other party requires that the analyst be called as a witness.[43] The magistrates are obliged to act on the certificate and convict if no evidence is tendered by the defence.[44] However, the defendant may call evidence to contradict the certificate.[45] Where the analyst is called to give evidence, the certificate then ceases to be regarded as evidence and the court must consider whether the analyst's oral evidence is sufficient in itself to prove the offence.[46]

Should a defendant decide to produce an analyst's certificate in evidence or call the analyst as a witness he must give three clear days' notice before the summons is returnable to the prosecutor. He must include a copy of the certificate with the notice if he intends to enter the certificate as evidence. If these procedures are not followed the court may adjourn the hearing on such terms as it thinks fit.[47]

If a sample of milk has been taken by a sampling officer of one authority at the request of an officer of another authority, a document which purports to be a certificate signed by the officer who took the sample and which states that the statutory requirements regarding the taking of the sample were complied with is sufficient evidence of that fact, unless the defendant requires the sampling officer to attend the hearing as a witness.[48]

Three rebuttable presumptions are contained in section 98 of the 1984 Act. Any article commonly used for human consumption shall, if sold or offered, exposed or kept for sale, be presumed, until the contrary is proved, to have been sold or, as the case may be, to have been or be intended for sale for human consumption. Likewise, any article commonly used for human consumption which is found on premises used for the preparation, storage or sale of that article and any article commonly used in the manufacture of products for human consumption which is found on premises used for the preparation, storage or sale of those products, shall be presumed, until the contrary is proved, to be intended for sale, or for manufacturing products for sale, for human consumption. Lastly, any substance capable of being used in the composition or preparation of any article commonly used for human consumption which is

---

[43] Food Act 1984, s.97(1).

[44] *Harrison* v. *Richards* (1881) 45 J.P. 552; *Elder* v. *Dryden* (1908) 72 J.P. 355; *Robinson* v. *Newman* (1917) 88 L.J.K.B. 814 J.P. 187; *Kings* v. *Merris* [1920] 3 K.B. 566.

[45] *Preston* v. *Fennell* [1951] 1 K.B. 16.

[46] *Stone and Sons (Hounslow)* v. *Pugh* [1949] 1 K.B. 240.

[47] Food Act 1984, s.97(3).

[48] *Ibid.* s.97(2). The same notice of intention to call the sampling officer must be given to the prosecutor as in the case of the analyst, and the court has the same power of adjournment if the procedures are not followed.

found on premises on which that article is prepared shall, until the contrary is proved, be presumed to be intended for such use.

The second presumption above was considered in *Hooper* v. *Petrou*,[49] in relation to a prosecution under section 8 of the Food and Drugs Act 1955.[50] A public health inspector, on a routine inspection of a restaurant, found a wire tray containing dried fruit puddings, which appeared to be contaminated by mice, in a part of the store-room not used for day-to-day storage. He removed the contents from the tray for further inspection and the owner was subsequently charged with an offence under section 8(1) of the Food and Drugs Act 1955, for having in his possession for the purposes of preparation for sale the puddings which were unfit for human consumption.

The charge was laid on the footing that the possession was for the purposes of preparation of sale because the puddings required to be cooked before they would be consumed. At magistrates' court level the justices had accepted the explanation of the defendant and considered that section 111 of the 1955 Act (the presumption section) was irrelevant to the operation of section 8 of the 1955 Act and dismissed the information.

The defendant's explanation was that the puddings were not immediately required, that they were put in a suitable place for long-term storage and that the intention was that before they were brought down and cooked for the consumption of the patrons of the restaurant, they would be inspected, and if on inspection a pudding or puddings was found to be contaminated, it would be rejected. The argument of the defence counsel was that his client did not at the relevant time have possession of these puddings for the purpose of preparation for sale, because, in so far as the puddings proved to be contaminated, they would never have been so prepared, but thrown away.

On appeal by way of case stated, the court held that section 111 of the Act of 1955 was relevant and section 8 had to be read in the light of the presumption contained in section 111 and unless the presumption was rebutted, the person charged with the offence under section 8 in circumstances such as the present, was presumed to intend to sell the articles in question for human consumption. Since the defendant was undoubtedly in possession of the contaminated puddings they must have been in his possession for the purpose of preparation for sale, and so the appeal was allowed.

SALE OF FOOD NOT OF THE NATURE, QUALITY OR SUBSTANCE DEMANDED
BY THE PURCHASER

Section 2 of the Food Act 1984 contains the offence of selling to the **8.08** prejudice of the purchaser food which is not of the nature, of the quality, or of the substance demanded by him. This is an offence of strict

[49] (1973) 71 L.G.R. 347.
[50] Now the Food and Drugs Act 1955, s.8.

liability as no *mens rea* is required to be proved in order to establish the offence.[51] It is an offence which is described by Wright J. in *Sherras* v. *De Rutzen*[52] as " . . . not criminal in any real sense, but are acts which in the public interest are prohibited under a penalty . . . " The prosecutor has only to prove that the purchaser has not received the food which he asked for and was entitled to receive. For example, a purchaser of "rum and butter toffee" is entitled to expect that all the fat in the confection will be butter fat.[53] Subsection (2) of the section states that the sale refers to sale for human consumption and that it is no defence to say that the purchaser was not prejudiced because he brought the food for analysis or examination.

Where food is supplied under a contract for sale and delivery which allows the purchaser to reject the food, the supply is a "sale" under section 2 since section 131(2)(*a*) provides that the supply of food in the course of business otherwise than by sale is deemed to be a sale. Accordingly, in *Fleming* v. *Edwards*,[54] a supplier of food that had been rejected under such a contract was liable to be prosecuted on the ground that he had sold, to the prejudice of the purchaser, food which was not of the quality demanded.

The owner of a shop is liable for the actions of his employee under section 2 if he has given authority to sell even though he may have expressly forbidden him to adulterate the food.[55] If, however, the employee acts completely outside the scope of his authority the employer will not be liable, for example, where he sells food which is not for sale.[56] In the first instance the employee as well as the employer may be prosecuted.

Where something which is sold is completely different to that which the purchaser requested and the purchaser is prejudiced, an offence is committed under this section. An example is the caustic soda sold for lemonade in *Meah* v. *Roberts*; *Lansley* v. *Roberts*.[57]

Prejudice of purchaser

8.09   A purchaser is normally prejudiced if he is sold unwholesome food or if the food causes him harm or he suffers a pecuniary disadvantage. It could be considered that a person with an expert knowledge of food who purchases food which is not of the nature, quality or substance demanded is not prejudiced. However, this is not the case; the test is

---

[51] *Betts* v. *Armstead* (1888) 20 Q.B.D. 771; *Pearks, Gunston and Tee* v. *Ward*; *Hennen* v. *Southern Counties Dairies Co.* [1902] 2 K.B. 1.

[52] [1895] 1 Q.B. 918 at 922; [1895–99] All E.R. 1167 at 1169.

[53] *Riley Brothers (Halifax)* v. *Hallimond* (1927) 44 T.L.R. 238.

[54] (1986) 150 J.P. 539.

[55] *Houghton* v. *Mundy* (1910) 103 L.T. 60; *Andrews* v. *Luckins* (1917) 117 L.T. 726.

[56] *Whittaker* v. *Forshaw* [1919] 2 K.B. 419; *Lindsay* v. *Dempster* (1912) S.C.(J) 110.

[57] [1977] 1 W.L.R. 1187 (see p. 000).

whether the sale would have been to the prejudice of a purchaser without that special knowledge.[58]

If the purchaser is sold food which is superior to that which he asked for then he is not prejudiced. Again there is no prejudice where he has noticed that the article is mixed with an ingredient, though he is not told the exact nature or effect of that ingredient and chooses to buy the article so mixed.[59]

Nature, quality or substance

There are three distinct offences. The food is either not of the nature, **8.10** not of the quality or not of the substance demanded and an information laid which charges all three would be bad for uncertainty.[60] Where there is uncertainty about which of the three categories should be used more than one information should be laid.[61]

If there is no recognised standard for a food it is a question of fact in each case whether it is not of the nature, quality or substance. In *Barber* v. *Co-operative Wholesale Society*,[62] milk was sold to a school where the schoolmaster noticed that an unopened bottle contained a green plastic straw. He contacted the Environmental Health Department and a prosecution was brought against the sellers charging them that they sold to the prejudice of the purchaser milk not of the quality demanded by the purchaser. The defendants argued that the fact that there was a foreign body in the milk did not mean that it necessarily moved from being of the quality demanded by the purchaser; that in the absence of contrary evidence there must be a presumption that the contents of the bottle were sterile; and that there was no evidence to show that the existence of the straw affected the "quality" of the milk.

The court did not accept this submission and held that in such a case as this, although it is true that the question was essentially one of fact for the justices to decide, where the case was concerned with the presence of extraneous matter, it was not necessary for the prosecution to prove that the extraneous matter was deleterious. It was sufficient if it was proved that the presence of the extraneous matter would give rise to the consequence, that a purchaser could, in the context of the particular transaction, reasonably object to the presence of the matter.

The case of *Southworth* v. *Whitewell Dairies*[63] decided that a sliver of glass sharp enough to penetrate the skin found in a bottle of milk affected its substance to the prejudice of the purchaser. The defendants had sold milk to an infants' school and one of the infants drinking the milk by straw sucked up the sliver of glass with the milk. The justices dis-

---

[58] *Pearks, Gunston and Tee* v. *Ward*; *Hennen* v. *Southern Counties Dairies Co.* [1902] 2 K.B. 1.
[59] *Williams* v. *Friend* [1912] 2 K.B. 471.
[60] *Bastin* v. *Davies* [1950] 2 K.B. 579.
[61] *Moore* v. *Ray* [1951] 1 K.B. 58.
[62] [1983] Crim.L.R. 476.
[63] (1958) 122 J.P. 322.

missed the information relying on *Edwards* v. *Llaethdy Mirion*,[64] where it was held that a clean and sterilised cap found in a bottle of milk did not affect its substance.

The court on appeal held that whereas the clean and sterilised cap of a bottle would not contaminate the milk in any way a sliver of glass sharp enough to penetrate the skin was in a different position and a potential source of danger and the case must be remitted to the justices with a direction that the offence was proved. It was pointed out in the *Edwards* v. *Llaethdy Mirion* judgment that whenever there is a milk bottle with the top on it the milk is always touching the top, just as in a bottle of wine the wine is always touching the cork.

Statutory defences

8.11   In addition to the defences of "passing over" under section 100 and warranty under section 102 there are three defences specifically applicable to this offence which are set out in section 3.

Subsection (2) of section 3 of the 1984 Act states that in respect of any food containing extraneous matter, it is a defence to prove that the presence of that matter was an unavoidable consequence of the process of collection or preparation. This defence was considered in *Smedleys* v. *Breed*,[65] where the defendants who manufactured tins of peas had installed a satisfactory system of manufacturing and spot checking the peas which they canned. In the 1971 canning season the defendants produced some $3\frac{1}{2}$ million tins of peas and only four complaints were received concerning the presence of extraneous matter in the tins. One complaint was that of a can of peas containing a caterpillar which was of a similar density, diameter and weight of the peas which allowed it to pass the mechanical screening process and of similar colour thereby causing it to be not noticed by the visual inspectors.

The point of law which had to be decided by the House of Lords was whether a defence was established, under section 3(3) of the Food and Drugs Act 1955,[66] if a defendant proves that he took all reasonable care to avoid the presence of extraneous matter in the food he manufactures. The defence is made out if the extraneous matter present in the food is as a result of an unavoidable consequence of the process of *collection* or *preparation*. However, the caterpillar was present in this case, despite the processes rather than because of them. In rejecting the arguments of the defence in this case, Lord Dilhorne stated:

> " . . . the unavoidable consequence of a process is, in my opinion, something that is bound to result from that process. It is something that cannot be prevented. That it should be there as a result of the process is inevitable . . . In the process of canning the peas we

[64] [1957] Crim.L.R. 402.
[65] [1974] A.C. 839.
[66] Now the Food Act 1984, s.3(2).

were told that hot brine was added so brine was in every tin of peas. The presence of the brine was the inevitable and unavoidable consequence of the appellant's process, so if they were prosecuted under section 2(1) of the 1955[67] Act for selling to the prejudice of the purchaser peas not of the nature or substance or quality demanded on account of the presence of the brine section 3(3) would provide them with a good defence. On this view of the meaning of section 3(3) the question whether the appellants had or had not taken reasonable care to exclude the caterpillar is irrelevant . . . "

It was held, therefore, that in order to establish a defence under section 3(3) it was necessary to show that the presence of the extraneous matter was a consequence of the process of collection or preparation of the food and that that consequence could not have been avoided by any human agency; it was not sufficient for the defendant to show that he had taken all reasonable care to avoid the presence of the extraneous matter.

This case was followed in *Greater Manchester Council* v. *Lockwood Foods*,[68] where a purchaser of a can of strawberries which contained a black-beetle complained to the food and drugs authority. The manufacturers successfully established the defence at magistrates' court level that the presence of the beetle was an unavoidable consequence of the process of collection or preparation. The authority appealed and it was held on appeal that the questions for consideration were whether the presence of the beetle had been a consequence of the process of preparation and collection and if so, whether it had been unavoidable. The presence of the beetle could not, in its ordinary meaning, be said to be a consequence of that process and the appeal was allowed.

The other two specific defences are contained in subsections (1) and (3) of section 3 of the 1984 Act.

Subsection (1) provides that in proceedings under section 2 for an offence consisting of the sale of food:

(a) to which any substance has been added; or
(b) in the preparation of which any substance has been used as an ingredient; or
(c) from which any constituent has been abstracted; or
(d) which has been subjected to any other process or treatment;

other than food thereby rendered injurious to health, it is a defence to prove that:

(1) the operation in question was not carried out fraudulently; and
(2) the article was sold with a notice attached to it of adequate size, distinctly and legibly printed and conspicuously visible,

---

[67] *Ibid.* s.2(1).
[68] [1979] Crim.L.R. 593.

stating explicitly the nature of the operation, or was sold in a wrapper or container displaying such a notice.

Subsection (3) states that in proceedings under section 2 in respect of diluted whisky, brandy, rum, or gin, it is a defence to prove that:

(a) the spirit in question had been diluted with water only; and
(b) its alcoholic strength by volume was still not lower than 37.2 per cent.

SALE, ETC. OF FOOD UNFIT FOR HUMAN CONSUMPTION

8.12   Any person who: (a) sells, offers or exposes for sale, or has in his possession for the purpose of sale or of preparation of sale; or (b) deposits with, or consigns to, any person for the purpose of sale or of preparation for sale any food intended for, but unfit for human consumption is guilty of an offence.[69] The person who sold the food to the offender under the first offence (a) may also be guilty of an offence.[70] *Mens rea* is not an element of the offence and, therefore, it is not essential to prove that the offender knew that the food was unfit or that he knew that the food was in his possession.[71]

Possession must be read in connection with the purposes of sale or preparation of sale and should be given a wide and not a narrow construction,[72] and section 8 has also to be read in the light of the presumption laid down in section 98 of the 1984 Act.[73]

Unfitness of food

8.13   It is important to distinguish between food which has become unfit for human consumption because it has become contaminated by the presence of an extraneous substance, and food which because of the extraneous substance has rendered it not of the nature, quality or substance demanded by the purchaser. Certain defences become available depending on which section the prosecutor decides is applicable in the circumstances.

In *Miller (J.)* v. *Battersea Borough Council,*[74] a customer purchased from the defendants four cream buns, one of which was eaten by her young son who found a small piece of metal in his mouth. An information was laid under a section of the 1938 Food and Drugs Act, which is now section 8 of the Food Act 1984. The defendants claimed that the bun, apart from the presence of the extraneous piece of metal, was sound and that the section used by the council was directed to the sale of

---

[69] Food Act 1984, s.8(1).
[70] *Ibid.* s.8(2).
[71] *Blaker* v. *Tillstone* [1894] 1 Q.B. 345; *Firth* v. *McPhail* [1905] 2 K.B. 300; *Hobbs* v. *Winchester Corpn.* [1910] 2 K.B. 471.
[72] *Webb* v. *Baker* [1916] 2 K.B. 753 at 759, *per* Lord Reading C.J.
[73] See p. 150 and *Hooper* v. *Petrou* (1973) 71 L.G.R. 347.
[74] [1956] 1 Q.B. 43.

food which was putrid and unwholesome. Lord Goddard C.J. stated in his judgment:

" . . . How can it be said that food becomes unsound, that is to say, putrid or dangerous, merely because there is a piece of extraneous matter in it which has no effect on the general composition of the food? Two illustrations have been given in the present case which seem to me to make the point perfectly clear, indeed unanswerable. A person who buys game finds some metal pellets in it. The fact that game has shot in it does not make it unfit for human consumption, although everyone who has eaten game knows that it is sometimes quite painful if one bites on the shot. That is probably not to the prejudice of the purchaser because one expects to find shot; but I point to that example in order to show that it is absurd to say that some lead shot in a bird, or hare makes the article of food unfit for human consumption. It is not unfit for human consumption. So also is the illustration which Ormerod J. put in the course of the argument. Everyone knows that when children are about at Christmas time threepenny pieces are put into plum puddings. That does not make the plum pudding unfit for human consumption because one says 'Look out, do not swallow the threepenny pieces.' The threepenny pieces are not fit for human consumption, but the pudding is . . . "

This reasoning was followed in *Turner & Son* v. *Owen*,[75] where a piece of string was found in a loaf of bread. The string had probably attached a label to the sack of flour from which the loaf of bread was made and had somehow dropped into the flour during the bread-making process. However, it was held that a seller was correctly charged with selling to the prejudice of the purchaser under section 2 of the Food and Drugs Act 1955[76] a bottle of milk not of the quality demanded by him when a fly was discovered in the unopened bottle.[77]

If there is a likelihood of the extraneous matter contaminating the food purchased then section 8 of the 1984 Act is the correct section under which the information should be laid. For example, in *Chibnall's Bakeries* v. *Cope Brown*[78] part of a dirty used bandage in a load of bread was held to render the bread unfit for human consumption, as was the remains of a mouse found in a bottle of milk in *Barton* v. *Unigate Dairies*.[79]

The sale of a pork pie with mould under the crust was considered in *Greig (David)* v. *Goldfinch*.[80] When the customer purchased the pie it

[75] [1956] 1 Q.B. 48.
[76] Now the Food Act 1984, s.2.
[77] *Newton* v. *West Vale Creamery Co.* (1956) 120 J.P. 318.
[78] [1956] Crim.L.R. 263.
[79] (1987) 151 J.P. 113.
[80] (1961) 105 S.J. 367.

was not contradicted at the trial that the pie contained a small patch of mould. It was purchased at 9.30 a.m. on Saturday and taken home and cut by the customer at 5.30 p.m. She noticed small patches of mould of the penicillin type (which of itself is not harmful to human beings) underneath the top crust, but did not take it to the public health inspector until the Monday by which time the mould had grown to an area about the size of a 10 pence piece. In the meantime she had stored it in a ventilated cupboard.

The defendants were charged with selling to the customer a pork pie intended for, but unfit for human consumption and the justices found the charge proved. The defendants appealed to the High Court which dismissed the appeal. They held that although the words "unfit for human consumption" in section 8 meant something more than that the food was unsuitable for human consumption, it was not necessary for the prosecution to prove in every prosecution under the section that it would be injurious to health or dangerous to eat the food, but that the words must be looked at in a broad sense and an article of food which was going mouldy was prima facie unfit for human consumption; and that, since it was a matter of degree and the justices had found that the pie was unfit for human consumption, the court could not say that they were wrong.

Statutory defences

8.14   Again, as with section 2 of the 1984 Act, the defences under sections 100 (default of another) and 102 (warranty) apply but additional specific defences are contained in section 8. With regard to the first offence in the section, *i.e.* section 8(1)(*a*), the person who sold the food to the offender is also guilty of the offence but both this person and the offender in the second offence, *i.e.* section 8(1)(*b*) have a defence if they can prove either that they gave notice to the person with whom they deposited or consigned the food that it was not intended for human consumption or that the food was fit for human consumption when delivered or dispatched or did not know, and could not with reasonable diligence have ascertained, that it was unfit for human consumption.[81]

Reasonable diligence is a question of fact in each case and in *Jordan* v. *White*[82] a person who consigned a bovine head and tongue affected with tuberculosis from an abattoir was held not to have made out a defence under this subsection after relying on an inspection of the meat by a sanitary inspector. He did not inspect the animal himself, but assuming that he was not a qualified inspector it is difficult to imagine any other reasonable course of action that he could have taken.

The onus of proof is on the defendant to establish on the balance of

---

[81] Food Act 1984, s.8(2), (3).
[82] (1945) 109 J.P. 229.

probabilities that he could not have ascertained that the food was unfit for human consumption by the exercise of reasonable diligence.[83]

Inspection and seizure of suspected food

An authorised officer of a council[84] may at all reasonable times exam- **8.15**
ine any food intended for human consumption which has been sold, or is offered or exposed for sale, or is in the possession of or has been deposited with or consigned to any person for the purpose of sale or of preparation for sale.[85]

There must be an intention to sell the food. If a person has in his possession food which although unfit to eat is for use by his family or friends he cannot be guilty of an offence.[86]

The food may be examined at all reasonable times which would appear to be the normal opening hours of a shop and working hours of a factory.

If the food appears to him to be unfit for human consumption then he may seize it and remove it in order to have it dealt with by a justice of the peace. He must inform the person who has possession of the food of his intentions, his liability to prosecution under section 8 of the 1984 Act and his right to be heard and call witnesses.[87]

The justice of the peace must condemn the food and order it to be destroyed if it appears to him to be unfit for human consumption but if he is not satisfied as to its unfitness and refuses to condemn it the council who employed the authorised officer must pay the owner of the food compensation.[88]

The question of whether or not the food is unfit for human consumption is independent of the condemnation by the justice of the peace and if a prosecution is brought later under section 8 of the 1984 Act, the defendant is entitled to bring forward evidence to prove that the food was not unfit. In *Wayne* v. *Thompson*,[89] meat was seized and condemned by the justices on the evidence of a sanitary inspector. Proceedings were then taken for selling unfit meat and the butcher submitted the evidence of a veterinary surgeon who testified to the effect that the sanitary inspector was mistaken. It was held on appeal that the butcher could adduce evidence as to the fitness of the meat in these proceedings as the question whether the food is unfit is a separate issue from the action taken under the section in dealing with seizure and condemnation by a justice of the peace.

There is also power under section 11 of the Food Act 1984 for an

[83] *Wilson (John) & Co. (Foods) of York* v. *Thomas* (1961) 59 L.G.R. 264.
[84] See p. 144.
[85] Food Act 1984, s.9(1)(*a*).
[86] *Rendell* v. *Hemingway* (1898) 14 T.L.R. 456.
[87] Food Act 1984, s.9(1)(*b*), (2).
[88] *Ibid.* s.9(3), (4).
[89] (1885) 15 Q.B.D. 342.

authorised officer in certain circumstances to examine, detain and seize food in transit.

Food offered as prizes or rewards

8.16   All the provisions relating to the examination, seizure and condemnation of unfit food and the offences concerning the sale of unfit food apply where food intended for human consumption is offered as prizes or rewards in connection with any entertainment to which the public are admitted whether on payment of money or not. Likewise, if the food which is intended for human consumption is offered as a prize or reward or given away for the purpose of advertisement, or in furtherance of any trade or business.

The aforementioned provisions also apply in either case if the food is deposited or exposed in any premises for the purpose of being so offered or given away. In such cases the position is as if the food were, or had been, exposed for sale by each person concerned in the organisation of the entertainment, or by the person offering or giving away the food or by the occupier of the premises respectively.[90]

CONTRAVENTION DUE TO ANOTHER'S DEFAULT

8.17   Any person against whom proceedings are brought under the Food Act 1984 is entitled under section 100 of the Act to have any other person who he alleges is responsible for the contravention in question brought before the court in the proceedings. He must lay information to this effect and give the prosecutor not less than three clear days' notice of his intention.

If the original defendant proves at the hearing after the contravention has been proved that the other person's act or default caused the contravention, the other person may be convicted of the offence and the original defendant shall be acquitted if he proves to the court that he used all due diligence to prevent the contravention.

Although in previous legislation which embodied these provisions the intention was to protect a master who had given direct instructions which are disobeyed, any person may now be brought before the court. However, proceedings against a third party for an offence against Regulations made under the Food and Drugs Act 1955 or the 1984 Act cannot be brought where the Regulations do not expressly incorporate the section.[91] The Food Hygiene (General) Regulations 1970 incorporates the section under regulation 29(4).

There is nothing to prevent both defendants being convicted. In order for the original defendant to escape conviction he must adduce evidence that he used all due diligence to comply with the relevant provision of

---

[90] Food Act 1984, s.10.
[91] *United Dairies (London)* v. *Beckenham Corporation*; *United Dairies (London)* v. *Fisher (E) & Sons* [1963] 1 Q.B. 434.

the Act. There is no legal standard of "due diligence"; it is a question of fact in each case.[92] If the original defendant proves due diligence and that the contravention was caused by the act or default of a third party and the third party cannot be convicted for some reason the original defendant is still entitled to be acquitted.[93]

The prosecuting authority, as well as the third party defending himself, in these proceedings has the right to cross-examine the original defendant and any witnesses called by him in support of his pleas. They may also call rebutting evidence.[94]

Where the authority is reasonably satisfied that a defence could be established under this section they may institute proceedings against the third party without first taking proceedings against the original person.[95] But where two summonses are issued they can validly exist contemporaneously and the justices have jurisdiction to hear the summons against those defendants whom the prosecuting authority believe to be guilty of the offence, provided that the first summons is dismissed before the hearing of that summons.

In *Macpherson Train & Co.* v. *Christchurch Borough Council,*[96] retailers International Stores Ltd. sold a can of grapefruit segments intended for human consumption but which it was alleged were unfit for human consumption. The local authority laid information under section 8 of the Food and Drugs Act 1955[97] and a summons was issued against International Stores Ltd. The company drew the authority's attention to certain considerations and the authority became reasonably satisfied that International Stores Ltd. could make out a defence under section 113(1)[98] and consequently preferred a second information and a second summons was issued against Macpherson Train and Co., the wholesalers to the retailers. Both summonses were listed for hearing on the same day and the local authority first asked the justices to dismiss the summons against International Stores Ltd. and to do so before proceeding with the summons against the wholesalers. This the justices did.

The wholesalers maintained that as the two summonses existed contemporaneously the justices had no jurisdiction to continue to hear and determine the second summons and relied on *Fisher* v. *Santovin,*[99] where there were three merchants in the chain. In this case summonses were issued against all three and although the local authority was reasonably convinced that the first and second merchants would be able to make out a defence they sought to have the best of all three worlds, left all three summonses in existence and allowed them all to be heard

[92] *Hammett R.C. Ltd.* v. *Crabb; Hammett R.C. Ltd.* v. *Beldam* (1931) 95 J.P. 180.
[93] *Malcolm* v. *Cheek* [1948] 1 K.B. 400.
[94] Food Act 1984, s.200(2).
[95] *Ibid.* s.100(3).
[96] [1976] Crim.L.R. 568.
[97] Now Food Act 1984, s.8.
[98] *Ibid.* s.100(1).
[99] (1953) 117 J.P. 437.

by the same stipendiary magistrate at the same time. It was held that the rights to prosecute are alternative and cannot go on contemporaneously.

Lord Widgery in distinguishing the *Fisher* case stated:

" . . . I can see nothing in the judgment of Lord Goddard C.J. to prevent two summonses as pieces of paper, as it were, being in existence at the same time, and indeed having the same return dates, provided that you get rid of all but one of the summonses, leaving only that one to be decided. This will of course be the summons against the defendant whom the local authority is prepared to say was really responsible for the alleged food and drugs offence . . . "

WARRANTY PLEADED AS A DEFENCE

8.18　Section 102 of the Food Act 1984 contains conditions whereby a warranty may be pleaded as a defence in any proceedings for an offence under the Act or any Regulation made thereunder being an offence consisting of selling or offering, exposing or advertising for sale, or having in possession for the purpose of sale, any article or substance. It is a defence for the defendant to prove:

    (a) that he purchased it as being an article or substance which could lawfully be sold or otherwise dealt with as aforesaid, or, as the case may be, could lawfully be so sold or dealt with under the name or description or for the purposes under or for which he sold or dealt with it, and with a written warranty to that effect; and

    (b) that he had no reason to believe at the time of the commission of the alleged offence that it was otherwise; and

    (c) that it was then in the same state as when he purchased it.

In order to take advantage of this defence the defendant must notify the prosecuting authority and the alleged warrantor that he intends to make use of this defence. He must send to the prosecutor not later than three clear days before the date of the hearing a copy of the warranty together with notice of his intention and the name and address of the person from whom he received it. A like notice must also be sent to that person.[1] The defendant will comply with the terms of the section even if the notice is not received by the prosecutor after the three days have elapsed as long as it is posted within the required time.[2]

If the defendant has a warranty which was given by a person resident outside the United Kingdom he must also prove that he had taken reasonable steps to ascertain, and in fact believe in, the accuracy of the statement contained in it. Also, in the case of a prosecution in respect of

---

[1] Food Act 1984, s.102(2)(*a*).
[2] *Retail Dairy Co.* v. *Clarke* [1912] 2 K.B. 388.

a sample of milk, the defendant must also either have within 60 hours after the sample was procured, served a notice requiring a sample to be procured from a corresponding milking, or, not having served such a notice, prove that such a notice would have been of no effect by reason of the fact that the milk was a mixture of milk produced on more than one dairy farm.[3]

No definition of "warranty" is contained in the Food Act 1984. In contract law, warranty is usually contrasted with a condition of a contract and under section 61 of the Sale of Goods Act 1979 is defined (as regards England, Wales and Northern Ireland) as meaning an agreement with reference to goods which are the subject of a contract of sale, but collateral to the main purpose of such contract, the breach of which gives rise to a claim for damages, but not to a right to reject the goods and treat the contract as repudiated. In practice, unless there is a clear intention to the contrary, a warranty is a minor term of the contract and a condition is a major term.

Section 102(5) of the 1984 Act clarifies the position of invoices in this respect. It states that a name or description entered in an invoice shall be deemed to be a written warranty that the article or substance to which the entry refers can be sold or otherwise dealt with under that name or description by any person without contravening any of the provisions of the 1984 Act or of Regulations made under the 1984 Act.

An invoice as a warranty was considered in *Rochdale Metropolitan Borough Council* v. *F.M.C. (Meat)*,[4] where a frozen chicken which was intended for, but unfit for human consumption, was sold to Rochdale Metropolitan Borough Council contrary to section 8(1) of the Food and Drugs Act 1955.[5] The chicken was sold through a succession of suppliers to the local authority and the immediate supplier relied on the "warranty" defence under section 115(1) of the 1955 Act[6] on the basis that the brand name "Saxon Chix" on the invoice amounted to a warranty by virtue of section 115(5) of the 1955 Act.[7]

All parties were agreed that the brand name came from a firm which enjoyed the highest of reputations and that the defendants had satisfied the magistrates that the name "Saxon Chix" was one of the major factors that determined their decision to purchase the chicken. The local authority, on the other hand, contended that the name "Saxon Chix" on the invoice was insufficient to amount to a warranty that the chicken in question was fit for human consumption. The court held on appeal that an invoice bearing the name of the article is deemed to be a written warranty that, so far as the provisions of the Act are concerned, that article could lawfully be sold under that name.

---

[3] Food Act 1984, s.102(2)(*b*), (*c*).
[4] [1908] 1 W.L.R. 461.
[5] Now the Food Act 1984, s.8(1).
[6] *Ibid.* s.102(1).
[7] *Ibid.* s.102(5).

In addition to this, however, the defendant must prove paragraphs (*b*) and (*c*) of the section, *i.e.* that he had no reason to believe at the time of the commission of the alleged offence that it was otherwise and that the product was then in the same state as when he purchased it.[7a] In many cases this will not be possible and the prosecution will succeed because of this, but in this particular case the defendant proved these points mainly because of the high reputation of the brand. It is contemporary market practice to frequently rely on a trade name as a guarantee of its quality. Where section 102(5) of the Food Act 1984 does not apply to the contract, and other documents are put forward as a warranty, the ordinary rules of law with regard to warranties are applicable.

A defendant who is the servant of the person who purchased the article or substance under a warranty is entitled to rely on the defence of warranty in the same way as his employer would have been entitled to do if he had been the defendant.[8]

There has been much litigation on the question whether or not the food is in the same state as when the defendant purchased it. For example, in *Hennen* v. *Long*[9] the respondent was summonsed for selling milk which was deficient in fat to the extent of at least 3 per cent. and contained added water to the amount of 5.2 per cent. He relied on a warranty under which he bought the milk by virtue of section 25 of the Sale of Food and Drugs Act 1875 but admitted that he had added one ounce of milk preservative to each 10 gallons of milk. It was held that the respondent could not rely on the warranty as a defence as he had not sold it "in the same state as when purchased." He had not done anything to encourage any deterioration but had changed the state of the goods.

In *United Dairies (London)* v. *Ealing Borough Council*,[10] a quantity of porridge oats had been bought by the retailer and a package of the oats had been sold to a retail customer who found that it contained flour moths. The eggs of the moths had got into the oats and by the time it reached the customer the eggs had turned into moths. Lord Parker C.J. said that he was quite unable to accept the argument that the porridge oats had become in a different state merely because the eggs had matured in that way. This case established that deterioration which occurs through natural causes between the acquisition of the article by the retailer and its subsequent sale to the customer is not such as to be regarded as changing the state of the article.

These cases were considered in *Tesco Stores* v. *Roberts*,[11] in which the defendants purchased a consignment of frozen pig's liver from a supplier and when it was sufficiently thawed out to enable it to be cut it was cut

---

[7a] See p. 162.
[8] *Ibid.* s.102(3).
[9] (1904) 68 J.P. 237.
[10] (unreported) February 29, 1968.
[11] [1974] 1 W.L.R. 1253.

into 40 to 45 pieces. Each piece was placed in a box, covered with polythene and the packs were put back into the refrigerator display cabinet. One was purchased by a customer who called in the public health inspector when she found that it turned green after defrosting. Nobody could say when the deterioration began.

The court found that the article, pig's liver, changed its state after it was cut. An analogy was drawn in cutting an orange. If, for example, a crate full of oranges was delivered to a shop and the oranges were taken out and placed individually on a shelf the state of the oranges is not changed in any way. However, if one of the oranges is cut with a knife then the orange has been changed. Also, when a liver is cut with a knife the opportunity for contamination is increased as the knife may be dirty.

The *Tesco* case was followed in *Walker* v. *Baxter's Butchers*,[12] where puff pastry was received by a shop in a refrigerated condition and immediately placed in a deep freeze. Eleven days later a customer bought two packs which were on a shelf where they had been placed to thaw and put them in a refrigerator when she got home. The next day when she took them out she noticed that they were mouldy.

The court considered that, for the purposes of the warranty defence section, goods might remain in the same state even though their organic content had changed by natural deterioration; that, therefore, notwithstanding there was mould on the pastry, since there was no evidence that the freezing and thawing to which the pastry had been subjected had had any effect on its state or that the defendants had otherwise physically tampered with the pastry, the pastry was in the same state when sold as when it was received by the defendant.

In proving paragraph 1(*b*) of section 102 of the 1984 Act, *i.e.* that the retailer had no reason to believe at the time of the commission of the alleged offence that the foodstuffs were unfit for human consumption, he must call evidence of the system he adopts to try to ensure that any defective article does not get passed on to the consumer.[13]

Section 103 of the Food Act 1984 lays down circumstances where the giving of a false warranty or certificate of analysis is an offence.

HYGIENE

The incidence of food poisoning notifications has dramatically increased **8.19** in the last 10 years. The true cause of this increase is unclear. It has been suggested that better diagnosis may be the reason but unhygienic premises and practices have certainly contributed towards this rise.

In recent years educating food handlers on proper food hygiene practices has been one of the main concerns of the Institution of Environmental Health Officers. Basic, intermediate and advanced food hygiene courses promoted by the Institution have been set up by many Environ-

[12] (1977) 121 S.J. 617.
[13] *London Borough of Camden* v. *Fine Fare* (1987), see "Food Law Monthly," July 1987.

mental Health Departments and these are to be applauded. This, however, must be balanced by the enforcement of food hygiene law.

The Institution has been campaigning for some form of prior approval or registration of food premises. At present any person may set himself up in the food business in insanitary premises and with no proper training in food hygiene, but as mentioned in the introduction to the book the recent government White Paper has proposed certain amendments to food law which includes registration of food premises and statutory regulation of the training of food handlers.

The Regulations concerned with food hygiene are the Food Hygiene (General) Regulations 1970 and the law regarding the enforced closing of insanitary food premises is contained in sections 21 to 25 of the Food Act 1984.

Scope of the Food Hygiene (General) Regulations 1970

8.20   The Regulations[14] are made under section 13 of the Food and Drugs Act 1955.[15] The enabling provisions are stated generally in subsection (1) and in particular subsection (2). Subsection (1), which was an important factor in the decision on the meaning of risk of contamination contained in *Mac Fisheries (Wholesale and Retail)* v. *Coventry Corporation*[16] (which is discussed later), states that the Ministers may make such Regulations as appear to them to be expedient for securing the observance of sanitary and clean conditions and practices in connection with:

(a) the sale of food for human consumption; or

(b) the importation, preparation, transport, storage, packaging, wrapping, exposure for sale, service or delivery of food intended for sale or sold for human consumption, or otherwise for the protection of the public health in connection with those matters.

"The Ministers" in this case means the Minister of Agriculture, Fisheries and Food and the Minister of Health, acting jointly.[17]

The Ministers shall from time to time take such steps as they think expedient for publishing codes of practice for the purpose of giving guidance on food hygiene.[18]

If any person, who has incurred, or is about to incur expenditure in securing that the requirements of the Regulations, being requirements of a structural character, are complied with in respect of any premises

---

[14] S.I. 1970 No. 1172.

[15] Now the Food Act 1984, s.13.

[16] [1957] 1 W.L.R. 1066.

[17] Food and Drugs Act 1955, s.135(1). Now under the Food Act 1984, s.132(1), "the Ministers" means the Minister of Agriculture, Fisheries and Food, the Secretary of State for Social Services, and the Secretary of State for Wales, acting jointly.

[18] Food and Drugs Act 1955, s.13(8). The following Food Hygiene Codes of Practice have been published and are available from H.M.S.O.: No. 3, Hygiene in the retail fish trade; No. 4, The hygienic transport and handling of fish; No. 5, Poultry dressing and

owned or occupied by him, claims that the whole or part of the expenditure ought to be borne by any other person having an interest in the premises, he may apply to the county court and the court may apportion the expenditure as it considers just and equitable.[19]

All premises where a food business is carried on are subject to the Regulations. Also affected are certain kinds of ship and moored craft upon which food is sold and some agricultural activities such as the packing or storing of eggs, fruit and vegetables.

The premises exempted from application of the Regulations are those subject to other special Regulations, *i.e.* slaughterhouses, cold stores, dock premises, carriers' premises, market stalls or delivery vehicles. Where, however, canteens are on these premises and made use of by the persons working in the premises, these have to comply with the 1970 Regulations. Food business means any trade or business for the purposes of which any person engages in the handling of food[20] and business includes the undertaking of a canteen, club, school, hospital or institution, whether carried on for profit or not, and any undertaking or activity carried on by a public or local authority.[21]

"Handling of food" covers any process or operation in the sale of food, wholesale or retail, or in the preparation, transport, storage, packaging, wrapping, exposure for sale, service or delivery of food, and includes the cleaning of articles or equipment with which the food comes into contact.[22]

The Regulations differentiate between "food" and "open food." "Open food" is defined as food not in a container of such materials and so closed as to exclude the risk of contamination. The Schedule to the Regulations lists certain foods, *i.e.* butter, margarine, cooking fat, meat (except cooked meat), fish, vegetables, flour, confectionery and bakery goods, ice-cream and ice lollies. These are not to be regarded as open food if they are wrapped in the manner described in the Regulations.[23]

The meaning of "risk of contamination"

Regulation 2(4) states that in determining for the purposes of these **8.21** Regulations whether any matter involves a risk of contamination to any food, regard shall be had to the extent to which such contamination is immaterial because of:

   (a) the nature of the food;
   (b) the manner in which the food is packed; or
   (c) any process to which the food is to be subjected before sale to

packing; No. 6, Hygiene in the bakery trade and industry; No. 7, Hygiene in the operation of coin operated food vending machines; No. 8, Hygiene in the meat trade. See p. 89 for the legal status of codes of practice.
[19] *Ibid.* s.13(4), (5).
[20] Food Hygiene (General) Regulations 1970, reg. 3.
[21] *Ibid.* reg. 2(1).
[22] *Ibid.* reg. 2(2).
[23] *Ibid.* reg. 2(1).

the consumer, being a process to which food of that nature is normally so subjected.

The term "risk of contamination" was considered in *Mac Fisheries (Wholesale and Retail)* v. *Coventry Corporation.*[24] The appellant company which was the largest retail fishmonger in the world, had opened a new retail outlet in Coventry and it was agreed by all parties that the company had spared no expense in order to provide the most modern and up-to-date premises of its kind in the country. Wet fish, cured fish, shell fish and sausages were displayed in open plastic trays on the two tiers forming the main counter extending along the whole length of the shop. Food was also displayed in the same way in the shop window and on a shelf fixed to the wall on the customer's side. It was contended by the council that because the clothing of customers came into contact with the food, particularly when they were handing over money, and the possibility of customers and assistants sneezing and coughing over the food, there was a risk of contamination and contravention of regulation 8 of the Food Hygiene Regulations 1955.[25]

Although the public health inspector giving evidence for the Corporation thought that the problem could be solved by the installation of glass screens, the company objected to this because the closing in of the shop would interfere with the free flow of air thereby causing the fish to deteriorate more rapidly. Also, the lack of screens speeded up sales and thereby prevented the fish remaining in the trays too long.

The justices were of the opinion that the risk of contamination referred to in regulation 8 was the risk of any contamination whether or not it was injurious to health. They considered that there was nothing in the Regulations from which it could be implied that contamination, if it occurred, must be injurious to health.

Lord Goddard C.J. on delivering judgment in the appeal by way of case said:

" . . . In order to interpret the regulations it is necessary and desirable, though it is very often forgotten, to have regard to what the Statute, under which the regulations are made, says . . . [26] It is therefore quite obvious to my mind that the object of the Statute, and therefore the object of the regulations, is to procure the protection of the public health . . . For the reasons I have pointed out it seems to me that the governing consideration in this case is the words of section 13, and therefore the whole task here is to see whether there was contamination which was injurious to health."

The magistrates had themselves found that the contamination was not injurious to health and, therefore, the court upheld the appeal and the conviction was quashed.

[24] [1957] 1 W.L.R. 1066.
[25] Now the Food Hygiene (General) Regulations 1970, reg. 9.
[26] See extract from the Food and Drugs Act 1955, s.13.

General requirements—insanitary premises, etc.

Regulation 6 states that no food business shall be carried on at any **8.22** insanitary premises or place or at any premises or place the condition, situation or construction of which is such that food is exposed to the risk of contamination. Under regulation 7, articles or equipment with which food comes, or is liable to come, into contact[27] must be kept clean and be so constructed, be of such materials and kept in such good order, repair and condition as to enable them to be thoroughly cleaned and to prevent absorption of matter. There is also a restriction under regulation 8 on preparing and packing food on domestic premises. Any person carrying on a food business must not give out food in order for it to be prepared and packed by another person at any domestic premises. An exception is made in respect of the peeling of shrimps and prawns in certain circumstances and the domestic premises of the person carrying on the business may be so used.

Food handlers—food to be protected from contamination, etc.

Food handlers must take all such steps as may be reasonably necess- **8.23** ary to protect the food from the risk of contamination. In particular no food must be placed lower than 18 inches from the ground in or about any forecourt or yard unless it is adequately protected. Also, open food, while exposed for sale or during sale or delivery, where reasonably necessary, must be kept covered or otherwise effectively screened against possible sources of contamination. Unfit food must be kept apart from any food being offered for sale, and any animal feed must not be kept in a food room[28] unless it is in a container of such material

---

[27] There is a possibility that a narrow interpretation of this provision could mean that only, for example, the top of a preparation table needs to be clean because that is the part likely to come into contact with food, whereas other parts such as the legs and framework can be ignored.

[28] "Food room" means any room (being, or being part of, any food premises) in which any person engages in the handling of food for the purpose of a food business, but does not include:

    (a) a room used as a sleeping place if the only handling of food which occurs in a room is in the course of serving food there to, or at the request of, any person occupying it as a sleeping place; or

    (b) a room communicating with a room used as a sleeping place if the only handling of food which occurs in the room is in the course of serving food there to, or at the request of, any person (not being a person carrying on a food business at the premises which include the room or a person employed by him) by whom the room is occupied as a sleeping place; or

    (c) a day room in a hospital or in a home for the reception of aged or disabled persons (reg. 2(1)).

Substantial evidence must be adduced in legal proceedings that the room in which the contravention occurs is a food room. For example, in *Cleethorpes Borough Council* v. *Charolambous* (1987) Food Enforcement Bulletin B, No. 7 (I.E.H.O.), the magistrates accepted the defence's contention that the room where the alleged contravention took place was not a food room because the commercial food mixer in the room was used to mix experimental batches of fish cakes and not used to manufacture a product intended for retail sale.

and so closed as to prevent the risk of contaminating the food in the room.[29]

In addition persons engaged in handling food shall, while so engaged:

(a) keep all parts of themselves and their clothing liable to come into contact with food as clean as reasonably practicable;

(b) keep open cuts or abrasions on any exposed part of their person covered with a suitable waterproof dressing;

(c) refrain from spitting; and

(d) refrain from the use of tobacco or any other smoking mixture or snuff while they are handling[30] open food or when in a food room where there is open food.[30a]

In *Pitt* v. *Locke*,[31] the stallholder was observed serving tomatoes from his stall when there was an unlighted cigarette in his mouth. The cigarette had been half smoked and had gone out. It was held that as one of the mischiefs at which the regulation was aimed was ash falling on food the respondent was found guilty and convicted.

Clean and washable overclothing must be worn by every food handler whilst handling open food other than raw vegetables, intoxicating liquor or soft drinks, and persons carrying meat where it is likely to come into contact with the head or neck must wear clean and washable neck and head covering. Waiters in the catering business, persons engaged only in the carrying of unskinned rabbits or hares or unplucked game or poultry and certain transporters of food are exempt from these provisions as long as they take reasonable precautions to prevent open food from coming into contact with exposed parts of the person or with clothing other than overclothing.[32]

Food must be protected from contamination from other articles when it is being carried. In particular, live animals or poultry must not be carried with food unless all such precautions are taken as are reasonably practicable to avoid the risk of contamination. Open food must not be wrapped in any paper or wrapping material which is not clean or liable to contaminate the food. No printed paper must be used unless designed exclusively for wrapping or containing food, except that printed paper can be used for wrapping uncooked vegetables or unskinned rabbits or hares or unplucked game or poultry.[33]

As soon as a person engaged in the handling of food becomes aware that he is suffering from, or is the carrier of, typhoid, paratyphoid or any

---

[29] reg. 9.

[30] The phrase "while he is handling open food" in relation to smoking was considered in *Cuckson* v. *Bugg* (1986) 150 J.P. 635. The offence was committed at a stall and the Food Hygiene (Markets Stalls and Delivery Vehicles) Regulations (S.I. 1966 No. 791) applied (see Chap. 9, p. 183).

[30a] Food Hygiene (General) Regulations 1970, reg. 10.

[31] (1960) 125 J.P. 93.

[32] Food Hygiene (General) Regulations 1970, reg. 11.

[33] *Ibid.* reg. 12.

other salmonella infection or amoebic or bacillary dysentery or any sta-phylococcal infection likely to cause food poisoning he must inform the person carrying on the food business who must in turn notify the medical officer of environmental health for the district.[34] In order to prevent the spread of disease, such as food poisoning, the proper officer of a council may by notice request any person to discontinue work. Where this is done compensation will be payable to that person.[34a]

Food premises—structural requirements, etc.

Food premises to which the Regulations apply have to comply with **8.24** certain structural requirements. Fresh air intakes of any ventilation pipe connected to the soil drainage system must not be placed in a food room and every inlet to the drainage system situated in any such room must be trapped.[35] No room which contains a sanitary convenience can be used as a food room and no open food can be handled in a room which communicates directly with a room containing a sanitary convenience.[36] Also food rooms must not be used as sleeping places and subject to the provision of any certificate of exemption no food room which communicates directly with a sleeping place can be used for handling open food.[37]

All sanitary conveniences in food premises must be kept clean and in efficient order and must be so placed as to prevent offensive odours penetrating into a food room. They must be kept clean and suitably and sufficiently lighted and ventilated. In addition, a clearly legible notice requesting users to wash their hands after using the convenience must be fixed and maintained in a prominent position near every sanitary convenience provided or made regularly available for use by persons employed in the handling of food.[38]

Subject to the provisions of any certificate of exemption an adequate supply of clean and wholesome water must be provided in all food rooms so that the requirements of the regulation can be complied with. The water supply must be constant if it is reasonably practicable and is in accordance with good practice at premises used for businesses of a similar class.[39] If water is supplied to the food room through a cistern that cistern must not supply water to a sanitary convenience except through a cistern of such design as will prevent risk of contamination of the water supply.[40]

Suitable and sufficient wash-hand basins must be provided and placed in a position conveniently accessible to food handlers, and at every

[34] *Ibid.* reg. 13.
[34a] See the Public Health (Control of Disease) Act 1984, s.20 and Public Health (Infectious Diseases) Regulation 1988. (S.I. 1988 No. 1546).
[35] Food Hygiene (General) Regulations 1970, reg. 14.
[36] *Ibid.* reg. 16.
[37] *Ibid.* reg. 24.
[38] *Ibid.* reg. 16.
[39] *Ibid.* reg. 17.
[40] *Ibid.* reg. 15.

wash-hand basin must be an adequate supply of hot and cold water or hot water at a suitably controlled temperature, or in the case of food premises where no open food is handled, a supply of cold water. The wash-hand basin must only be used for the purpose of personal hygiene and be kept clean and in good working condition and an adequate supply of soap, or other suitable detergent, nail-brush and clean towels or other suitable drying facilities must also be provided.[41]

Where open food is handled, sinks or other washing facilities suitable and sufficient for any necessary washing of food and equipment must be provided together with an adequate supply of hot and cold water or hot water at a suitably controlled temperature. Cold water need only be supplied where the sink is used for washing fish, fruit or vegetables or for washing with a suitable bactericidal agent only drinking vessels, or only ice-cream formers or servers. The sink must be kept clean and in good working condition.[41a]

Food rooms must have suitable and sufficient means of lighting and must be suitably and sufficiently lighted.[42] Ventilation must be of a similar standard except where the humidity or temperature is controlled.[43]

Walls, floors, doors, windows, ceilings, woodwork and all other parts of the structure of every food room must be kept clean and in such good order, repair and condition as to enable them to be effectively cleaned and prevent, so far as is reasonably practicable, any risk of infestation by rats, mice or insects.[44-45]

The layout of the food premises must be such as to allow enough space for removing waste from food and for storing such waste until removal and for separating food fit for human consumption from unfit food. No waste, whether liquid or solid, must be deposited or allowed to accumulate in a food room except so far as may be unavoidable for the proper carrying on of the trade or business.[46]

Suitable and sufficient accommodation for outdoor or other clothing and footwear not being worn during working hours by food handlers must be provided in food premises where open food is handled. Such clothing must not be kept in and around the food premises but must be placed in the accommodation provided and where this facility is situated in a food room it must be in the form of lockers and cupboards. This requirement is subject to the provision of any certificate of exemption.[47]

A sufficient supply of suitable bandages, dressings (including water-

---

[41] *Ibid.* reg. 18.

[41a] *Ibid.* reg. 21.

[42] *Ibid.* reg. 22.

[43] *Ibid.* reg. 23.

[44-45] reg. 25. The laying of information under the Regulations was considered in *George* v. *Kumar* (1982) 80 L.G.R. 525. It was held that since the primary object of reg. 25 was to impose an obligation to keep the structure of every food room clean, it was not necessary for the prosecution to lay information separately in respect to particular items in the structure of the room.

[46] Food Hygiene (General) Regulations 1970, reg. 26.

[47] *Ibid.* reg. 20.

proof dressings) and antiseptic for first-aid treatment of persons engaged in the handling of food must be available in food premises and readily accessible to food handlers.[48]

Temperature at which certain foods are to be kept

Generally, bacterial growth in food is slow at high and low tempera- **8.25** tures and when food is cooked, although most of the bacteria are killed, some will survive and will multiply rapidly below 63°C until a temperature of about 5°C is obtained. The optimum temperature for the growth of pathogenic organisms is around 37°C.

Temperature control of food is therefore one of, if not the, most important consideration in preventative measures to be taken to combat the increasing incidence of food poisoning and regulation 27 contains details of temperatures at which certain susceptible foods have to be kept.

These are foods consisting of meat, fish, gravy, imitation cream or prepared from or containing any of those substances or any egg or milk. Apart from exceptions listed in the regulation,[49] this type of food (examples are cooked meats, meat pies and those made from eggs and milk such as cream cakes and trifle), if brought on to any food premises on or from which is carried on a catering business, if not already at a temperature of 62.7°C or above on the one hand or below 10°C on the other hand, be brought to one or other of those temperatures without any avoidable delay after arrival.

In a catering establishment where such food has been cooked or partly cooked on the premises, it shall be kept at a temperature of not less than 62.7°C until it is required for serving for immediate consumption. Alternatively, if the temperature is brought or allowed to fall below 62.7°C, it is to be cooled to a temperature below 10°C under hygienic conditions as quickly as is reasonably practicable and thereafter kept below 10°C until it is required for servicing or is further cooked or is reheated for service.

The requirements regarding temperature control do not apply in a situation where the food falls below 62.7°C or rises above 10°C as a result of a step in preparing the food or if the food is moved from one part of the premises to another as long as the food is restored as quickly

---

[48] *Ibid.* reg. 19.

[49] The provisions of reg. 27 do not apply to: (a) bread, biscuits, cakes or pastry by reason only of the use of egg or milk as an ingredient thereof introduced prior to baking; (b) chocolate or sugar confectionery; (c) ice-cream to which the provisions of any regulations with respect of heat treatment of ice-cream in force under the Food and Drugs Act 1955, s.4 apply; (d) food canned, bottled or otherwise preserved in an effectively closed container of a metal, glass or other impermeable material, so long as the container remains effectively closed; (e) butter, margarine, lard, shortening, cooking fats or beef suet; (f) cheese, uncooked bacon, uncooked ham, dry pasta, dry pudding mixes, dry soup mixes or dry mixtures for the preparation of beverages; or (g) any unskinned rabbits or hares or unplucked game or poultry.

as reasonably practicable to the temperature limits on completion of the process.

Likewise the requirements do not apply to any food which is exposed for sale, or which will be exposed for sale, if it is brought on to catering premises within four hours before they are open for business; also where food is kept to replenish food of a similar kind if the keeping available of such a supply is in accordance with good practice on such premises and the quantity so kept is not greater than is reasonably necessary.

Exemptions

8.26 Under regulation 28, if the local authority is satisfied that by reason of restricted accommodation or other special circumstances affecting food premises it is reasonable that a certificate of exemption be granted they may grant such a certificate. A certificate may be granted in respect of regulation 17 (water supply), regulation 20 (accommodation for clothing, etc.) and regulation 24(2) (food room not to be or communicate with a sleeping place).

A certificate of exemption may be withdrawn by the local authority if at any time they cease to be satisfied as to the conditions mentioned above. If the person carrying on a food business is aggrieved by the refusal or withdrawal of a certificate of exemption he may appeal to a magistrates' court and that court may make such order concerning the certificate as the court considers just and equitable.

Offences and penalties

8.27 Where the Regulations impose an obligation on a person engaged in handling food and that person fails to comply with the obligation he shall be guilty of an offence. A person carrying on a food business shall be guilty of an offence if he fails to take all reasonable steps to secure compliance with regulations 10 and 13 (*i.e.* personal cleanliness and notification of infectious diseases respectively) by a person employed by him or under his control, and also if any of the other regulations are contravened.[50]

In addition, an offence is committed by any person for the time being having the control or management of persons engaged in the handling of food not being himself a person carrying on a food business, if he fails to take all reasonable steps to secure the compliance by any person under his control or management with any provision of the Regulations which imposes an obligation on a person engaged in the handling of food.[51]

The defence under section 100 of the Food Act (contravention due to another person[52]) is available in respect of an offence under the Regulations.[53]

[50] Food Hygiene (General) Regulations 1970, reg. 29(1), (2).
[51] *Ibid.* reg. 29(3).
[52] See p. 160.
[53] Food Hygiene (General) Regulations 1970, reg. 29(4).

Any person guilty of an offence against the Regulations is liable on summary conviction to a fine not exceeding level 5 on the standard scale and on indictment to an unlimited fine and/or a maximum of two years' imprisonment.[54]

The closure of food premises and stalls dangerous to health

Sections 21 to 25 of the Food Act 1984 outline the legal methods by **8.28** which a local authority can ensure that extremely unhygienic and dangerous food premises are closed so as not to cause a danger to the health of the public. There is also an informal practical way whereby these types of premises can be closed almost immediately they come to the notice of the environmental health officer without the need to enter the matter into court. This is by means of a written agreement.[54a]

Under section 21 of the 1984 Act, a local authority may apply to the magistrates' court for an order (called a "closure order") prohibiting the preparation, storage, sale or offer or exposure for sale of food from any premises or stall. Before an application can be made the person carrying on the food business must have been convicted of an offence under Regulations made under section 13 of the 1984 Act on information laid by the local authority.

Where premises are the subject of the order, the offence referred to above must include the carrying on of a food business at any insanitary premises or at any premises the condition, situation or construction of which is such that food is exposed to the risk of contamination. Where it is a stall, the offence must include the carrying on of a food business on, at or from a stall which is insanitary, or which is also so situated or constructed, or is in such a condition, that the food is exposed to the risk of contamination.

The court may make the order on the local authority's application but it must be satisfied that the sale, etc., of food is continuing or likely to continue and by reason of the situation, construction or insanitary or defective condition of the premises or stall or the insanitary or defective condition of the fittings or fixtures or equipment or the infestation of vermin or the accumulation of refuse, the carrying on of a food business at those premises or on, at or from that stall would be dangerous to health.

Fourteen days' written notice of intention to apply for the order must be given to the person against whom the information was laid and the owner of the premises or stall (assuming that he is not the same person). The notice must include measures which, in their opinion, should be taken to remove any danger to health.

---

[54] Criminal Justice Act 1982, ss.38, 46.

[54a] If the shop opens in contravention of the agreement the local authority will have to revert to either the closure order or emergency closure order procedure depending on the condition of the shop. However, it is almost certain that the magistrates will take this into account in any prosecution that may follow.

An application may be made to resume the business of selling, etc., food, where a closure order is in force, to the local authority who if they are satisfied that the measures specified in the closure order have been carried out, shall as soon as practicable and not in more than 14 days give to the applicant a certificate to that effect and such certificate shall be conclusive evidence of the matters stated in it.

Where there is an imminent risk of danger to health the court may, under section 22 of the 1984 Act, make an order called "an emergency order." The order is made where information is, or has been laid by a local authority in respect of the offences mentioned under section 21 of the 1984 Act and they are satisfied an application by the local authority for an emergency order that the use of the premises or stall for the preparation, storage, sale or offer or exposure for sale of food involves imminent risk of danger to health. Before making the decision the court must afford, if he appears, the person against whom the information is or was laid and the owner of the premises or stall (assuming he is not the same person) an opportunity to be heard and to tender evidence.

Three clear days' written notice of intention to apply for an emergency order must be given to the aforementioned person otherwise the court cannot consider the application, and the notice must specify the measures to be taken to remove the danger to health. A copy of the emergency order must be sent to the aforementioned persons and a copy fixed in a conspicuous position to the premises or stall if practicable.

Again, application may be made to the local authority to resume preparing or selling food, etc. on such a stall or premises and if they are satisfied that there is no longer a risk of danger to health they must as soon as practicable and in not more than 14 days issue a certificate to that effect.

Compensation may be payable by order of the court if, on trial of the information of the offences mentioned in section 21 of the 1984 Act, the court determines that at the date of any emergency order the use of the premises or stall did not involve imminent risk of danger to health and they were satisfied that loss occurred as a result of the emergency order being granted.[55]

Both the local authority and the person on whom the notice of application is served have a right of appeal to the Crown Court. They have a right of appeal on the granting or otherwise of a closure order and in the case of an emergency order in respect of the granting or refusal of compensation.[56]

Contravention of a closure order or an emergency order will make the person responsible liable on summary conviction to a fine not exceeding level 5 on the standard scale.[57]

[55] Food Act 1984, s.23.
[56] *Ibid.* s.24.
[57] *Ibid.*

CHAPTER 9

MOBILE SHOPS, STALLS, DELIVERY VEHICLES AND STREET TRADING

Mobile shops and stalls are deserving of special consideration because of **9.01** their very nature. They are treated separately from premises in the Shops Act 1950 and in some legislation such as the Offices Shops and Railway Premises Act 1963, they are omitted altogether. Other areas of law which must be considered are planning, which is dealt with in Chapter 1,[1] and the procedure for registration of food hawkers, which is contained in Chapter 3.[2]

APPLICATION OF HIGHWAY LAW TO MOBILE SHOPS

Mobile snackbars are frequently seen at the side of roads, in lay-bys and **9.02** on verges. They provide a service particularly where there are no other facilities available but unfortunately they can be an eyesore, cause litter problems and a danger to other road users.

There are a number of sections in the Highways Act 1980 that can be implemented by the appropriate authorities to remove such a mobile shop if a nuisance or danger exists. The appropriate authorities in this case are the Minister of Transport, county councils, metropolitan district councils and councils of the London boroughs who are the principal highway authorities.[3] District councils may, however, have responsibilities under the Act on an agency basis.

Offences may take place on a highway and mobile shops are found in places that may or may not be part of the highway, and so it is imperative to define a highway. No definition is contained in the 1980 Act and so the common law must be considered. In *ex parte Lewis*,[4] Willis J. stated that a highway is a way over which there exists a public right of passage and re-passage without hindrance and in *Attorney-General* v. *Beynon*,[5] Goff J. laid down the principle that the highway extends to the whole space between the fences enclosing a highway and is not confined to such part as may have been made up. In *Rodgers* v. *Ministry of Transport*,[6] lorry drivers had the habit of driving onto the grass verge of a trunk road out of the way of the traffic in order to park and call into a roadside cafe. This churned up the grass leaving the area in a mess and

---

[1] See pp. 4 to 6.
[2] See pp. 49 to 51.
[3] Highways Act 1980, s.1.
[4] (1888) 21 Q.B.D. 191.
[5] [1970] Ch. 1.
[6] (1952) 116 J.P. 200.

the local authority decided to construct a proper parking area but a local resident objected to this and claimed that the verge was not part of the highway. The court, however, ruled that the local authority was within its rights as the grass verge was part of the highway. The relevant section of the 1980 Act will apply therefore to grass verges and lay-bys.

Section 137 of the 1980 Act states that it is an offence for any person without lawful authority or excuse wilfully to obstruct in any way the free passage along a highway. A seller of hot dogs was prosecuted under a similar section in the 1959 Highways Act[7] in *Pitcher* v. *Lockett*.[8] He had set up his van on two occasions on a busy road, selling hot dogs to members of the public. He was convicted and on appeal to the High Court the appellant contended that the mere fact of selling from a vehicle did not make the presence of that vehicle an unreasonable user of a highway. It was held, however, that the right of the public in regard to a highway was a right of passage to and fro and that the setting up of a stationary shop for the purposes of selling to the public, which had nothing to do with passage to and fro, was an unreasonable use of the highway. In dismissing the appeal Lord Parker of Waddington C.J. stated that it was a question of fact in each case as it depended on all the circumstances including the length of time the obstruction continues, the place it occurs, the purpose for which it is done, and of course whether it does in fact cause an actual obstruction as opposed to a potential obstruction. A milkman who delivers milk on his rounds is making use of the free passage to and fro on the highway for the purpose of delivering his commodities and, therefore, does not cause an obstruction.

To secure a conviction under section 137 an obstruction must be proved to exist and therefore this section would be inappropriate in the case of a mobile shop operating from a lay-by as an obstruction in that situation would very often be difficult to prove. Section 143 of the 1980 Highways Act gives power to a competent authority to serve a notice in order to remove a structure from the highway where it has been set up or erected other than under a provision of the 1980 Act or some other enactment. There is no need to prove obstruction and for that reason it can be used to remove a snack bar from a lay-by. But the snack bar must be a structure and it is doubtful that a mobile shop would come under the definition of "structure" unless it had some degree of permanence.[9]

It is also an offence under section 148 of the Highways Act 1980 for any hawker or other itinerant trader, without lawful authority, to pitch a booth, stall or stand, or encamp on a highway. This would not apply to a mobile shop unless it was a trailer which could be separated from the towing vehicle. In *Divito* v. *Stickings*,[10] Humphrey J. thought that it was

[7] Highways Act 1959, s.121(1).
[8] (1966) 64 L.G.R. 477.
[9] See *Kingston Plastics* v. *Esher Urban District Council* (1969) 68 L.G.R. 401.
[10] (1948) 112 J.P. 166.

an extravagant use of language to say that a man driving a motor van who stops for the purpose of making a sale thereby pitches a stall, *i.e.* his motor van on the highway.

Different circumstances prevailed in *Waltham Forest London Borough Council* v. *Mills*[11] where a mobile snack bar was parked in a lay-by; the snack bar consisted of a trailer stall coupled to a pick-up lorry but was capable of being uncoupled. It was held that this was a hawker pitching a stall on the highway. It was a stall because it was capable of being separated from the vehicle which was towing it and it was pitched because it was placed in a definite place, always the same on each of five days.

Section 147A of the 1980 Act, which was inserted by the Local Government (Miscellaneous Provisions) Act 1982, section 23, provides that no person shall, for the purpose of selling anything or offering or exposing anything for sale, use any stall or similar structure or any container or vehicle, kept or placed on the verge of a trunk or principal road or a lay-by on any such road or on unenclosed land within 15 metres of any part of any such road. Its presence must be likely to cause danger on the road or interrupt or likely to interrupt any user of the road and there is a defence if the person charged can prove that he took all reasonable precautions and exercised all due diligence to avoid commission of the offence. The sale or offer or exposure for sale of newspapers, the sale or offer or exposure for sale on a vehicle for itinerant trading with occupiers of premises, anything done at a market where rents, etc. are payable and street trading authorised under the Local Government (Miscellaneous Provisions) Act 1982 are exempt activities under the section.

APPLICATION OF THE SHOPS ACT 1950

The bulk of the Shops Act 1950 is concerned with the hours of closing, **9.03** Sunday trading and the employment of persons in "Shops."[12] There are some sections that deal with retail trading elsewhere than in shops but with regard to mobile shops, the applicability of the 1950 Act has been restricted somewhat by case law.

Hours of closing

Section 12 of the 1950 Act provides that it shall not be lawful in any **9.04** locality to carry on in any place not being a shop retail trade or business of any class at any time when it would be unlawful in that locality to keep a shop open for the purposes of retail trade or business of that class. Exempted from this stipulation are the sale of newspapers, cutting hair in a customer's house, and holding an auction in a private dwelling house. Also, with regard to any day other than the weekly half-holiday,

[11] (1979) 78 L.G.R. 248.
[12] See p. 55 for definition of "shop."

where a closing order is in force the prohibition in the section shall be subject to any exemptions and conditions contained in the order.

All the provisions applying to shops regarding weekly half closing, the general closing hours and closing orders made by local authorities in accordance with section 8 of the 1950 Act are extended by this section to retail trade and businesses carried on elsewhere than in shops. Case law has restricted the application of section 12 and other corresponding provisions in the Act to mobile shops in England and Wales but not in Scotland.

In *Kahn* v. *Newberry*,[13] the appellant had been convicted of selling apples, contrary to section 2 of the 1950 Act, from a costermonger's barrow which was stationary at the time in Great Windmill Street, London. Section 2 of the 1950 Act makes it unlawful for a shop to keep open for the serving of customers after certain hours, after 9 p.m. on the "late day" and 8 p.m. on any other. The appellant had been serving apples from his barrow in Great Windmill Street between 10.20 p.m. and 10.25 p.m.

The costermonger's barrow was obviously not a shop and the court had to decide whether section 12 of the 1950 Act applies, that is whether the barrow could be regarded as a "place" not being a shop where a retail trade or business was being carried on. In reversing the conviction the court considered *Eldorado Ice Cream Co. Ltd.* v. *Keating*[14] and *Stone* v. *Boreman*,[15] two English cases, and *Nixon* v. *Capaldi*[16] and *Cowlairs Co-Operative Society* v. *Glasgow Corporation*,[17] two Scottish cases.

The *Eldorado* Case was in regard to Sunday trading contravening the Shops (Sunday Trading Restrictions) Act 1936. Ice-Cream had been sold from a moveable box tricycle and it was contended by the prosecutions that as section 13 of the same Act provided that the provisions of the Act shall extend to any place where any retail trade or business is carried on as if that place was a shop, the tricycle from which the sales were made was "a place" where retail trade or business was being carried on. However, the court held that for section 13 to apply the "place" must be premises akin to a shop. The box tricycle was part of a moveable and peripatetic apparatus by means of which sales were enabled to be made at every sort of point in streets and roads over a large area—no fixed position, no fixed locality, no identifiable place.

There is a different interpretation in Scottish law. The *Nixon* Case was concerned with the selling of ice-cream from a mobile shop outside permitted hours under section 9 of the Shops Act 1912, and the court

---

[13] [1959] 2 Q.B. 1.
[14] [1938] 1 K.B. 715.
[15] [1959] 1 Q.B. 1.
[16] 1949 S.C.(J) 155.
[17] 1957 S.C.(J) 51.

distinguished *Eldorado* and held that the word "place" was not limited to places of a permanent or quasi-permanent nature with a definite location. In the *Cowlairs* case where one co-operative society was prosecuted under section 12 of the 1950 Act, there was no argument that a van (which was a mobile shop and towed to vacant land each morning and towed back to its garage at night) was a "place" from which a retail trade or business was carried on. This had already been decided in the *Nixon* Case and the society argued that there was sufficient permanence about the arrangement to constitute the van "a shop" and it was therefore not within the scope of section 12. This was rejected by the court. The fundamental idea in the definition of a shop was that trading must be carried on from premises.

The final case which the court considered was *Stone* v. *Boreham*,[18] an English case. This was a prosecution under the Sunday trading provisions of the 1950 Act in relation to a mobile shop which was stocked with a variety of goods, and sold on a Sunday a packet of tea to a customer standing on the roadway. Section 58 provides that the law regarding Sunday trading shall extend to any place where any retail trade or business is carried on as if that place were a shop. The prosecution argued that in the *Eldorado* Case the court was only concerned with the box tricycle and this could be distinguished as in the present case they were to consider the ground upon which the mobile shop stood as being the "place" from which the retail trade or business was being carried on. Lord Goddard said it would be really fanciful to distinguish the *Eldorado* Case on that ground and in his opinion the *Eldorado* decision was binding on the court. Devlin J. said:

> " . . . I think it is very undesirable that this court should strain to give meanings to a section of the Act which would be to produce a result incomprehensible to the traders who have to deal with it. The result is, I think, that it must now be taken as definitely decided in these courts that a mobile van is not a shop within the meaning of the Shops Act 1950, and if Parliament desire to make it so it must introduce new legislation for that purpose . . . "

The fact that the costermonger's barrow is something on wheels and could be pushed about meant that there was no relevant distinction between this case and *Stone* v. *Boreham*. The court therefore followed the English view and allowed the appeal.

Devlin J. however, stated in his judgment that this case is not the case where a stall is regularly erected on the same piece of land so that an aspect of some permanency is given to the site as one where goods are regularly sold by retail. It may be that such a place would be within the language of sections 12 and 58 of the Shops Act 1950.

---

[18] [1959] 1 Q.B. 1.

Sunday trading

9.05   Section 58 of the Shops Act 1950 extends the provision of the Act relating to Sunday trading (with some small exceptions)[19] to any place where any retail trade or business is carried on as if that place were a shop. The scope of this section, however, is restricted in its application to mobile shops by the cases referred to above.

This means that all kinds of goods can be sold on Sunday with impunity from a mobile shop or from a stall without the necessary degree of permanence to make it a place within section 58 of the 1950 Act.[20]

Employed persons

9.06   Section 33 of the Shops Act 1950 extends to a place not being a shop where any retail trade or business is carried on, the provisions of sections 24 and 27 to 32 relating to hours of employment, power to regulate, employment in spells, night employment and the keeping of records. Also, section 22 of the 1950 Act (Sunday employment) is extended by section 23 to any place where any retail trade or business is carried on but in this case it only applies to persons wholly or mainly employed in connection with retail trade or business.

It appears that the same restrictions as outlined above on the application of these sections to mobile shops also apply in respect of the provision relating to Sunday employment and the hours of employment, etc. Although it must be said that the issue has not been tested in the courts.

APPLICATION OF HEALTH AND SAFETY LEGISLATION

9.07   The Offices, Shops and Railway Premises Act 1963 does not apply to mobile shops. Section 1(3)(*a*) of the 1963 Act defines "shop premises" as meaning, *inter alia*, "a shop."[21] As a shop is a species of the genus

---

[19] The exceptions are: (a) those provisions of ss.52, 54 which relate to the approval by occupiers of shops of orders made under those sections; (b) the provisions of s.53(1), (2); and (c) the provision of s.57.

[20] See *Jarmain* v. *Wetherell* (1977) 121 S.J. 153, where a coin and stamp fair was held on a Sunday at hotel where stalls had been erected in the morning and were removed in the evening at the conclusion of the fair. An occupier of a stall who sold a stamp album was prescribed but it was held on appeal that the period during which the stall was open was so short that the stall lacked the degree of permanence necessary to make it a "place" for the purposes of the Act. Also, *Newark District Council* v. *E. & A. Market Promotions* (1978) 77 L.G.R. 6, where Sunday markets were held on successive Sundays on three different sites. The court held that whether the business carried on at a place had a sufficient degree of permanence justifying the place being described as "a place where a retail trade or buisness was carried on" was a question of fact and degree and that any trader who regularly or frequenlty rented a stall each Sunday at markets, wherever they were held, showed a sufficient continuity of the trade or business carried on by him to fall within the meaning of s.58 of the 1950 Act.

[21] See p. 111.

"shop premises" in this definition, it would appear there must be premises before anything is entitled to come under the definition of shop for the purposes of the 1963 Act. Therefore a mobile shop, stall or any structure that has not a sufficient degree of permanency to be regarded as premises does not come within the definition.

On the other hand, the general purpose of the Health and Safety at Work etc. Act 1974 is to secure the health, safety and welfare of persons at work and to protect members of the public from the risks to health and safety arising out of or in connection with activities of persons at work. The definition of a person at work in the 1974 Act embraces both an employee and self-employed persons. The provisions of the 1974 Act applies to an employee throughout the time when he is in course of his employment, but not otherwise, and to a self-employed person throughout such time as he devotes to his work as a self-employed person.

The general duties laid down in the 1974 Act cover those persons working in a mobile shop as well as other people likely to be affected by their activities. Although no prosecution may be brought under the Offices, Shops and Railway Premises Act 1963, the standards laid down in the 1963 Act can be used for assessing, where applicable, if a breach of duty has occurred.

SALE AND DELIVERY OF FOOD

The hygiene requirements in respect of the sale of food from mobile   **9.08** shops, stalls, markets and the delivery of food are contained in the Food Hygiene (Market Stalls and Delivery Vehicles) Regulations 1966[22] which are enforced by each local authority[23] in its district.

The Regulations were made by the Minister of Agriculture, Fisheries and Food and the Minister of Health, acting jointly under the powers laid down in sections 13 and 123 of the Food and Drugs Act 1955. The Regulations are basically sectionalised into:

(a) general requirements;
(b) requirements relating to food handlers and the handling of food;
(c) requirements relating to markets and stalls and delivery vehicles; and
(d) administrative provisions that deal with exemption.

The section on the requirements relating to food handlers and the handling of food is almost exactly the same as that contained in the Food

---

[22] S.I. 1966 No. 791.
[23] "local authority" in: (a) as respects the city of London, the common council; (b) as respects the Inner Temple and the Middle Temple, the respective overseers thereof; and (c) as respects any borough and any urban district.

Hygiene (General) Regulations 1970 which is outlined in the chapter on the preparation, sale and storage of food.[24] Included in this section is the regulation which states the temperature at which certain foods are to be kept. This particular regulation is under that part dealing with requirements relating to food premises in the Food Hygiene (General) Regulations 1970.[25] It is unnecessary to repeat these requirements here but it must be borne in mind that they apply to food handlers and the handling of food in mobile shops, stalls, markets and delivery vehicles. For the purposes of the Food Hygiene (Markets, Stalls and Delivery Vehicles) Regulations 1966, a "stall" is defined as including any stand, marquee, tent, mobile canteen, vehicle (whether moveable or not), vending machine, site or pitch, from which food is sold, not being food premises or a food room to which the 1970 Regulations apply.[26] A "delivery vehicle" means a vehicle used for the delivery of food in the course of a trade or business, but does not include any vehicle which, being used for the sale of food, falls within the definition of "stall." As with the General Regulations, these Regulations differentiate between "food" and "open food" in regulation 2.[27]

General requirements

9.09   If a stall is insanitary or so situated or constructed or in such a condition that the food is exposed to the risk of contamination,[28] no food business must be carried on at that stall. In addition, no delivery vehicles must be used in the course of a food business that are insanitary or so constructed, or in such a condition, that the food is exposed to the risk of contamination.[29]

The stall or delivery vehicle must be kept clean and in such good order, repair and condition as to enable it to be effectively cleaned. Any person or authority who provides a market or permits land to be used for the erection of any stall and in each case food is to be sold, stored, exposed or deposited for sale, must take account of the nature and packing of the food to be handled and must ensure the land, market premises or stall are clean and in proper repair. He must not permit the use of the land, stall or market premises if they are in such a condition as to expose the food to the risk of contamination or prevent the observance of clean practices in handling the food.[30]

---

[24] See p. 166.
[25] See p. 172.
[26] Food Hygiene (Market, Stalls and Delivery Vehicles) Regulations 1966 (S.I. 1966 No. 791), reg. 2.
[27] See p. 167.
[28] "Contamination" includes contamination by odour, and "contaminating" shall be construed accordingly (reg. 2.) As regards the meaning of "risk of contamination," see p. 167.
[29] Food Hygiene (Market, Stalls and Delivery Vehicles) Regulations 1966, reg. 4.
[30] *Ibid.* reg. 5.

Under regulation 6, articles or equipment with which food comes, or is liable to come, into contact must be kept clean and be so constructed as to enable them to be thoroughly cleaned and to prevent absorption of matter. Containers intended for keeping food whether or not they come into contact, or are liable to come into contact with food must, so far as is reasonably practicable, be protected and kept free from contamination. Regard must be had to the nature and packing of food and the use which is made of the article or equipment in determining whether any article or equipment is clean.

Requirements relating to markets and stalls and delivery vehicles

Every stall or delivery vehicle used in the carrying on of a food busi-   **9.10**
ness must bear conspicuously the name and address of the person carrying on the business and (except in the case of a vending machine) any other address at which it is normally kept or garaged, unless it bears a fleet number and is kept or garaged on that person's premises. There are restrictions on the storage of food with delivery vehicles and stalls when not in use. The food must be kept clean and free from contamination and the delivery vehicles and stalls themselves must not be stored in any place liable to render it insanitary or incapable of being properly cleaned. No person may sleep in stalls or delivery vehicles except where a driving compartment has a division separating it from the area where the food is carried.[31]

All sanitary conveniences situated in a market or used regularly in connection with a stall must be kept clean and in efficient order and the room containing the sanitary conveniences suitably and sufficiently ventilated and lighted. Food rooms where open food is handled or the equipment for use with open food is handled must not communicate directly with a room containing a sanitary convenience and no room which contains a sanitary convenience can be used as a food room. A "now wash hands" notice must be fixed in a prominent position.[32]

A supply of clean and wholesome water sufficient in quantity to enable the Regulations to be complied with must be provided and maintained in connection with every market or stall at or from which a food business is carried on and in every delivery vehicle. This is subject to an exemption certificate that may be issued under regulation 24, and it should be noted that there is no mention in this regulation about the water being a constant supply.[33]

Every stall where a food business is being carried on and every delivery vehicle used for the delivery of food must have a wash hand basin and in addition to this a sink for washing food and equipment used

---

[31] *Ibid.* reg. 13.
[32] *Ibid.* reg. 14.
[33] *Ibid.* reg. 15.

in the food business. The wash hand basin must be in a position conveniently accessible to persons engaged in handling the food, be suitable and sufficient, have an adequate supply of hot water at a suitably controlled temperature and soap or other suitable detergent, nail brush and adequate drying facilities must be provided. The wash hand basin must be kept clean and in efficient working order.[34]

Where the sink is used only for the washing of fish, fruit or vegetables or is only used for washing drinking vessels with a suitable bactericidal agent the provision of cold water is sufficient. Adequate supplies of soap or other suitable detergent and of clean cloths or other adequate and suitable drying facilities must be available and maintained for use at the sink.[35]

The provision of a sink and wash hand basin, etc., is subject to an exemption certificate which can be obtained from the local authority in certain circumstances,[36] and no sink is needed for washing soft ice-cream freezers if such facilities are provided at the premises from which the stall or delivery vehicle operates and the freezer is not dismantled in the stall or delivery vehicle except for washing at such premises.[37]

Every stall must have space suitable and sufficient for the separation of unsound food and for the disposal of waste and every stall and delivery vehicle must have first aid materials (including waterproof dressings) and antiseptics in a readily accessible position.[38]

Stalls must have suitable and sufficient lighting[39] and, unless in an enclosed and covered market, must be properly covered and screened at the sides and back to prevent mud, dust, etc. from depositing on any open food that is sold. The latter requirements do not apply to stalls that sell only raw vegetables and no other open food. Also, there is no need for screening if the stall is so designed, constructed and operated that the food in the stall is completely enclosed until it is taken from its enclosure to be sold or cooked for immediate consumption.[40]

No accumulation of refuse or filth, whether solid or liquid, is allowed in any stall or market or delivery vehicle used for the carrying of food unless it is unavoidable in carrying on the business.[41] Sufficient covered receptacles constructed of impervious materials must be provided at every stall for receiving waste trimmings and rubbish which must be kept apart from open food. This requirement does not apply if there is a contractual arrangement existing for the removal of refuse from the stall at sufficient intervals. All waste must be placed in the receptacles and

---

[34] *Ibid.* reg. 16.
[35] *Ibid.* reg. 18.
[36] See p. 188.
[37] Food Hygiene (Markets, Stalls and Delivery Vehicles) Regulations 1966, reg. 18.
[38] Food Hygiene (Markets, Stalls and Delivery Vehicles) Regulations 1966, reg. 17.
[39] *Ibid.* reg. 19.
[40] *Ibid.* reg. 21.
[41] *Ibid.* reg. 20.

these must be sited in in accordance with any reasonable direction given by the local authority.[42]

Transportation of meat

Regulation 23 stipulates the hygienic precautions necessary when **9.11** meat which is open food (other than unskinned rabbits or hares or unplucked game or poultry) is transported by vehicle. The Code of Practice No. 8, "Hygiene in the Meat Trades," (H.M.S.O.) should be consulted for guidance on complying with this regulation, although it must be remembered that the code has no statutory force. Also included in this code is advice on the hygienic requirements in mobile butchers' shops and stalls.

The 1966 Regulations provide that (except where meat is transported on isolated occasions in the course of the business of a carrier and the meat is adquately protected by suitable material from the risk of contamination) the floor of the vehicle must be impervious and fitted with removable duckboards and if the vehicle is an open vehicle it must be completely enclosed by canvas or other washable material. That part of the vehicle where the meat is placed must be completely enclosed and, so far as is reasonably practicable, the cover must not be allowed to come into contact with the meat.

In any case whenever meat is transported all receptacles, duckboards, slings, etc. that are likely to come into contact with the meat must be kept clean and in such good order, repair and condition as to enable them to be thoroughly cleaned.

All offal (other than skinned heads, scalded heads and offal that has not been detached from the carcase) transported by vehicle must be in separate receptacles from joints of meat. A sufficient number of covered receptacles must be provided. These receptacles must be constructed of impervious materials and kept clean and in such good order, repair and condition as to enable them to be thoroughly cleaned. There are exceptions to these requirements in that there is no need to provide or use separate receptacles for the transport of:

(a) packaged or wrapped frozen offal so long as such offal remains frozen hard;

(b) giblets of game or poultry which are carried in or attached to the carcase from which they have been removed;

(c) uncleaned tripe, uncleaned stomachs, uncleaned intestines or uncleaned feet in a vehicle in which no other meat other than offal of these descriptions is being carried; and

(d) unskinned or unscalded heads in a vehicle in which no meat other than offal of these descriptions or uncleaned feet is being carried.

---

[42] *Ibid.* reg. 22.

Exemptions

9.12   Regulation 24 contains a list of certain trades that are exempt from the requirement of providing a water supply, wash hand basin, first aid materials or a sink for washing food and equipment.

There is no need to provide any of the afore-mentioned facilities at a stall where the food business consists wholly of, (a) the preparation and supply of roast chestnuts or hot potatoes; and (b) the sale of covered food, where the person carrying on the food business has notified the appropriate local authority in writing that he is so engaged.

A bread van or any delivery vehicle used solely for the delivery of covered food is also exempt from providing these facilities so long as the vehicle operates from premises where the corresponding facilities are provided under the Food Hygiene (General) Regulations 1970 or other Regulations.[43] Any delivery vehicle, whether delivering covered food or not, is exempt from providing facilities for *washing food or equipment* so long as the vehicle operates from premises where the corresponding facilities are provided under the Food Hygiene (General) Regulations 1970 or other Regulations.[44]

Where a stall is used for a food business consisting wholly of that of a fruiterer, wholesaler of fruit, greengrocer or wholesaler of raw vegetables and the person carrying on the business has notified the local authority in writing that he is so engaged, there is no necessity for him to provide at the stall facilities for washing food and equipment, etc.

Schedule 2 to the 1966 Regulations sets out situations where a local authority may issue certificates of exemption. A person carrying on any food business from a stall in a market is entitled to a certificate of exemption in respect of providing water supply, a wash hand basin, first aid kit and a sink for washing food and equipment if these factilities are made available by any authority for that market. Also, if a person carrying on a food business from a stall can satisfy the local authority that these facilities are conveniently and readily available without payment he will also be entitled to a certificate of exemption. But he will not be entitled if he carries on one or more of the following types of trade:

(a) a catering business;

(b) the sale of bakery goods and flour confectionery prepared at the stall;

(c) the sale of fried fish and chips;

(d) the sale of sugar confectionery prepared at the stall; or

(e) the sale of ice-cream and ice lollies prepared at the stall and the sale of ice-cream which is open food.

A person will only be entitled to exemption from the requirement of

---

[43] Where the premises are occupied by a carrier of goods the relevant Regulations are the Docks and Carrier Regulations.

[44] *Ibid.*

providing facilities for washing food or equipment when carrying on a food business of the following class:

(a) a butcher or poulterer;
(b) a fishmonger;
(c) the sale of groceries and provisions which are open food;
(d) the sale of bakery goods and flour confectionery which are open food;
(e) the sale of cooked meat and butchers' small goods; and
(f) the sale of sugar confectionery which is open food.

Where the business is a combination of the two classes it is deemed to fall in the first class of business and where it is a combination of either class and some other then it is deemed to fall within the class specified in the Schedule to the Regulations.

Noise from Mobile Shops and Stalls in Streets

The legislation concerned with pollution by noise is contained in Part III **9.13** of the Control of Pollution Act 1974. A duty is placed on local authorities in inspect their districts from time to time to ascertain whether any action ought to be taken under this part of the Act.[45] The action that can be taken includes the service of a notice where the noise amounts to a nuisance,[46] control of noise on construction sites by prior consent or the service of a notice,[47] or by the designation of any part of the district as a noise abatement zone.[47a] Noise in streets is specifically dealt with under section 62 of the 1974 Act.

Noise in streets can be the most upsetting of experiences for most people and the difficulty in controlling it lies in the fact that it is usually transient in nature. Examples include noisy vehicles and motor cycles, loudspeakers, chimes on ice cream vans, pneumatic drills and transistor radios. This section is concerned with noise from mobile shops and stalls and the provisions of section 62 must be considered.

The operation of loudspeakers in a street between the hours of nine in the evening and eight the following morning for any purpose whatsoever is prohibited. At any other time, *i.e.* between 8 a.m. and 9 p.m., the operation of loudspeakers in a street for the purpose of advertising any entertainment, trade or business only is not allowed. Section 62 lists certain exceptions:

(a) for police, fire brigade or ambulance purposes, by a water authority in the exercise of any of its functions, or by a local authority within its area;

---

[45] Control of Pollution Act 1974, s.57.
[46] *Ibid.* s.58.
[47] *Ibid.* ss.60, 61.
[47a] *Ibid.* ss.63–67.

   (b) for communicating with persons on a vessel for the purpose of directing the movement of that or any other vessel;

   (c) if the loudspeaker forms part of a public telephone system;

   (d) if the loudspeaker:

      (i) is in or fixed to a vehicle; and

      (ii) is operated solely for the entertainment of or for communicating with the driver or a passenger of the vehicle or, where the loudspeaker is or forms part of the horn or similar warning instrument of the vehicle, solely for giving warning to other traffic; and

      (iii) is so operated as not to give reasonable cause for annoyance to persons in the vicinity;

   (e) otherwise than on a highway, by persons employed in connection with a transport undertaking used by the public in a case where the loudspeaker is operated solely for making announcements to passengers or prospective passengers or to other persons so employed;

   (f) by a travelling showman on land which is being used for the purposes of a pleasure fair;

   (g) in case of emergency.

In addition, where perishable food is being conveyed on a vehicle a loudspeaker can be operated between the hours of noon and seven on the same day to inform members of the public (otherwise than by means of words) that the commodity is on sale from the vehicle as long as it is so operated as not to give reasonable cause for annoyance to persons in the vicinity. Ice-cream vendors may, therefore, use their chimes quite legitimately between these hours as long as the use does not cause unreasonable annoyance.

"Street" is defined in section 62 as meaning a highway and any other road, footway, square or court which is for the time being open to the public. This definition was considered in *Tower Hamlets London Borough Council* v. *Creitzman*.[48] A stall in Petticoat Lane Market which was situated on the ground floor below a building which was supported by pillars and which was open on three sides was held by the court to be a "square" under this definition. The public had access to the market, therefore it was open to the public.

The control of noise in streets is rather limited under section 62 of the 1974 Act because although the use of loudspeakers is prohibited between 9 p.m. and 8 a.m., it is only prohibited between 8 a.m. and 9 p.m. for the purpose of advertising any entertainment, trade or business. The use of loudspeakers for any other purpose between these times is not caught by the section.

In *Tower Hamlets London Borough Council* v. *Manzoni and*

---

[48] (1984) 148 J.P. 630, D.C.

Walder,[49] the selling of pets in a market stall offended certain members of the public and they chanted slogans in the market using megaphones. This caused annoyance and nuisance and the London Borough of Tower Hamlets decided to take statutory action. Section 62 could not be used because the loudspeakers were not being used to advertise entertainment, trade or business, and therefore opted for the service of a notice under section 58 of the 1974 Act.

Section 58(1) states that where a local authority is satisfied that noise amounting to a nuisance exists or is likely to occur or recur in the area of a local authority, it shall serve a notice requiring the abatement of the nuisance, etc. Section 58(2) provides that the notice shall be served on the person responsible for the nuisance or if that person cannot be found or the nuisance has not yet occurred, on the owner or occupier of the premises from which the noise is emitted or would be emitted.

On appeal by way of case stated to the Divisional Court the respondents relied on the argument that for a notice to be legally effective the noise nuisance must be emitted from premises. They contended that section 58(1) must not be read in isolation. Section 58(2) allows service of the notice on either the person responsible for the noise or on the owner or occupier of the premises and in a situation where the noise has not occurred but is likely to occur the notice may only be served on the owner or occupier of premises. In addition, if section 59 is taken into consideration where a neighbouring occupier may make a complaint direct to a magistrates' court, this section provides that the magistrates can only act if they are "satisfied that the alleged nuisance exists, or . . . is likely to recur on the same premises."

The court accepted this argument and held that the appeal be dismissed and that section 58 of the 1974 Act only applied to noise emitted from premises and not from the highway.

This decision has left a big loophole in the statutory law relating to noise nuisance and restricts the enforcement powers of local authorities. Any noise from mobile shops and stalls that are situated in a street and outside the scope of section 62 of the 1974 Act cannot be controlled by any powers available in the Control of Pollution Act 1974.

STATUTORY CONTROL OF STREET TRADING

A district council has power under section 3 of the Local Government **9.14** (Miscellaneous Provisions) Act 1982 to resolve that Schedule 4 to the 1982 Act shall apply to their district. The Schedule refers to the methods of control over street[50] trading, and if such a resolution is made the

---

[49] (1984) 148 J.P. 123.

[50] "Street" includes: (a) any road, footway, beach or other area to which the public have access without payment; and (b) a service area as defined in (Sched. 4, para. 1) the Highways Act 1980, s.329.

Schedule shall come into force in the district council's area on such a day as may be specified in the resolution.

"Street trading" means the selling or exposing or offering for sale of any article (including a living thing) in a street. However, there are certain activities that are not regarded as street trading for the purposes of the Act:

(a) trading by a person acting as a pedlar under the authority of a pedlar's certificate granted under the Pedlar's Act 1871;

(b) anything done in a market or fair, the right to hold which was acquired by virtue of a grant (including a presumed grant) or acquired or established by virtue of an enactment or order;

(c) trading in a trunk road picnic area provided by the Secretary of State under the Highways Act 1980, section 112;

(d) trading as a news vendor;

(e) trading which:

   (i) is carried on at premises used as a petrol filling station;

   (ii) is carried on at premises used as a shop or in a street adjoining premises so used as a part of the business of the shop;

(f) selling things, or offering or exposing them for sale as a roundsman;

(g) the use for trading under Part VIIA of the Highways Act 1980 of an object or structure placed on, in or over a highway;

(h) the operation of facilities for recreation or refreshment under Part VIIA of the Highways Act 1980;

(i) the doing of anything authorised by Regulations made under the Police, Factories, etc. (Miscellaneous Provisions) Act 1916, section 5.

Most notable among these is the selling, offering or exposing of articles for sale as a roundsman and trading as a newsvendor as long as he only sells newspapers and periodicals and they are sold etc. without a stall or frame which does not exceed one metre in length or width or two metres high, occupy a ground area not exceeding 0.25 square metres or stand on a carriageway of a street.[51] Where a mobile shop calls on regular customers and occasionally sells to passers by or other customers it would be a question of fact in each case whether the number of customers who are not regular customers would place the operator outside the category of "roundsman." It is to be noted that the fact that a person is registered as a food hawker under section 19 of the 1982 Act does not entitle him to an exemption from control under this part of the Act.

The council may designate any street in their district under paragraph 2 of Schedule 4 as:

---

[51] Sched. 4, para. 1(4).

(a) a prohibited street which means that no street trading shall be carried on at all;

(b) a licensed street where street trading is prohibited without a licence granted by the council; and

(c) a consent street where street trading is prohibited without the consent of the council.

Although it does not state specifically in the Act, it appears that a licensed street would be applicable in cases where control is required in respect of trading carried on from stalls and a consent street where the control of mobile shops is required.

Street trading licences

Paragraph 3 of Schedule 4 lists the procedure for making an appli- **9.15** cation for a street trading licence. The applicant must be over 17 years old and it is the duty of the council to grant the licence unless they consider that it ought to be refused on one or more of the following grounds:

(a) that there is not enough space in the street for the applicant to engage in the trading in which he desires to engage without causing undue interference or inconvenience to persons using the street;

(b) that there are already enough traders trading in the street from shops or otherwise in the goods in which the applicant desires to trade;

(c) that the applicant desires to trade on fewer days than the minimum number specified in a resolution under paragraph 2(11) of the Schedule[52];

(d) that the applicant is unsuitable to hold the licence by reason of having been convicted of an offence or for any other reason;

(e) that the applicant has at any time been granted a street trading licence by the council and has persistently refused or neglected to pay fees due to them for it or charges due to them under paragraph 9(6) for services rendered by them to him in his capacity as licence holder;

(f) that the applicant has at any time been granted a street trading consent by the council and has persistently refused or neglected to pay fees due to them for it; and

(g) that the applicant has without reasonable excuse failed to avail himself to a reasonable extent of a previous street trading licence.

---

[52] Sched. 4, para. 2(11) states that where a street is designated as a licenced street, the council may resolve: (a) in the resolution which so designates the street; or (b) subject to sub-paragraph (12), by a separate resolution at any time; that a street trading licence is not to be granted to any person who proposes to trade in the street for a number of days in every week less than a number specified in the resolution.

From the wording of the paragraph it is clear that the above grounds are the only grounds upon which a council may refuse an application for a street trading licence. Where, however, a person is licensed or authorised to trade in a street under the provision of any local Act and the street then becomes a licensed street, he can only be refused a street trading licence under grounds (d) to (g) (above) inclusive.[53]

Paragraph 4 of the Schedule contains details about the contents of the licence and paragraph 5 specifies reasons for revocation of the licence. If the council are satisfied that there are grounds for refusing the licence the procedure laid out in paragraph 6 must be followed. The council must serve a notice on the applicant specifying the grounds upon which they intend refusing the licence and give the applicant an opportunity to make representations, within seven days of receiving the notice, to satisfy the council otherwise. If the licence is refused after hearing the representation, the applicant has a right of appeal under sub-paragraph (5) of paragraph 6 of Schedule 4 to the magistrates' court with a further right of appeal against the decision of that court to the Crown Court.

Street trading consents

9.16   The granting of consent to trade in a street designated as a consent street involves different considerations. Paragraph 7 of the Schedule states that an application for a street trading consent or the renewal of such a consent shall be made in writing to the district council and the council may grant a consent if they think fit, except that a consent may not be granted:

(a) to a person under the age of 17 years; or

(b) for any trading in a highway to which a control order under section 7 of the Local Government (Miscellaneous Provisions) Act 1976 is in force, other than trading to which the central order does not apply.

Whereas under the provision relating to the granting of street trading licences, the grounds upon which a council may refuse a licence are clearly specified, there are no grounds which the council need to take into account when considering whether to grant or to refuse a street trading consent. There is also no procedure laid down for the making by the applicant of any representations and no right of appeal.

Reasonable conditions may be attached to the consent under paragraph 7(4) and the holder of a street trading consent shall not trade from a van or other vehicle or from a stall or cart unless the council have included in the consent permission to do so. If the council have included such a permission they may make the consent subject to conditions as to where and at what times he may trade. The consent may be granted for any period not exceeding 12 months but may be revoked at any time.[54]

[53] Sched. 4, para. 3(8).
[54] Sched. 4, para. 7.

The only way an aggrieved applicant can reverse a decision of a council to refuse a consent or granting a consent subject to conditions is by application for an order of judicial review. Such an order will only be granted if either the council has failed to take account of relevant consideration, or has taken account of irrelevant considerations, or has acted perversely or contrary to natural justice.[55]

In *R.* v. *Bristol City Council, ex p. Pearce*,[56] it was held that a local authority was perfectly entitled, if it thought fit, to decide that there were too many mobile traders operating in the area generally or in a particular street, and if it did, to refuse some applications for consent and grant others but the exercise of their powers to grant or refuse a street trading consent was one to which the rules of natural justice applied in that the local authority had a duty to act fairly. The authority was, however, not obliged to hear oral representations or to give reasons for the refusal to grant a consent. Where they heard objections or representations from persons other than their own officers, officers of the police or county highway authority, the authority have a duty to tell the applicant the substance of the objections and allow him to comment on them.

Offences

A person is guilty of an offence if he engages in street trading in a prohibited street, in a licence street or consent street without being authorised to do so under Schedule 4, or contravenes any of the principal terms of a street trading licence. He will also be guilty of an offence if, being authorised by a street trading consent to trade in a consent street, trades in that street from a stationary van, cart, barrow or other vehicle or from a portable stall without receiving the necessary permission to do so or if he contravenes a condition attached to a consent regarding the place and times of trading.[57] **9.17**

Any person charged with any of these offences will have a defence if he is able to prove that he took all reasonable precautions and exercised all due diligence to avoid commission of the offence.[58]

A person is also guilty of an offence, in relation to street trading licences and consents, if he knowingly makes a false statement which is false in any material respect, or which he does not believe to be true. The above defence of "due diligence" is not applicable to this offence.[59]

A person guilty of any of the above offences is liable on summary conviction to a fine not exceeding level 3 on the standard scale.[60]

[55] *Council of Civil Service Unions* v. *Minister for the Civil Service* [1984] 3 W.L.R. 1174.
[56] (1984) 83 L.G.R. 711.
[57] Sched. 4, para. 10(1).
[58] *Ibid.* para. 10(2).
[59] *Ibid.* para. 10(3).
[60] *Ibid.* para. 10(4).

HOME OFFICE MODEL BYELAWS ON SKIN PIERCING

EAR PIERCING AND ELECTROLYSIS

1. Interpretation:
a. In these byelaws, unless the context otherwise requires:

"The Act" means the Local Government (Miscellaneous Provisions) Act 1982;

"Client" means any person undergoing treatment;

"Operator" means any person giving treatment;

"Premises" means any premises registered under Part VIII of the Act;

"Proprietor" means any person registered under Part VIII of the Act;

"Treatment" means any operation in effecting ear-piercing or electrolysis;

"The treatment area" means any part of premises where treatment is given to clients.

b. The Interpretation Act 1978 shall apply for the interpretation of these byelaws as it applies for the interpretation of an Act of Parliament.

2. For the purpose of securing the cleanliness of premises and fittings therein a proprietor shall ensure that:

a. All internal walls, doors, windows, partitions, floors and floor coverings and ceilings in any part of the premises used by clients and operators are kept clean and in such good repair as to enable them to be cleaned effectively;

b. All waste material and other litter, arising from the treatment, is placed in suitable covered receptacles, which are washable and leakproof, or use a leakproof liner bag. The receptacles shall be emptied, or the bags changed, at least once every working day, or more frequently as necessary and the material disposed of safely. Where liners are not used, the receptacles shall then be cleaned;

c. All needles used in treatment are placed after use in separate covered and leakproof washable boxes, or disposable needle boxes designed for the purpose. When washable boxes are used they shall be emptied at least once very working day or more frequently as necessary and the contents disposed of safely or sterilised for re-use, as appropriate. The box shall then be cleaned. Where needle boxes are used they shall be disposed of safely at suitable intervals;

d. All furniture and fittings in the treatment area are kept clean and in such good repair as to enable them to be cleaned effectively;

e. All tables, couches and seats used by clients in the treatment area and any surface on which the items specified in 3b below are placed immediately prior to treatment have a smooth impervious surface which is wiped down regularly with a suitable disinfectant;

f. Where tables or couches are used, they shall be covered by a disposable paper sheet which shall be changed for each client;

g. A notice or notices reading "No Smoking" are prominently displayed within the treatment area.

3. For the purpose of securing the cleansing and so far as is appropriate, the sterilisation of instruments, towels, materials and equipment used in connection with the treatment:

a. An operator shall ensure that, before use in connection with treatment, any gown, wrap or other protective clothing, paper or other covering, cloth or other such articles used in the treatment:

    i. is clean and in good repair and so far as is appropriate, is sterile;

    ii. has not previously been used in connection with any other client unless it consists of a material which can be and has been adequately cleaned and so far as is appropriate sterilised;

b. An operator shall ensure that any needle, metal instrument, or other item of equipment used in treatment or for handling instruments and needles used in treatment, is in a sterile condition and kept sterile until it is used;

c. A proprietor shall provide:

    i. adequate facilities and equipment for the purpose of sterilisation (unless pre-sterilised items are used) and of cleansing, as required in pursuance of these byelaws;

    ii. sufficient and safe gas points and/or electrical socket outlets to enable compliance with these byelaws;

    iii. an adequate constant supply of clean hot and cold water readily available at all times on the premises;

    iv. adequate storage for all items mentioned in byelaw 3a and b above, so that those items shall be properly stored in a clean and suitable place so as to avoid, as far as possible, the risk of contamination.

4. For the purpose of securing the cleanliness of operators:

a. An operator whilst giving treatment shall ensure that:

    i. his hands are clean;

    ii. he is wearing clean clothing;

    iii. he keeps any open boil, sore, cut or open wound on an exposed part of his body effectively covered by an impermeable dressing;

    iv. he does not smoke or consume food or drink;

b. A proprietor shall provide;

    i. suitable and sufficient washing facilities for the use of operators, such facilities to have hot and cold water, sanitising soap or detergent and a nail brush;

    ii. suitable and sufficient sanitary accommodation for operators.

NOTE—The following does not form part of the byelaws

A. Proprietors shall take all reasonable steps to ensure compliance with these byelaws by persons working on the premises. Section 16(9) of the Act lays down that a registered person shall cause to be prominently displayed on the premises a copy of these byelaws and a copy of any certificate of registration issued to him under Part VIII of the Act.

B. Section 16(1) and (2) of the Local Government (Miscellaneous Provisions) Act 1982 provides that any person who offends against any of these byelaws shall be guilty of an offence and liable on summary conviction to a fine not exceeding £200. If the convicted person is registered under Part VIII of the Act, the court may, instead of or in addition to imposing a fine, order the suspension or cancellation of his registration and of the registration of the premises in which the offence was committed if such premises are occupied by the person so convicted. Section 16(11) of the Act provides that it shall be a defence for the person charged to prove that he took all reasonable precautions and exercised all due diligence to avoid the commission of the offence.

C. Nothing in these byelaws shall extend to the carrying on of the business of ear piercing or of electrolysis as the case may be by or under the supervision of a person who is registered as a medical practitioner or to premises on which any such business is carried on by or under the supervision of such a person.

TATTOOING

1. Interpretation:
a. In these byelaws, unless the context otherwise requires:

"The Act" means the Local Government (Miscellaneous Provisions) Act 1982;
"Client" means any person undergoing treatment;
"Operator" means any person giving treatment;
"Premises" means any premises registered under Part VIII of the Act;
"Proprietor" means any person registered under Part VIII of the Act;
"Treatment" means any operation in effecting tattooing;
"The treatment area" means any part of premises where treatment is given to clients.

b. The Interpretation Act 1978 shall apply for the interpretation of these byelaws as it applies for the interpretation of an Act of Parliament.

2. For the purpose of securing the cleanliness of premises and fittings therein a proprietor shall ensure that:
a. All internal walls, doors, windows, partitions, floors and floor coverings, and ceilings are kept clean and in such good repair as to enable them to be cleaned effectively;

b. The treatment area is used solely for giving treatment;

c. The floor of the treatment area is provided with a smooth impervious surface;

d. All waste material, and other litter, arising from the treatment, is placed in suitable covered receptacles, which are washable and leakproof, or use a leakproof liner bag. The receptacles shall be emptied, or the bags changed, at least once every working day, or more frequently as necessary, and the material disposed of safely. Where liners are not used, the receptacles shall then be cleaned;

e. All needles used in treatment are placed after use in separate covered and leakproof washable boxes, or disposable needle boxes designed for the purpose. Where washable boxes are used they shall be emptied at least once every working day or more frequently as necessary, and the contents disposed of safely or sterilised for re-use, as appropriate. The box shall then be cleaned. Where needle boxes are used they shall be disposed of safely at suitable intervals;

f. All furniture and fittings in the premises area are kept clean and in such good repair as to enable them to be cleaned effectively;

g. All tables, couches and seats used by clients in the treatment area, and any surface on which the items specified in 3b below are placed immediately prior to treatment, have a smooth impervious surface which is wiped down with a suitable disinfectant between the treatment of different clients, and thoroughly cleaned at the end of each working day;

h. Where tables or couches are used they shall be covered by a disposable paper sheet which shall be changed for each client.

i. A notice or notices reading "No Smoking" are prominently displayed within the treatment area.

3. For the purpose of securing the cleaning and, so far as is appropriate, the sterilisation of instruments, materials and equipment used in connection with the treatment:

a. An operator shall ensure that, before use in connection with treatment, any gown, wrap or other protective clothing, paper or other covering, towel, cloth or other such articles used in the treatment:

    i. is clean and in good repair, and, so far as is appropriate, is sterile;

    ii. has not previously been used in connection with any other client unless it consists of a material which can be and has been adequately cleaned and, so far as is appropriate, sterilised;

b. An operator shall ensure that:

    i. any needle, metal instrument, or other item of equipment, used in treatment or for handling instruments and needles used in treatment, is in a sterile condition and kept sterile until it is used;

    ii. All dyes used for tattooing are bacteriologically clean and inert;

    iii. the containers used to hold the dyes for each customer are either disposed of at the end of each session of treatments, or are sterilised before re-use;

c. A proprietor shall provide:

    i. adequate facilities and equipment for the purpose of sterilisation (unless pre-sterilised items are used) and of cleansing, as required in pursuance of these byelaws;

    ii. sufficient and safe gas points and/or electrical socket outlets to enable compliance with these byelaws;

    iii. an adequate constant supply of clean hot and cold water readily available at all times on the premises;

    iv. adequate storage for all items mentioned in byelaw 3a and b above, so that those items shall be properly stored in a clean and suitable place so as to avoid, as far as possible, the risk of contamination.

4. For the purpose of securing the cleanliness of operators:

a. An operator whilst giving treatment shall ensure that:

    i. his hands and nails are clean, and nails kept short;

    ii. he is wearing clean and washable clothing, or alternatively a disposable covering that has not previously been used in connection with any other client;

    iii. he keeps any open boil, sore, cut or open wound on an exposed part of his body effectively covered by an impermeable dressing;

    iv. he does not smoke or consume food or drink;

b. A proprietor shall provide:

    i. suitable and sufficient washing facilities for the sole use of operators, such facilities to have hot and cold water, sanitising soap or detergent, and a nail brush;

  ii. suitable and sufficient sanitary accommodation for operators.

NOTE—The following does not form part of the byelaws

A. A proprietor shall take all reasonable steps to ensure compliance with these byelaws by persons working on the premises. Section 16(9) of the Act lays down that a registered person shall cause to be prominently displayed on the premises a copy of these byelaws and a copy of any certificate of registration issued to him under Part VIII of the Act.

B. Section 16(1) and (2) of the Local Government (Miscellaneous Provisions) Act 1982 provides that any person who offends against any of these byelaws shall be guilty of an offence and liable on summary conviction to a fine not exceeding £200. If the convicted person is registered under Part VIII of the Act, the court may, instead of or in addition to imposing a fine, order the suspension or cancellation of his registration, and of the registration of the premises in which the offence was committed if such premises are occupied by the person so convicted. Section 16(11) of the Act provides that it shall be a defence for the person charged to prove that he took all reasonable precautions and exercised all due diligence to avoid the commission of the offence.

C. Nothing in these byelaws shall extend to the carrying on of the business of tattooing by or under the supervision of a person who is registered as a medical practitioner or to premises on which any such business is carried on by or under the supervision of such a person.

ACUPUNCTURE

1. Interpretation:
  a. In these byelaws, unless the context otherwise requires:

    "The Act" means the Local Government (Miscellaneous Provisions) Act 1982;
    "Client" means any person undergoing treatment;
    "Operator" means any person giving treatment;
    "Premises" means any premises registered under Part VIII of the Act;
    "Proprietor" means any person registered under Part VIII of the Act;
    "Treatment" means any operation in the practice of acupuncture;
    "The treatment area" means any part of premises where treatment is given to clients.

  b. The Interpretation Act 1978 shall apply for the interpretation of these bye-laws as it applies for the interpretation of an Act of Parliament.

2. For the purpose of securing the cleanliness of premises and fittings therein a proprietor shall ensure that:
  a. All internal walls, doors, windows, partitions, floors and floor coverings, and ceilings are kept clean and in such good repair as to enable them to be cleaned effectively;

  b. The treatment area is used solely for giving treatment;

  c. All waste material, and other litter, arising from the treatment, is placed in suitable covered receptacles, which are washable and leakproof, or use a leak-proof liner bag. The receptacles shall be emptied, or the bags changed, at least

201

once every working day, or more frequently as necessary, and the material disposed of safely. Where liners are not used, the receptacles shall then be cleaned;

d. All needles used in treatment are placed after use in separate covered and leakproof washable boxes, or disposable needle boxes designed for the purpose. Where washable boxes are used they shall be emptied at least once every working day or more frequently as necessary, and the contents disposed of safely or sterilised for re-use, as appropriate. The box shall then be cleaned. Where needle boxes are used they shall be disposed of safely at suitable intervals;

e. All furniture and fittings in the premises are kept clean and in such good repair as to enable them to be cleaned effectively;

f. All tables, couches and seats used by clients in the treatment area, and any surface on which the items specified in 3b below are placed immediately prior to treatment, have a smooth impervious surface which is wiped down at least daily with a suitable disinfectant;

g. Where tables or couches are used they shall be covered by a disposable paper sheet which shall be changed for each client;

h. A notice or notices reading "No Smoking" are prominently displayed within the treatment area.

3. For the purpose of securing the cleansing and, so far as is appropriate, the sterilisation of instruments, materials and equipment used in connection with the treatment:

a. An operator shall ensure that, before use in connection with treatment, any gown, wrap or other protective clothing, paper or other covering, towel, cloth or other such articles used in the treatment:

    i. is clean and in good repair, and, so far as is appropriate, is sterile;
    ii. has not previously been used in connection with any other client unless it consists of a material which can be and has been adequately cleaned and, so far as is appropriate, sterilised;

b. An operator shall ensure that any needle, metal instrument, or other item of equipment, used in treatment or for handling instruments and needles used in treatment, is in a sterile condition and kept sterile until it is used;

c. A proprietor shall provide:

    i. adequate facilities and equipment for the purpose of sterilisation (unless pre-sterilised items are used) and of cleansing, as required in pursuance of these byelaws;
    ii. sufficient and safe gas points and/or electrical socket outlets to enable compliance with these byelaws;
    iii. an adequate constant supply of clean hot and cold water readily available at all times on the premises;
    iv. adequate storage for all items mentioned in byelaw 3a and b above, so that those items shall be properly stored in a clean and suitable place so as to avoid, as far as possible, the risk of contamination.

4. For the purpose of securing the cleanliness of operators:
a. An operator whilst giving treatment shall ensure that:

    i. his hands and nails are clean and nails kept short;
    ii. he is wearing clean and washable clothing, or alternatively a disposable

covering that has not previously been used in connection with any other client;

iii. he keeps any open boil, sore, cut or open wound on an exposed part of his body effectively covered by an impermeable dressing;

iv. he does not smoke or consume food or drink;

b. A proprietor shall provide:

i. suitable and sufficient washing facilities for the sole use of operators, such facilities to have hot and cold water, sanitising soap or detergent, and a nail brush;

ii. suitable and sufficient sanitary accommodation for operators.

NOTE—The following does not form part of the byelaws

A. Proprietors shall take all reasonable steps to ensure compliance with these byelaws by persons working on the premises. Section 16(9) of the Act lays down that a registered person shall cause to be prominently displayed on the premises a copy of these byelaws and a copy of any certificate of registration issued to him under Part VIII of the Act.

B. Section 16(1) and (2) of the Local Government (Miscellaneous Provisions) Act 1982 provides that any person who offends against any of these byelaws shall be guilty of an offence and liable on summary conviction to a fine not exceeding £200. If the convicted person is registered under Part VIII of the Act, the court may, instead of or in addition to imposing a fine, order the suspension or cancellation of his registration, and of the registration of the premises in which the offence was committed if such premises are occupied by the person so convicted. Section 16(11) of the Act provides that it shall be a defence for the person charged to prove that he took all reasonable precautions and exercised all due diligence to avoid the commission of the offence.

C. Nothing in these byelaws shall extend to the practice of acupuncture by or under the supervision of a person who is registered as a medical practitioner or a dentist or to premises on which the practice of acupuncture is carried on by or under the supervision of such a person.

NAMES AND ADDRESSES OF ACUPUNCTURE ORGANISATIONS

British Acupuncture Association and Register
34 Alderney Street,
London SW1V 4EU

Register of Oriental Medicine,
16 Cottenham Park Road,
Wimbledon,
London SW20

Traditional Acupuncture Society,
115 Loxley Road,
Stratford-on-Avon,
Warwickshire CV37 7DS

SHOPS ACT 1950, SCHEDULE 5

TRANSACTIONS FOR THE PURPOSES OF WHICH A SHOP MAY BE OPEN IN
ENGLAND AND WALES FOR THE SERVING OF CUSTOMERS ON SUNDAY

1. The sale of—

(a) intoxicating liquors;

(b) meals or refreshments whether or not for consumption at the shop at
which they are sold, but not including the sale of fried fish and chips at a
fried fish and chip shop;

(c) newly cooked provisions and cooked or partly cooked tripe;

(d) table waters, sweets, chocolates, sugar confectionery and ice-cream
(including wafers and edible containers);

(e) flowers, fruit and vegetables (including mushrooms) other than tinned
or bottled fruit or vegetables;

(f) milk and cream, not including tinned or dried milk or cream, but including clotted cream whether sold in tins or otherwise;

(g) medicines and medical and surgical appliances—
   (i) at any premises registered under section twelve of the Pharmacy
   and Poisons Act, 1933; or
   (ii) by any person who has entered into a contract with an Executive
   Council for the supply of drugs and appliances;

(h) aircraft, motor, or cycle supplies or accessories;

(i) tobacco and smokers' requisites;

(j) newspapers, periodicals and magazines;

(k) books and stationery from the bookstalls of such terminal and main line
railway or omnibus stations, or at such aerodromes as may be approved
by the Secretary of State;

(l) guide books, postcards, photographs, reproductions, photographic
films and plates, and souvenirs—
   (i) at any gallery, museum, garden, park or ancient monument under
   the control of a public authority or university; or
   (ii) at any other gallery or museum, or any place of natural beauty or
   historic interest, or any zoological, botanical or horticultural gar-
   dens, or aquarium, if and to the extent that the local authority cer-
   tify that such sale is desirable in the interests of the public; or
   (iii) in any passenger vessel within the meaning of Part II of the
   Finance (1909–1910) Act, 1910, while engaged in carrying passengers;

(m) photographs for passports;

(n) requisites for any game or sport at any premises or place where that
game or sport is played or carried on;

(o) fodder for horses, mules, ponies and donkeys at any farm, stables, hotel
or inn.

2. The transaction of—

(a) post office business;

(b) the business carried on by a funeral undertaker.

REPORTING OF INJURIES, DISEASES AND DANGEROUS OCCURRENCES REGULATIONS 1985
(S.I. 1985 No. 2023)

REGULATION 2(1)

. . . "Responsible person" means—

(*a*) in the case of—
    (i) a mine, the manager of that mine;
    (ii) a quarry, the owner of that quarry;
    (iii) a closed tip, the owner of the mine or quarry with which that tip is associated;
    (iv) a pipe-line within the meaning of section 65 of the Pipe-lines Act 1962, the owner of that pipe-line;
    (v) a vehicle to which paragraph 13 or 14 of Schedule 1, Part I applies, the operator of the vehicle;

(*b*) where sub-paragraph (*a*) above does not apply, in the case of any event (other than a dangerous occurrence) reportable under Regulation 3, or any case of disease reportable under Regulation 5, involving—
    (i) an employee at work (including any person who is to be treated as an employee by virtue of any relevant statutory provision), his employer;
    (ii) a person (excluding one who is to be treated as an employee by virtue of any relevant statutory provision) undergoing training for employment, the person whose undertaking makes the immediate provision of that training;

(*c*) in any other case, the person for the time being having control of the premises in connection with the carrying on by him of any trade, business or other undertaking (whether for profit or not) at which, or in connection with the work at which, the accident or dangerous occurrence reportable under Regulation 3, or case of disease reportable under Regulation 5, happened; . . .

REPORTING OF INJURIES, DISEASES AND DANGEROUS OCCURRENCES REGULATION 1985
(S.I. 1985 No. 2023)

Regulation 3

Notification and reporting of injuries and dangerous occurrences

3.—(1) Subject to Regultion 10, where any person as a result of an accident arising out of or in connection with work, dies or suffers any of the injuries or conditions specified in paragraph (2) or where there is a dangerous occurrence, the responsible person shall—

(a) forthwith notify the enforcing authority thereof by the quickest practicable means; and

(b) within 7 days send a report thereof to the enforcing authority on a form approved for the purposes of this Regulation.

(2) The injuries and conditions referred to in paragraph (1) are—

(a) fracture of the skull, spine or pelvis;

(b) fracture of any bone—
   (i) in the arm or wrist, but not a bone in the hand; or
   (ii) in the leg or ankle, but not a bone in the foot;

(c) amputation of—
   (i) a hand or foot; or
   (ii) a finger, thumb or toe, or any part thereof if the joint or bone is completely severed;

(d) the loss of sight of an eye, a penetrating injury to an eye, or a chemical or hot metal burn to an eye;

(e) either injury (including burns) requiring immediate medical treatment, or loss of consciousness, resulting in either case from an electric shock from any electrical circuit or equipment, whether or not due to direct contact;

(f) loss of consciousness resulting from lack of oxygen;

(g) decompression sickness (unless suffered during an operation to which the Diving Operations at Work Regulations 1981 apply) requiring immediate medical treatment;

(h) either acute illness requiring medical treatment, or loss of consciousness, resulting in either case from the absorption of any substance by inhalation, ingestion or through the skin;

(i) acute illness requiring medical treatment where there is reason to believe that this resulted from exposure to a pathogen or infected material;

(j) any other injury which results in the person injured being admitted immediately into hospital for more than 24 hours.

(3) Subject to Regulation 10, where a person at work is incapacitated for work of a kind which he might reasonably be expected to do, either under his contract of employment, or, if there is no such contract, in the normal course of his work, for more than 3 consecutive days (excluding the day of the accident but including any days which would not have been working days) because of an injury

(other than one specified in paragraph (2)) resulting from an accident at work the responsible person shall within 7 days of the accident send a report thereof to the enforcing authority on a form approved for the purposes of this Regulation.

REPORTING OF INJURIES, DISEASES AND DANGEROUS OCCURRENCES REGULATIONS 1985
(S.I. 1985 No. 2023)

SCHEDULE 1

Regulation 2(1)

DANGEROUS OCCURRENCES

PART I—GENERAL

Lifting machinery etc.
1. The collapse of, the overturning of, or the failure of any load bearing part of—

   (a) any lift, hoist, crane, derrick or mobile powered access platform, but not any winch, teagle, pulley block, gin wheel, transporter or runway;
   (b) any excavator; or
   (c) any pile driving frame or rig having an overall height, when operating, of more than 7 metres.

Passenger carrying amusement device
2. The following incidents at a fun fair (whether or not a travelling fun fair) while the relevant device is in use or under test—

   (a) the collapse of, or the failure of any load bearing part of, any amusement device provided as part of the fun fair which is designed to allow passengers to move or ride on it or inside it; or
   (b) the failure of any safety arrangement connected with such a device, which is designed to restrain or support passengers.

Pressure vessels
3. Explosion, collapse or bursting of any closed vessel, including a boiler or boiler tube, in which the internal pressure was above or below atmospheric pressure, which might have been liable to cause the death of, or any of the injuries or conditions covered by Regulation 3(2) to, any person, or which resulted in the stoppage of the plant involved for more than 24 hours.

Electrical short circuit
4. Electrical short circuit or overload attended by fire or explosion which resulted in the stoppage of the plant involved for more than 24 hours and which, taking into account the circumstances of the occurrence, might have been liable to cause the death of, or any of the injuries or conditions covered by Regulation 3(2) to, any person.

Explosion or fire
5. An explosion or fire occurring in any plant or place which resulted in the stoppage of that plant or suspension of normal work in that place for more than

24 hours, where such explosion or fire was due to the ignition of process materials, their by-products (including waste) or finished products.

Escape of flammable substances

6. The sudden, uncontrollable release of one tonne or more of highly flammable liquid, within the meaning of Regulation 2(2) of the Highly Flammable Liquids and Liquefied Petroleum Gases Regulations 1972, flammable gas or flammable liquid above its boiling point from any system or plant or pipe-line.

Collapse of scaffolding

7. A collapse or partial collapse of any scaffold which is more than 5 metres high which results in a substantial part of the scaffold falling or over-turning; and where the scaffold is slung or suspended, a collapse or partial collapse of the suspension arrangements (including any outrigger) which causes a working platform or cradle to fall more than 5 metres.

Collapse of building or structure

8. Any unintended collapse or partial collapse of—

(*a*) any building or structure under construction, reconstruction, alteration or demolition, or of any false-work, involving a fall of more than 5 tonnes of material; or

(*b*) any floor or wall of any building being used as a place of work, not being a building under construction, reconstruction, alteration or demolition.

Escape of a substance or pathogen

9. The uncontrolled or accidental release or the escape of any substance or pathogen from any apparatus, equipment, pipework, pipe-line, process plant, storage vessel, tank, in-works conveyance tanker, land-fill site, or exploratory land drilling site, which having regard to the nature of the substance or pathogen and the extent and location of the release or escape, might have been liable to cause the death of, any of the injuries or conditions covered by Regulation 3(2) to, or other damage to the health of, any person.

Explosives

10. Any ignition or explosives, where the ignition or explosion was not intentional.

Freight containers

11. Failure of any freight container or failure of any load bearing part thereof while it is being raised, lowered or suspended and in this paragraph "freight container" means a container within the meaning of Regulation 2(1) of The Freight Containers (Safety Convention) Regulations 1984.

Pipe-lines

12. Either of the following incidents in relation to a pipe-line as defined by section 65 of the Pipe-lines Act 1962—

(*a*) the bursting, explosion or collapse of a pipe-line or any part thereof; or

(*b*) the unintentional ignition of anything in a pipe-line, or of anything which immediately before it was ignited was in a pipe-line.

Conveyance of dangerous substances by road

13.—(1) Any incident—

(a) in which a road tanker or tank container used for conveying a dangerous substance by road—

    (i) overturns; or

    (ii) suffers serious damage to the tank in which the dangerous substance is being conveyed; or

(b) in which there is, in relation to such a road tanker or tank container—

    (i) an uncontrolled release or escape of the dangerous substance being conveyed; or

    (ii) a fire which involves the dangerous substance being conveyed.

(2) In this paragraph, "conveyance by road," "road tanker," "tank container" and "dangerous substance" has in each case the meaning assigned to it by Regulation 2(1) of the Dangerous Substances (Conveyance by Road in Road Tankers and Tank Containers) Regulations 1981.

14.—(1) Any incident involving a vehicle conveying a dangerous substance by road, other than a vehicle to which paragraph 13 applies, where there is—

(a) an uncontrolled release or escape from any package or container of the dangerous substance being conveyed; or

(b) a fire which involves the dangerous substance being conveyed.

(2) In this paragraph "dangerous substance" means a substance which is dangerous for conveyance as defined in Regulation 2(1) of the Classification, Packaging and Labelling of Dangerous Substances Regulations 1984.

Breathing apparatus

15. Any incident where breathing apparatus, while being used to enable the wearer to breathe independently of the surrounding environment, malfunctions in such a way as to be likely either to deprive the wearer of oxygen or, in the case of use in a contaminated atmosphere, to expose the wearer to the contaminant, to the extent in either case of posing a danger to his health, except that this paragraph shall not apply to such apparatus while it is being—

(a) used in a mine; or

(b) maintained or tested.

Overhead electric lines

16. Any incident in which plant or equipment either comes into contact with an uninsulated overhead electric line in which the voltage exceeds 200 volts, or causes an electrical discharge from such an electric line by coming into close proximity to it, unless in either case the incident was intentional.

Locomotives

17. Any case of an accidental collision between a locomotive or a train an any other vehicle at a factory or at dock premises which might have been liable to cause the death of, or any of the injuries or conditions covered by Regulation 3(2) to, any person.

PRESCRIBED DANGEROUS MACHINES ORDER 1964
(S.I. 1964 No. 971)

Dated June 25, 1964, made by the Minister of Labour by virtue of the powers conferred on him by section 19 of the Offices, Shops and Railway Premises Act 1963 (hereafter in this Order referred as as "the Act") and of all other powers enabling him in that behalf.

1.—(1) This Order may be cited as the Prescribed Dangerous Machines Order 1964 and shall come into operation on 1st August 1964.

(2) The Interpretation Act 1889 shall apply to the interpretation of this Order as it applies to the interpretation of an Act of Parliament.

2. The machines specified in the Schedule to this Order are hereby prescribed as being machines which in the opinion of the Minister of Labour are of such a dangerous character that persons ought not to work at them unless the requirements of section 19(1) of the Act are complied with.

SCHEDULE

Article 2

PART I

The following machines when worked with the aid of mechanical power—

1. Worm-type mincing machines.
2. Rotary knife bowl-type chopping machines.
3. Dough brakes.
4. Dough mixers.
5. Food mixing machines when used with attachments for mincing, slicing, chipping or any other cutting operation, or for crumbing.
6. Pie and tart making machines.
7. Vegetable slicing machines.
8. Wrapping and packing machines.
9. Garment presses.
10. Opening or teasing machines used for upholstery or bedding work.
11. Corner staying machines.
12. Loose knife punching machines.
13. Wire stitching machines.
14. Machines of any type equipped with a circular saw blade.
15. Machines of any type equipped with a saw in the form of a continuous band or strip.
16. Planing machines, vertical spindle moulding machines and routing machines, being, in any case, machines used for cutting wood, wood products, fibre-board, plastic or similar material.

Part II

The following machines whether worked with the aid of mechanical power or not—

17. Circular knife slicing machines used for cutting bacon and other foods (whether similar to bacon or not).
18. Potato chipping machines.
19. Platen printing machines, including such machines when used for cutting and creasing.
20. Guillotine machines.

STORAGE OF LIQUID PETROLEUM GAS

Extract from Guidance Note CS 8 from the Health and Safety Executive

Small Scale Storage and Display of LPG at Retail Premises

Chemical Safety Series 8 (June 1985)
These Guidance Notes are published under five subject headings: Medical, Environmental Hygiene, Chemical Safety, Plant and Machinery and General.

Introduction
1. Over the past few years there has been a considerable increase in the number of retail premises selling cylinders and cartridges of liquefied petroleum gas (LPG). In many cases there have been difficulties in complying with the standards set out in paragraphs 61 and 62 of Health and Safety Executive (HSE) Guidance Note CS 4 (Feb 1981). This new guidance note gives supplementary guidance relating solely to the small scale storage and display of LPG at retail premises.

Scope
2. This guidance note shows how the general duties under the Health and Safety at Work, etc., Act 1974 may be met at retail premises where LPG is sold. The note is not exhaustive, however, and there may be other ways of meeting these duties. Advice may be obtained from HSE Area Offices.
3. The standards given in this guidance note are appropriate to the storage and display of more than 15 kg, but less than 400 kg, of LPG at retail premises, provided the LPG is kept in containers with individual capacities of not more than 20 kg. It replaces the advice in paragraphs 61 and 62 of HSE Guidance Note CS 4 (Feb 1981), which is to be revised.
4. Quantities of LPG in excess of 400 kg, or containers of more than 20 kg capacity, should be kept only on premises that comply fully with the recommendations in Guidance Note CS 4. For the purposes of calculating the total quantity of LPG present on the premises, all containers should be regarded as full, irrespective of the quantity of LPG actually in them.
5. A cylinder which has held LPG and is nominally empty will still contain LPG vapour. If the valve is left open, air will diffuse into the cylinder and may form a dangerous mixture. Only dummy containers and containers that have been subjected to appropriate gas-freeing procedures and are clearly marked gas free can be regarded as safe.
6. This guidance note does not apply to the storage of aerosol products in which LPG is used as a propellant, nor to cylinders fitted to a vehicle to provide fuel, nor to aluminium cylinders.
7. The storage of LPG may be subject to additional requirements:

  (a) if the premises are subject to the Factories Act 1961, The Highly Flammable Liquids and Liquefied Petroleum Gases Regulations 1972 (Statutory Instrument 1972 No. 917) will apply;

(b) although LPG itself is not subject to the Petroleum (Consolidation) Act 1928 the Petroleum Licensing Authority may take its presence into account in determining the conditions to any licence that may be issued under the Act.

8. In premises subject to the Fire Precautions Act 1971, the fire authority may take the presence of LPG into account when making any requirements for a fire certificate.

9. The guidance note does not deal with container filling because REFILL-ING CONTAINERS IN RETAIL PREMISES IS NOT PERMITTED.

Paragraphs 10 to 26 inclusive contain details of the properties of liquefied petroleum gas and definitions for the purpose of the guidance note.

Display and keeping for use

General

27. Display stands should not be located on staircases, near exit doors, next to flammable materials or in any other place where they are likely to hinder or endanger a means of escape. In addition steps should be taken to prohibit smoking or naked lights from around the display area.

28. Only dummy or certified gas-free containers should be used for permanent display in windows, on advertising stands, etc.

Cylinders

29. No more than five cylinders should be allowed on display. Where the largest cylinder capacity does not exceed 3 kg the number on display may be increased to 20. The total contents available including cartridges should not exceed 70 kg. (Table 1).

30. No more than four cylinders should be connected for demonstration purposes at any one time. The total quantity of LPG in both connected cylinders and cartridges should not exceed 50 kg (Table 1).

Cartridges

31. The number of cartridges on display and available in the retail area for sale should be as low as reasonably practicable, but the total contents available on display including cylinders should not exceed 70 kg. All other LPG containers should be placed in the LPG storage area. No more than six cartridges should be connected for demonstration purposes. The total quantity of LPG connected for demonstration purposes in both cylinders and cartridges should not exceed 50 kg (Table 1).

32. Cartridges have a finite shelf life and retailers should ensure adequate stock rotation. It is essential that cartridges are stored in dry, well ventilated conditions.

Welding kits

33. Small kits, *i.e.* with a single 500-g (max) LPG cartridge and a single 50-g (max) oxygen cartridge or 500-g (max) container or oxygen-generating pellets may be displayed with other LPG containers but not more than ten kits may be displayed at a time. The total number of replacement cartridges of LPG and oxygen (or oxygen-generating pellets) on display should be kept as low as is reasonably practicable but in any case should not exceed five containers of each (*i.e.* LPG and oxygen or pellets).

Table 1 Maximum quantities of LPG displayed or kept for use

	Max number of containers	Max quanitity of LPG	Total LPG (including any used for heating and lighting: paragraph 35)
Display Cylinders (Paragraph 29) Cartridges (paragraph 31) including small welding kits	5 or 20 if max capacity 3 kg	70 kg	100 kg (but see also paragraph 36 where a 15 kg max limit may apply out of business hours when premises are shared with residential accommodation)
Demonstration Cylinders (paragraph 30) Cartridges (paragraph 31)	4 6	50 kg	

34. Larger welding kits should not be displayed with other LPG containers but they may be displayed separately with not more than one unit out at a time.

LPG used for heating or lighting

35. If LPG is to be used on the premises for heating or lighting the LPG containers in use should be kept in a safe place secure against interference and preferably in the open air. The supply should be connected to the applicances in a suitably safe manner, *e.g.* by permanent rigid piping, protected to prevent physical damage. The pipework should terminate at a suitable gas tap and where necessary short flexible hoses may be used for the connections between the cylinder and the pipe and the pipe and the appliance. If it is not reasonably practicable to provide a piped system, the total quantity of LPG used for heating, lighting, display and demonstration purposes in cylinders or cartridges should not exceed 100 kg, subject to paragraphs 29 to 31. Heating appliances should be sited away from escape routes and any combustible material. Retailers should ensure that when appliances are used adequate provisions is made for the ventilation of the room. In emergencies such as a heating or power failure additional LPG may, in agreement with the local enforcing authority, be used for heating or lighting. This should be used only for the duration of the emergency and should be removed from the premises as soon as the emergency is over.

36. Where retail premises selling LPG are occupied together with or under residential premises, 60-minute fire resisting separation should be provided between the two occupancies with, where possible, no connecting doors or direct access. Otherwise no more than 15 kg of LPG, which should include stock for sale and LPG used for demonstration, heating or lighting purposes, should be left in the retail areas of the buildings out of business hours. All other stocks of LPG should be returned to the main LPG storage area.

Paragraphs 37 to 58 inclusive cover the general requirements for storage (other than rooftop storage) of LPG.

Paragraphs 59 to 96 inclusive explain in detail and in diagrammatical form the requirements with regards to open-air storage, storage in separate buildings, storage in places within part of buildings and storage in cabinets and cupboards. Fire precautions and emergency procedures are covered in paragraphs 97 to 108 inclusive.

Further information
This Guidance Note is produced by the Health and Safety Executive. Further advice on this or any other publication produced by the Executive is obtained from the general enquiry point, St Hugh's House, Stanley Precinct, Bootle, Merseyside L20 3QY, or from Area Offices of HSE.

Reproduced with the kind permission of H.M.S.O.

SMALL-SCALE STORAGE OF LPG AT RETAIL PREMISES

THE BRITISH RETAILERS' ASSOCIATION ADVICE

To Directors/Chief Environmental Health Officers of District and Islands Councils (With copy for Chief Executive) and Chief Executive Officers of County, Regional and Islands Councils for the attention of Chief Fire Officers/Fire Masters and/or Directors of Consumer Protection, or other appropriate Officers

1. This Circular informs L/A Inspectors that the British Retailers' Association (BRA) has produced advice for its members (see Appendix). The statements sets out to expand on the practical advice and guidance contained in HSE Guidance Notes CS 4 "The keeping of LPG in cylinders and similar containers" and CS 8 "Small-scale Storage and Display of LPG at Retail Premises." Whilst the Association has issued the guidance to members, it is anxious that Inspectors also are aware of the position.

2. Inspectors are requested to take account of the "Statement of Advice" when visiting premises where the Guidance is relevant. If retailers have any queries concerning the statement they should be advised to raise these with the BRA, Commonwealth House, 1–19 New Oxford Street, London WC1A 1PA.

LAU/RPD A2

(HSD B2)

Appendix
THIS STATEMENT HAS BEEN PRODUCED BY THE BRITISH RETAILERS ASSOCIATION IN CONJUNCTION WITH THE HEALTH AND SAFETY EXECUTIVE. IT IS DESIGNED TO ASSIST RETAILERS IN UNDERSTANDING THE GUIDANCE NOTES PRODUCED BY THE HEALTH AND SAFETY EXECUTIVE AND ALSO TO SHARE THE COMMON EXPERIENCE GAINED BY MEMBERS IN THEIR USE OF LPG IN ITS VARIETY OF FUNCTIONS.

Statement of advice on the small-scale storage of liquefied petroleum gas at retail premises

1. Introduction
This statement should be read in conjunction with HSE Guidance Notes CS 4 and CS 8. Whilst HSE Guidance is a distillation of informed opinion reminder is made that employers have duties under section 2 and 3 of the Health and Safety at Work, etc., Act 1974. In practice the person in charge of the premises has the major responsibility concerning the safety of all persons in the building.

2. Small primary containers

Cigarette lighters and similar small containers such as those containing less than 10 g liquefied petroleum gas (LPG) intended for domestic use, for example independent gas-powered hair-styling wands, are outside the scope of HSE Guidance Note CS8. Nevertheless, storage in line with the following sensible general practice is recommended, *i.e.*:

In an adequately ventilated location above-ground (not in basements) that would not obstruct or prejudice an escape route from the premises in case of fire, away from potential sources of ignition, *e.g.* smoking.

Location in potential local "hotspots" such as shop windows or under flood-lighting should be avoided.

Any makers separate advice should be respected and good rotation of stock practised. Containers should be inspected regularly for signs of leakage or deterioration.

The quantity of LPG should be maintained at the lowest practicable level.

Other containers above this size up to and including 20 kg LPG individual capacity where the total LPG quantity exceeds 15 kg should be kept in accordance with the advice in HSE Guidance Note CS 8. Where less than 15 kg LPG is maintained the sensible general practice described above should be respected.

Note: Storage of containers capacity above 20 kg LPG or total quantity exceeding 400 kg should be in accordance with HSE Guidance Note CS4.

The storage of small welding kits (*i.e.* those with LPG and oxygen sources packaged together) should be in accordance with the HSE Guidance Note CS 8.

3. Emergencies

(a) General   In an emergency the temporary use of LPG for lighting or heating purposes may be an expedient remedial measure. It is advisable that organisations should have pre-emergency contingency plans drawn up for dealing with such situations and consideration should be given to alternative supplies of energy.

Advice on safe temporary marginal increase in LPG holdings for emergencies in retail areas should be obtainable from within the organisation's resources such as its fire, safety, operational or engineering functions. Advice may also be obtainable from the local environmental health officer, or the nearest Health and Safety Executive Office, if appropriate.

The following guidance is directed to use of heaters and lighting units:

(b) Heaters   Only the minimum number of heaters commensurate with the emergency need should be used and the number of cylinders restricted to those attached to the appliances.

Spare cylinder storage should be in compliance with HSE Guidance Notes CS 4 and CS 8.

Heaters in operation should be sited so that people will not inadvertently contact them or knock them over. They should not be used in close proximity to combustible or flammable materials or oxygen cylinders. They should be sited in well-ventilated positions to prevent dangerous accumulation of toxic products of combustion.

(c) Lighting Units   The number of units should be the minimum commensurate with the provision of an acceptable standard of overall illumination of the area.

The same considerations as apply to siting of heaters above should apply to the siting of lighting units.

If the LPG is contained in a disposable non-refillable cartridge, care should be

218

exercised to ensure that it is empty before removal from the unit and exchange should be carried out in the open air. "Empties" should not be allowed to accumulate in the sales area but should be removed to a safe place in the open air without delay because they will still contain some gas.

Storage of spare LPG containers should be in accordance with HSE Guidance Notes CS 4 and CS 8.

Reproduced with the kind permission of the British Retailers Association.

SANITARY CONVENIENCES REGULATIONS 1964
(S.I. 1964 No. 966)

Dated June 25, 1964, made by the Minister of Labour by virtue of the powers conferred on him by sections 9 and 80(3) of the Offices, Shops and Railway Premises Act 1963 (hereafter in these Regulations referred to as "the Act") and of all other powers enabling him in that behalf.

Citation, commencement and interpretation

1.—(1) These Regulations may be cited as the Sanitary Conveniences Regulations 1964 and shall come into operation on 1st January 1966.

(2) The Interpretation Act 1889 shall apply to the interpretation of these Regulations as it applies to the interpretation of an Act of Parliament.

(3) In these Regulations, unless the context otherwise requires, the following expressions have the meanings hereby assigned to them respectively, that is to say:

"chemical closet" means a closet having a receptacle for the reception of faecal matter and its deodorisation by the use of suitable chemicals;

"drainage system" means a drainage system connected to a sewer, to a cesspool or to a settlement tank or other tank for the reception or disposal of foul matter;

"urinal" means a urinal which is connected to a drainage system and which has provision for flushing from a supply of clean water either by the operation of mechanism or by automatic action; and

"watercloset" means a closet which has a separate fixed receptable connected to a drainage system and separate provision for flushing from a supply of clean water either by the operation of mechanism or by automatic action.

Application of Regulations

2.—(1) Subject to paragraph (2) of this Regulation, these Regulations shall apply to all office premises, shop premises and railway premises to which the Act applies.

(2) Nothing in these Regulations shall apply to any premises to which the Act applies which are aggregated in a market, being either—

(a) a market held by virtue of a grant from the Crown or of prescription or under statutory authority and which is maintained or regulated by a local or other authority;

(b) any market (other than as aforesaid) held in a market place of which the sole or principal use is for and in connection with the sale of horticultural produce by wholesale; or

(c) any market (other than a market specified in sub-paragraph (a) or (b) of this paragraph) which is a covered market place to which section 51 (power to adapt Act in relation to covered markets) of the Act relates.

Provision of sanitary conveniences

3.—(1) Except as otherwise provided in these Regulations, in the case of premises to which these Regulations apply the provision of sanitary conveniences for the use of persons employed to work therein shall not be suitable and sufficient provision for the purposes of section 9(1) of the Act—

   (*a*) unless provision is made—
      (i) in the case of premises other than those to which sub-paragraph (ii) of this paragraph applies, in accordance with the appropriate provisions of Part I of the Schedule to these Regulations (which relates to the provision of waterclosets and urinals); or
      (ii) where it is not reasonably practicable in the case of any premises to provide a drainage system for, and a supply of clean water for flushing, waterclosets and urinals, in accordance with the appropriate provisions of Part II of the said Schedule (which relates to the provision of chemical closets); and
   (*b*) unless the following provisions of these Regulations are observed.

(2) Sanitary conveniences available for use by all members of the public (or all members of the public of the same sex) and provided by a county council or local authority by virtue of powers contained in any enactment shall not constitute the provision of suitable and sufficient sanitary conveniences for the purposes of section 9(1) of the Act.

(3) Subject to paragraph 4 of this Regulation, in reckoning, for the purposes of Regulations 4, 5 and 9 and paragraphs 1(*a*), 2, 4(*a*) and 5 of the said Schedule, a number of persons, no account shall be taken of any person whose daily hours of work in the premises do not normally exceed two.

(4) In its application to persons employed by railway undertakers, who, by virtue of section 90(3) of the Act, are deemed to be employed to work in the premises at which the general control of the doing of their work is exercised, the last foregoing paragraph shall have effect as if the expression "in the premises" were omitted.

Sanitary conveniences the use of which is shared

4.—(1) Where in the case of any premises to which these Regulations apply—

   (*a*) there are in operation arrangements made in pursuance of section 9(5) of the Act for enabling all or any of the persons employed to work in the premises to have the use of sanitary conveniences provided for the use of others; or
   (*b*) sanitary conveniences provided for the use of all or any of the persons employed to work in the premises are made available for regular use by other persons (not being members of the public);

then in either of such cases, in determining the number of sanitary conveniences required by these Regulations to be provided in the case of the said premises for the said employed persons, the total number of persons for whose regular use the said sanitary conveniences are made available during the periods during which persons are employed to work in the said premises shall be treated as if that were the number of persons regularly employed to work in the said premises at any one time.

(2) Where in any of the following cases, that is to say—

   (*a*) in the case of a building to which section 42 of the Act applies containing two sets or more of premises to which the Act applies;
   (*b*) in the case of a part in single ownership of a building to which section 43

of the Act applies containing two sets or more of premises to which the Act applies; or

(c) in the case of a parcel of land in single ownership containing two sets or more of fuel storage premises to which section 44 of the Act applies;

all or any of the persons employed to work in any two sets or more of any such premises have the use of the same sanitary conveniences provided in pursuance of section 9 of the Act, the total number of the persons regularly so employed at any one time for whose use the conveniences are provided shall, for the purposes of applying these Regulations, be treated as if that were a number of persons all of whom are employed to work in one set of premises to which the Act applies.

Sanitary conveniences used by the public

5. Where in the case of any premises to which these Regulations apply in which the number of persons employed to work therein at any one time regularly exceeds ten, the sanitary conveniences provided for the use of, or used by arrangements by, all or any of such persons are also ordinarily made available for general use by members of the public resorting to the premises, the number of waterclosets or chemical closets (as the case may be) required by other provisions of these Regulations to be provided, or to be provided separately according to their sex (as the case may be), for the use of those persons shall in every case be increased by one.

Situation of sanitary conveniences

6.—(1) No sanitary convenience provided in pursuance of these Regulations shall be situated in any room in which any person (other than a lavatory attendant) is employed to work.

(2) Except as provided in paragraph (3) of this Regulation, no watercloset and chemical closet, no accommodation in which a urinal is provided and no accommodation containing a watercloset or chemical closet which, in either case, is not wholly enclosed shall be so situated that access to it is obtained directly from any room in which any person (other than a lavatory attendant) is employed to work.

(3) The requirements of paragraph (2) of this Regulation shall not apply where—

(a) it is not reasonably practicable to comply with such requirements in the case of any watercloset, chemical closet or accommodation of any kind referred to in the said paragraph (as the case may be); and

(b) the watercloset, chemical closet or accommodation (as the case may be) was first installed or constructed before the date of the making of these Regulations in a building for use therein;

and in any such case the watercloset, chemical closet or accommodation shall be provided with effective mechanical means of ventilation which shall discharge directly into the open air and which shall be kept in operation during the periods during which any person is employed to work in the room from which access is obtained directly to the watercloset, chemical closet or accommodation (as the case may be).

(4) Any enclosed space between a watercloset, chemical closet or accommodation where a urinal is provided and any room in which any person (other than a lavatory attendant) is employed to work shall be provided with effective means of ventilation.

Protection and privacy of sanitary conveniences

7.—(1) All accommodation where any watercloset, chemical closet or urinal is provided in pursuance of these Regulations shall be covered to an extent sufficient to ensure protection from the weather for persons using it.

(2) Every watercloset and chemical closet provided in pursuance of these Regulations shall be enclosed to an extent sufficient to ensure privacy and be fitted with a suitable door and door fastening.

(3) Every urinal provided in pursuance of these Regulations shall be so placed or so screened as not to be visible from outside the accommodation where the urinal is situated.

Marking of sanitary accommodation

8. Where in accordance with these Regulations separate accommodation is provided for persons of each sex, the accommodation shall be clearly marked to show for persons of which sex it is so provided.

Disposal of sanitary dressings

9.—(1) Where in any case the total number of female persons (not being members of the public) for whose regular use sanitary conveniences are made available exceeds ten, suitable and effective means for the disposal of sanitary dressings shall be provided.

(2) All means provided for the disposal of sanitary dressings in accordance with the foregoing paragraph of this Regulation shall be constantly maintained in proper condition and where the means provided consist of or include bins the contents of the bins shall be disposed of at suitable intervals.

SCHEDULE

Regulation 3

PART I

WATERCLOSETS AND URINALS TO BE PROVIDED IN ACCORDANCE WITH
SECTION 9 OF THE ACT

1. In the case of premises (whether or not persons of both sexes are employed to work therein) where—

(*a*) the number of persons employed to work therein does not regularly exceed five at any one time; or

(*b*) of the number of persons regularly employed to work therein there is none whose daily hours of work in the premises normally exceed two;

one watercloset.

2. In the case of premises to which paragraph 1 of this Schedule applies—accommodation in accordance with the following scales, which accommodation shall be provided separately for persons of each sex—

(*a*) for females, and

(*b*) for males (where urinal accommodation is not provided in accordance with the scale set out in sub-paragraph (*c*) of this paragraph)—

Number of persons of each sex regularly employed to work in the premises at any one time	Number of waterclosets
1 to 15	1
16 to 30	2
31 to 50	3
51 to 75	4
76 to 100	5
Exceeding 100	5, with the addition of one for every unit of 25 persons by which the number of persons exceeds 100 (any fraction of a unit of 25 persons being treated as one).

(c) for males (where urinal accommodation is provided)—

Number of male persons regularly employed to work in the premises at any one time	Number of waterclosets	Units of urinal accommodation
1 to 15	1	—
16 to 20	1	1
21 to 30	2	1
31 to 45	2	2
46 to 60	3	2
61 to 75	3	3
76 to 90	4	3
91 to 100	4	4
Exceeding 100	4	4

with the addition of one sanitary convenience (being either a watercloset or a unit of urinal accommodation) for every unit of 25 persons by which the number of persons exceeds 100 (any fraction of a unit of 25 persons being treated as one) of which additional number of sanitary conveniences not less than three-quarters shall be waterclosets (any fraction being treated as one).

3. For the purposes of this Part of this Schedule, the expression "unit of urinal accommodation" means one stall of a urinal or, where stalls are not provided, two feet of space of a urinal.

PART II

CHEMICAL CLOSETS TO BE PROVIDED IN ACCORDANCE WITH SECTION 9 OF THE ACT

4. In the case of premises (whether or not persons of both sexes are employed to work therein) where—

(a) the number of persons employed to work therein does not regularly exceed five at any one time; or

(b) of the number of persons regularly employed to work therein there is none whose daily hours of work in the premises normally exceed two;

224

one chemical closet.

5. In the case of premises other than premises to which paragraph 4 of this Schedule applies—accommodation in accordance with the following scales, which accommodation shall be provided separately for persons of each sex—

Number of persons of each sex regularly employed to work in the premises at any one time	*Number of waterclosets*
1 to 15	1
16 to 30	2
31 to 50	3
51 to 75	4
76 to 100	5
Exceeding 100	5, with the addition of one for every unit of 25 persons by which the number of persons exceeds 100 (any fraction of a unit of 25 persons being treated as one).

WASHING FACILITIES REGULATIONS 1964
(S.I. 1964 No. 965)

Dated June 25, 1964, made by the Minister of Labour by virtue of the powers conferred on him by sections 10 and 80(3) of the Offices, Shops and Railway Premises Act 1963 (hereafter in these Regulations referred to as "the Act") and of all other powers enabling him in that behalf.

Citation, commencement and interpretation

1.—(1) These Regulations may be cited as the Washing Facilities Regulations 1964 and shall come into operation on 1st January 1966.

(2) The Interpretation Act 1889 shall apply to the interpretation of these Regulations as it applies to the interpretation of an Act of Parliament.

(3) In these Regulations, unless the context otherwise requires, the following expressions have the meanings hereby assigned to them respectively, that is to say:—

"trough" means a trough measuring internally at least four feet over its longest or widest part with a smooth impervious surface and fitted with an unplugged waste pipe and having a supply of warm water laid on at points above the trough and at suitable intervals of not more than two feet;

"unit of trough or washing fountain accommodation" means two feet of length of a trough or, in the cases of circular or oval troughs and washing fountains, two feet of the circumference of the trough or fountain;

"wash-basin" means a fixed basin with a smooth impervious surface, having a supply of clean running hot and cold or warm water and fitted with a waste pipe and (except where the supply of water is from a spray tap) with a plug;

"wash-bowl" includes any water container suitable for use as a washing facility; and

"washing fountain" means a washing fountain measuring internally at least three feet over its widest part, with a smooth impervious surface and fitted with an unplugged waste pipe and having a supply of running warm water.

Application of Regulations

2.—(1) Subject to paragraph (2) of this Regulation, these Regulations shall apply to all office premises, shop premises and railway premises to which the Act applies.

(2) Nothing in these Regulations shall apply to any premises to which the Act applies which are aggregated in a market, being either—

(a) a market held by virtue of a grant from the Crown or of prescription or under statutory authority and which is maintained or regulated by a local or other authority;

(b) any market (other than as aforesaid) held in a market place of which the sole or principal use is for and in connection with the sale of horticultural produce by wholesale; or

(c) any market (other than a market specified in sub-paragraph (a) or (b) of this paragraph) which is a covered market place to which section 51 (power to adapt Act in relation to covered markets) of the Act relates.

Provision of washing facilities

3.—(1) Except as otherwise provided in these Regulations, in the case of premises to which these Regulations apply the provision of washing facilities for the use of persons employed to work therein shall not be suitable and sufficient provision for the purposes of section 10(1) of the Act—

    (*a*) unless, in addition to the provision of the facilities specified in the said section 10(1), provision is made—

        (i) in the case of premises other than those to which sub-paragraph (ii) of this paragraph applies, in accordance with the appropriate provisions of Part I of the Schedule to these Regulations (which relates to the provision of wash-basins, troughs and washing fountains); or

        (ii) in the case of premises to which Part II of the said Schedule applies, in accordance with the appropriate provisions of that Part of the said Schedule (which relates to the provision of fixed or portable wash-bowls); and

    (*b*) unless the following provisions of these Regultions are observed.

(2) The premises to which Part II of the said Schedule applies are—

    (*a*) premises of a class which by virtue of an order of the Minister of Labour pursuant to section 45 of the Act is for the time being exempted from so much of section 10(1) of the Act as requires the water supplied to be running water; and

    (*b*) premises which by virtue of section 46 of the Act are for the time being exempted from so much of section 10(1) of the Act as requires the water supplied to be running water.

(3) Where in the case of any premises to which these Regulations apply—

    (*a*) the number of persons employed to work therein regularly exceeds five at any one time;

    (*b*) persons of each sex are regularly employed to work therein; and

    (*c*) the circumstances affecting the premises are such that it is reasonably practicable to provide washing facilities in proper separate accommodation for persons of each sex;

the provision of washing facilities shall be deemed not to be suitable for the purposes of section 10(1) of the Act unless it affords proper separate accommodation for persons of each sex.

(4) Subject to paragraph 5 of this Regulation, in reckoning, for the purposes of this Regulation, Regulations 4 and 5 and paragraphs 1(*a*), 2, 3(*a*) and 4 of the said Schedule, a number of persons, no account shall be taken of any person whose daily hours of work in the premises do not normally exceed two.

(5) In its application to persons employed by railway undertakers, who, bur virtue of section 90(3) of the Act, are deemed to be employed to work in the premises at which the general control of the doing of their work is exercised, the last foregoing paragraph shall have effect as if the expression "in the premises" were omitted.

Washing facilities the use of which is shared

4.—(1) Where in the case of any premises to which these Regulations apply—

    (*a*) there are in operation arrangements made in pursuance of section 10(5) of the Act for enabling all or any of the persons employed to work in the premises to have the use of washing facilities provided for the use of others; or

(b) washing facilities provided for the use of all or any of the persons employed to work in the premises are made available for regular use by other persons (not being members of the public);

then in either of such cases, in determining the number of wash-basins, wash-bowls or units of trough or washing fountain accommodation (as the case may be) required by these Regulations to be provided in the case of the said premises for the said employed persons, the total number of persons for whose regular use the said washing facilities are made available during the periods during which persons are employed to work in the said premises shall be treated as if that were the number of persons regularly employed to work in the said premises at any one time.

(2) Where in any of the following cases, that is to say—

(a) in the case of a building to which section 42 of the Act applies containing two sets or more of premises to which the Act applies;

(b) in the case of a part in single ownership of a building to which section 43 of the Act applies containing two sets or more of premises to which the Act applies; or

(c) in the case of a parcel of land in single ownership containing two sets or more of fuel storage premises to which section 44 of the Act applies;

all or any of the persons employed to work in any two sets or more of any such premises have the use of the same washing facilities provided in pursuance of section 10 of the Act, the total number of the persons regularly so employed at any one time for whose use the facilities are provided shall, for the purpose of applying these Regulations, be treated as if that were a number of persons all of whom are employed to work in one set of premises to which the Act applies.

Washing facilities used by the public

5. Where in the case of any premises to which these Regulations apply in which the number of persons employed to work therein at any one time regularly exceeds ten, the washing facilities provided for the use of, or used by arrangements by, all or any of such persons are also ordinarily made available for general use by members of the public resorting to the premises, the total number of wash-basin, wash-bowls and units of trough and washing fountain accommodation (as the case may be) required by the other provisions of these Regulations to be provided, or to be provided separately according to their sex (as the case may be), for the use of those persons shall in every case be increased by one.

Protection of washing facilities

6. All accommodation where washing facilities are provided in pursuance of section 10(1) of the Act and of these Regulations shall be covered and enclosed to an extent sufficient to ensure protection from the weather for persons using them.

Ventilation of washing accommodation

7. Effective provision shall be made, as far as reasonably practicable, for ventilating rooms in which washing facilities are situated.

228

Marking of washing accommodation

8. Where in accordance with these Regulations separate accommodation is provided for persons of each sex, the accommodation shall be clearly marked to show for persons of which sex it is so provided.

SCHEDULE

Regulation 3

PART I

WASH-BASINS, TROUGHS OR WASHING FOUNTAINS TO BE PROVIDED AS WASHING FACILITIES IN ACCORDANCE WITH SECTION 10 OF THE ACT IN THE CASE OF PREMISES NOT EXEMPTED FROM THE REQUIREMENT TO SUPPLY RUNNING WATER

1. In the case of premises (whether or not persons of both sexes are employed to work therein) where—

(*a*) the number of persons employed to work therein does not regularly exceed five at any one time; or

(*b*) of the number of persons regularly employed to work therein there is none whose daily hours of work in the premises normally exceed two;

one wash-basin or trough or washing fountain.

2. In the case of premises other than premises to which paragraph 1 of this Schedule applies—wash-basins, troughs or washing fountains in accordance with the following scale—

Number of persons regularly employed to work in the premises at any one time (or, where separate accommodation for the sexes is required to be provided, number of such persons of each sex)	*Number of wash-basins or units of trough or washing fountain accommodation*
1 to 15	1
16 to 30	2
31 to 50	3
51 to 75	4
76 to 100	5
Exceeding 100	5, with the addition of one for every unit of 25 persons by which the number of persons exceeds 100 (any fraction of a unit of 25 persons being treated as one).

PART II

FIXED OR PORTABLE WASH-BOWLS TO BE PROVIDED AS WASHING FACILITIES IN ACCORDANCE WITH SECTION 10 OF THE ACT IN THE CASE OF PREMISES EXEMPTED FROM THE REQUIREMENT TO SUPPLY RUNNING WATER

3. In the case of premises to which this Part of this Schedule applies (whether or not persons of both sexes are employed to work therein) where—

(*a*) the number of persons employed to work therein does not regularly exceed five at any one time; or

(*b*) of the number of persons regularly employed to work therein there is none whose daily hours of work in the premises normally exceed two;

one fixed or portable wash-bowl.

4. In the case of premises to which this Part of this Schedule applies, other than premises to which paragraph 3 of this Schedule applies—facilities on the scale of one fixed or portable wash-bowl for every unit of five persons (or, where separate accommodation for the sexes is required to be provided, for every unit of five persons of each sex) regularly employed at any one time to work therein (any fraction of a unit being treated as one).

INDEX

231